Google Compute Engine

Marc Cohen, Kathryn Hurley, and Paul Newson

Beijing · Cambridge · Farnham · Köln · Sebastopol · Tokyo

Google Compute Engine

by Marc Cohen, Kathryn Hurley, and Paul Newson

Printed in the United States of America.

Published by O'Reilly Media, Inc. , 1005 Gravenstein Highway North, Sebastopol, CA 95472.

O'Reilly books may be purchased for educational, business, or sales promotional use. Online editions are also available for most titles (*http://safaribooksonline.com*). For more information, contact our corporate/institutional sales department: 800-998-9938 or corporate@oreilly.com .

Editor: Rachel Roumeliotis
Production Editor: Shiny Kalapurakkel
Copyeditor: Jasmine Kwityn
Proofreader: Amanda Kersey

Indexer: Angela Howard
Interior Designer: David Futato
Cover Designer: Karen Montgomery
Illustrator: Rebecca Demarest

December 2014: First Edition

Revision History for the First Edition
2014-12-08: First Release

See *http://oreilly.com/catalog/errata.csp?isbn=9781449360887* for release details.

978-1-449-36088-7

[LSI]

Table of Contents

Preface

Today's most advanced computing technology exists in large buildings containing vast arrays of low-cost servers. Enormous computing resources are housed in well-fortified, secure areas, maintained by teams of highly trained technicians. The photograph in Figure P-1 depicts Google's 115,000-square-foot data center in Council Bluffs, Iowa, taken from an interactive website describing Google's amazing network of data centers (see *http://www.google.com/about/datacenters/gallery*).

Figure P-1. Google Data Center (Photograph by Google/Connie Zhou)

In the mainframe era, if you outgrew the capacity of a single computer, you needed to come up with millions of dollars to buy another computer. Modern data centers achieve scalable capacity by allocating tasks across large numbers of commodity servers. In the data center era, you allocate as many inexpensive servers as you need and then relinquish those resources when you're done.

Until recently, data center resources were accessible by the few engineers fortunate enough to work for a new generation of technology companies. However, over the past few years, a revolution has taken place. Just as earlier revolutions in computer hardware made it feasible for more people to access larger numbers of smaller computers, cloud computing enables even greater access, via the public Internet, to vast clusters of computers in modern state-of-the-art data centers. And just as it did in the past, this expanded accessibility is stimulating tremendous innovation.

In its short history, Google has pioneered many of the techniques and best practices used to build and manage cloud computing services. From Search to Gmail to YouTube to Maps, Google services provide secure, scalable, reliable cloud computing to millions of users and serve billions of queries every day. Now, with Google Compute Engine, the infrastructure that supports those services is available to everyone.

Compute Engine offers many advantages: leading-edge hardware, upgraded regularly and automatically; virtually unlimited capacity to grow or shrink a business on demand; a flexible charging model; an army of experts maintaining computing and networking resources; and the ability to host your resources in a global network engineered for security and performance.

This book provides a guided tour of Google Compute Engine, with a focus on solving practical problems. At a high level, Google Compute Engine is about giving you access to the world's most advanced network of data centers—the computing resources that power Google itself. Practically speaking, this means providing APIs, command-line tools and web user interfaces to use Google's computing and networking resources.

In succeeding chapters, we'll explain the detailed product capabilities, along with some best practices for getting the most out of Google Compute Engine. We'll provide numerous examples, illustrating how to access Compute Engine services using all of the supported access methods. Although the programming examples in this book are all written in a combination of Python and JavaScript, the underlying RESTful API and the concepts presented are language independent.

Contents of This Book

Figure P-2 shows how all of Compute Engine's components fit together. At a high level, Compute Engine instances, networks, and storage are all owned by a Compute Engine project. A Compute Engine project is essentially a named collection of information about your application and acts as a container for your Compute Engine resources. Any Compute Engine resources that you create, such as instances, networks, and disks, are associated with, and contained in, your Compute Engine project. The API offers a way to interact with Compute Engine components and resources programmatically.

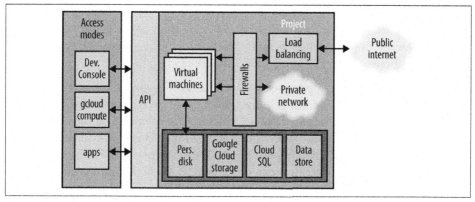

Figure P-2. Overview of Google Compute Engine's components

We'll explore the following Google Compute Engine components and resources:

- Projects, access modes, and the API (Chapter 1)
- Virtual machines (Chapter 2 and Chapter 7)
- Persistent disk (Chapter 3)
- Google Cloud Storage (Chapter 4)
- Cloud SQL and Cloud Datastore (Chapter 5)
- Firewalls, load balancing, and the private network (Chapter 6)
- A complete application (Chapter 8)

What Each Chapter Covers

Chapter 1, Getting Started

We'll take a look at how to get started using Compute Engine. We begin by creating a Compute Engine project using the Google Developers Console, a web UI. We then explore various means of accessing and managing Compute Engine resources via the Developers Console; gcloud compute, a command-line interface; and the Compute Engine API, a RESTful interface.

Chapter 2, Instances

Instances are customizable Linux machines and represent the core of Google Compute Engine. You have root access to any instance you create, which allows you to download and install packages and customize disk, hardware, or other configuration options. Chapter 2 covers the basics of working with Compute Engine instances and explains instance attributes in detail.

Chapter 3, Storage: Persistent Disk; Chapter 4, Storage: Cloud Storage; and Chapter 5, Storage: Cloud SQL and Cloud Datastore

Most applications require a location for storing their data. The storage available to Compute Engine comes in many flavors, including persistent disks, Google Cloud Storage, Cloud SQL, and Cloud Datastore.

As the name implies, a persistent disk stores data beyond the life of any associated instance(s). Cloud Storage allows you to store, access, and manage objects of any size on Google's infrastructure. Cloud Storage offers an excellent option for highly durable, high availability data storage. Your data is accessible both inside and outside the scope of Compute Engine via a variety of mechanisms and tools, including the Developers Console, the gsutil command, and the Cloud Storage API.

Cloud SQL provides a MySQL service in the cloud, managed by Google, while Cloud Datastore provides a Google scale NoSQL data service. Both of these services are available inside and outside the scope of Compute Engine.

Chapter 3, Chapter 4, and Chapter 5 explain all of these storage options in depth, and provide detailed examples illustrating how to exercise all supported access methods.

Chapter 6, Networking

Every project has its own private network with an integrated DNS service, numbering plan, and routing logic. A project can have multiple networks, and each network can include multiple instances. Firewall rules can be applied to a network to allow or prohibit incoming traffic to any or all instances and the internet. Load balancing provides advanced and responsive scalable traffic distribution. Chapter 6 provides a short primer on TCP/IP networking and covers Compute Engine's advanced networking features in depth.

Chapter 7, Advanced Topics

In Chapter 7, we'll cover a variety of advanced topics that provide additional ways to customize your Compute Engine resources. Topics include custom images, startup scripts, and the metadata server.

Chapter 8, A Complete Application

In Chapter 8, we present a guided tour of an application that ties together several of the topics covered earlier. Using an example application, this chapter builds a simple but comprehensive cloud computing application, step by step.

Conventions Used in This Book

The following typographical conventions are used in this book:

Italic

Indicates new terms, URLs, email addresses, filenames, and file extensions.

`Constant width`

Used for program listings, as well as within paragraphs to refer to program elements such as variable or function names, databases, data types, environment variables, statements, and keywords.

`Constant width bold`

Shows commands or other text that should be typed literally by the user.

`Constant width italic`

Shows text that should be replaced with user-supplied values or by values determined by context.

 This element signifies a tip or suggestion.

 This element signifies a general note.

 This element indicates a warning or caution.

Using Code Examples

This book is here to help you get your job done. In general, if example code is offered with this book, you may use it in your programs and documentation. You do not need to contact us for permission unless you're reproducing a significant portion of the code. For example, writing a program that uses several chunks of code from this book does not require permission. Selling or distributing a CD-ROM of examples from O'Reilly books does require permission. Answering a question by citing this book and quoting example code does not require permission. Incorporating a significant amount of example code from this book into your product's documentation does require permission.

We appreciate, but do not require, attribution. An attribution usually includes the title, author, publisher, and ISBN. For example: "*Book Title* by Some Author (O'Reilly). Copyright 2012 Some Copyright Holder, 978-0-596-xxxx-x."

If you feel your use of code examples falls outside fair use or the permission given above, feel free to contact us at *permissions@oreilly.com*.

Safari® Books Online

 *Safari Books Online* is an on-demand digital library that delivers expert content in both book and video form from the world's leading authors in technology and business.

Technology professionals, software developers, web designers, and business and creative professionals use Safari Books Online as their primary resource for research, problem solving, learning, and certification training.

Safari Books Online offers a range of plans and pricing for enterprise, government, education, and individuals.

Members have access to thousands of books, training videos, and prepublication manuscripts in one fully searchable database from publishers like O'Reilly Media, Prentice Hall Professional, Addison-Wesley Professional, Microsoft Press, Sams, Que, Peachpit Press, Focal Press, Cisco Press, John Wiley & Sons, Syngress, Morgan Kaufmann, IBM Redbooks, Packt, Adobe Press, FT Press, Apress, Manning, New Riders, McGraw-Hill, Jones & Bartlett, Course Technology, and hundreds more. For more information about Safari Books Online, please visit us online.

How to Contact Us

Please address comments and questions concerning this book to the publisher:

O'Reilly Media, Inc.
1005 Gravenstein Highway North
Sebastopol, CA 95472
800-998-9938 (in the United States or Canada)
707-829-0515 (international or local)
707-829-0104 (fax)

We have a web page for this book, where we list errata, examples, and any additional information. You can access this page at http://shop.oreilly.com/product/0636920028888.do.

To comment or ask technical questions about this book, send email to *bookquestions@oreilly.com*.

For more information about our books, courses, conferences, and news, see our website at http://www.oreilly.com.

Find us on Facebook: http://facebook.com/oreilly

Follow us on Twitter: http://twitter.com/oreillymedia

Watch us on YouTube: http://www.youtube.com/oreillymedia

Acknowledgments

Marc, Kathryn, and Paul would like to thank their expert editor, Rachel Roumeliotis, for her patience and guidance throughout this project. They'd also like to thank their many helpful reviewers and colleagues, who provided invaluable feedback on many revisions: Andrew Kadatch, Ankur Parikh, Benson Kalahar, Dan Miller, Danielle Aronstam, Dave Barth, Elizabeth Markman, Eric Johnson, Greg DeMichillie, Ian Barber, Jay Judkowitz, Joe Beda, Joe Faith, Johan Euphrosine, Jonathan Burns, Julia Ferraioli, Laurence Moroney, Martin Maly, Mike Trinh, Nathan Herring, Nathan Parker, Phun Lang, Rebecca Ward, Renny Hwang, Scott Van Woudenberg, Simon Newton, and Sunil James.

Marc would like to thank his dedicated, talented, and supportive coauthors for their hard work and inspiration. Marc is also grateful for the love and support of his family, including his wife Kimberly and daughter Maya, who tolerated many long hours spent completing this project.

Kathryn would like to thank her husband, James, and daughter, Violet, for their love and support and her coauthors, Marc and Paul, for being awesome.

Paul would like to thank Marc and Kathryn for the opportunity to collaborate on this project, even though he got to the party late.

## CHAPTER 1

Getting Started

Google Compute Engine is a service that provides virtual machines (VMs) that run on Google's infrastructure. You can create VMs with a variety of configurations using a number of available operating systems. The instance's data is stored and maintained on persistent block storage that is replicated for redundancy and persists beyond the life cycle of the VM. Network access can be configured to allow your virtual machines to talk to each other, the Internet, or your own private network.

Google Compute Engine provides a variety of tools you can use to interact with and manage your Compute Engine instances and configurations; for example, you can start and stop instances, attach disk storage, and configure network access using each of these access points. The tools include the Google Developers Console (*http://console.developers.google.com*), which provides a web-based user interface (UI) with HTML forms for instance creation and configuration; `gcloud compute`, a command-line interface that can be used interactively or in scripts for simple automation; and the Compute Engine API, a RESTful API for integration into your own code and cloud-management applications.

To start working with Google Compute Engine, you first need to create a Compute Engine project in the Developers Console. A Compute Engine project is a collection of information about your application and acts as a container for your Compute Engine resources and configurations. Disks, firewalls, networks, and instances are all associated with and contained within a single project. Billing is applied to a project based on the amount of resources used. Team members can be added to the project with specific permissions for access to the project's Compute Engine resources.

In this chapter, we'll show you how to use the Developers Console to create a new Compute Engine project, enable billing on the project, and add team members to the project. We'll then take a high-level look at Compute Engine's resources. Finally, we'll show you how to get started working with Compute Engine's tools and API.

Creating a Compute Engine Project

To access the Google Developers Console, first open up your favorite browser and go to the following URL:

http://console.developers.google.com

 This book does not cover all features of the Developers Console. To learn more about the console, see the online documentation: *https://developers.google.com/console/help/new/*.

Log in with your Gmail account if prompted, and read and accept the terms of use.

If this is your first time visiting the Developers Console, your project list will be empty. Create a new project by clicking on the Create Project button. This new project will be your Compute Engine project. The Developers Console opens a dialog box asking for a project name and project ID (see Figure 1-1). These fields default to My Project and a random, unique Project ID. Specify a new name and ID or keep the defaults, read and accept any terms of service, and click Create. Your new project will now be created.

 Please note that the Developer Console's UI may change over time, and the screenshots in this book might not exactly match the UI.

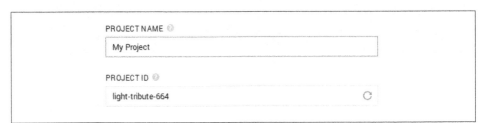

Figure 1-1. Form displayed when creating a new project via the Developers Console

If you've worked with Google's APIs before and are familiar with the Google Developers Console, feel free to use an existing project. Note that billing must be enabled on the project before you can start using Compute Engine, which we'll cover in the next section.

Enabling Billing

Now that you have a project, billing must be enabled before you can start working with Compute Engine.

 Completing the examples in this book may incur charges. Please review the pricing documentation of the various products used in the examples. To limit your expenses, *make sure to delete any resources you do not need.*

To enable billing, select Billing in the lefthand navigation. Then, follow the steps in the UI to create a new billing account.

Adding Team Members

All new projects have three existing members: one member associated with your Google Account and two special identities called service accounts, which are useful when developing server-to-server applications. Using a service account, an application can identify itself to a Google API on behalf of itself without any end-user involvement. Service accounts will be covered in more detail in Chapter 2, and you can also learn more online: *https://developers.google.com/accounts/docs/OAuth2Serv iceAccount.*

The console allows you to add team members to your project with view, edit, or ownership permissions. To add team members, select Permissions in the lefthand navigation.

Click the Add Member button at the top of the screen. Enter the email address of the team member you want to add, and select the appropriate permission level for that member (see Figure 1-2). "Can view" gives the team member read access to your project settings and Compute Engine resources. "Can edit" gives the team member write access to your project settings and Compute Engine resources (including adding and deleting resources). "Is owner" gives the team member all edit permissions, plus the ability to manage project settings and team members.

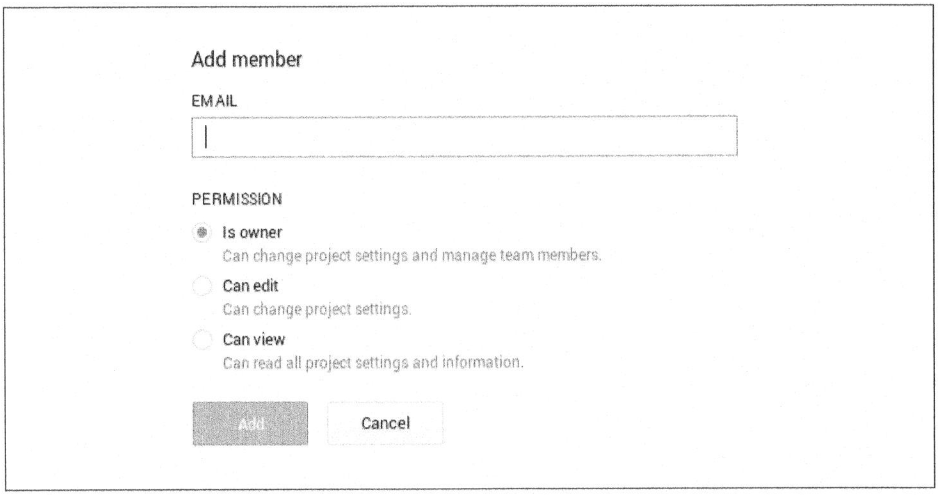

Figure 1-2. Add member form

Compute Engine Resources

Now that you created a Compute Engine project, let's take a look at the Compute Engine resources with which you'll be working.

To understand Compute Engine's resources, you must first understand the *instance* resource (i.e., your virtual machine, or VM). The instance resource utilizes all of Compute Engine's other resources, such as disks, networks, and images, for additional functionality. For example, disk resources provide storage to your instance, and network resources route traffic to and from your instance. Resources available for instance configuration include:

Image
> The base software for a hosted virtual machine, including the operating system and all associated system and application software

Disk
> A disk provides storage for your Compute Engine instances

Snapshot
> A copy of the contents of an existing persistent disk (i.e., an image copy)

Network
> Set of rules defining how an instance interacts with other instances, other networks, and the Internet

Firewall
> A single rule defining how an instance can accept incoming traffic[1]

Route
> A table which determines how traffic destined for a certain IP should be handled

Address
> A static IP address for your instances

Machine type
> A hardware configuration dictating the number of cores and available memory for a given instance

All resources are owned by a single project. Within that project, resources are available at different hierarchical levels (a.k.a. scopes). Currently, there are three scopes: global, regional, and zonal. Resources within the global scope are available to resources within the same project (in other words, they are globally available within that project). Resources within the regional scope are available to other resources within the same region. Finally, resources within the zonal scope are available to other resources within the same zone. The current breakdown of resource levels is as follows:

Global resources
> Image, snapshot, network, firewall, route

Regional resources
> Address

Zone resources
> Instance, machine type, disk

Manage Compute Engine Resources

Now that you have an understanding of Compute Engine's resources, let's take a look at the tools and access points available for managing these resources. Compute Engine offers several options for resource management that fit your specific needs. If you prefer using a rich user interface, the Google Developers Console offers a web UI to start, configure, and stop your VMs. If bash scripting is your preference, `gcloud compute` provides a command-line interface to manage your GCE resources. Finally, the Compute Engine API provides a RESTful interface for all your programming needs. In this section, we'll take a look at how to get started using each tool.

---

1 A Compute Engine "firewall" setting consists of a single rule defining how an instance accepts incoming traffic. This is a bit different than a typical firewall, which is usually the entire collection of rules around which ports can accept or reject traffic. Be sure to note that your configuration in GCE will have multiple firewalls, with each firewall being a single rule.

Google Developers Console

The Google Developers Console provides a web interface (see Figure 1-3) through which you can manage your Compute Engine instances and resources. To get started, click Compute > Compute Engine > "VM instances" in the lefthand navigation.

Figure 1-3. Compute Engine UI in the Developers Console

The lefthand navigation should now be displaying links to various Compute Engine resources. We'll take a closer look at the VM instances, zones, operations, and quotas sections.

VM Instances. Once you have started your first instance, you will have the option to view usage graphs showing your instances' CPU utilization, network traffic, and disk traffic (see Figure 1-4). You can also create a new instance by clicking the "New instance" button at the top of the screen. We'll cover instances in more detail in Chapter 2, including how to create a new instance using the Developers Console.

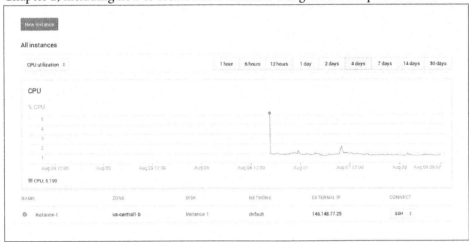

Figure 1-4. VM instances section in the Developers Console

Zones. The Zones section provides valuable information about planned outages for the zones available to your project (see Figure 1-5). You can also see how many instances you have running in each zone to help you manage your resources appropriately.

Zones					
REGION		ZONES	INSTANCES	DISKS	PLANNED OUTAGES
asia-east1	⊘	Zone A	0	0	No maintenance windows
	⊘	Zone B	0	0	No maintenance windows
	⊘	Zone C	0	0	No maintenance windows
europe-west1	⊘	Zone A	0	0	Aug 15, 2014 12:00:00 PM - Sep 1, 2014 12:00:00 PM
	⊘	Zone B	0	0	No maintenance windows
us-central1	⊘	Zone A	0	2	No maintenance windows
	⊘	Zone B	1	1	No maintenance windows
	⊘	Zone F	0	0	No maintenance windows

Figure 1-5. Zones section in the Developers Console

Operations. Every request submitted via the API generates an asynchronous transaction, called an operation. Examples include adding or deleting instances, reserving static IP addresses, or attaching persistent disks instances. The Operations tab of the Developers Console can be used to examine your completed and in-progress operations, which can be useful for debugging. If an operation failed for any reason, a red exclamation mark is displayed next to the operation, and the status will display the error message (see Figure 1-6).

Operations

Operation resources are asynchronous REST requests. Each operation resource represents a REST request. Learn more

OPERATION SUMMARY	TARGET	USER	TIME	STATUS
Automatically migrate an instance	my-instance	system	Start: Jul 28, 2014 11:50:02 AM End: Jul 28, 2014 11:50:02 AM	Done
Automatically migrate an instance	metadata-test	system	Start: Jul 29, 2014 5:43:23 AM End: Jul 29, 2014 5:43:23 AM	Done
Delete an instance	test-vm	gce.oreilly@gmail.com	Start: Aug 6, 2014 1:46:45 PM End: Aug 6, 2014 1:47:25 PM	Done
Delete an instance	my-instance	gce.oreilly@gmail.com	Start: Aug 6, 2014 1:46:51 PM End: Aug 6, 2014 1:47:16 PM	Done
Delete an instance	metadata-test	gce.oreilly@gmail.com	Start: Aug 6, 2014 1:46:56 PM End: Aug 6, 2014 1:47:16 PM	Done
Delete an instance	custom-image-reference	gce.oreilly@gmail.com	Start: Aug 6, 2014 1:47:02 PM End: Aug 6, 2014 1:47:25 PM	Done
Delete an instance	cloud-datastore-test	gce.oreilly@gmail.com	Start: Aug 6, 2014 1:47:07 PM End: Aug 6, 2014 1:47:36 PM	Done
Delete an instance	apache-server	gce.oreilly@gmail.com	Start: Aug 6, 2014 1:47:11 PM End: Aug 6, 2014 1:47:36 PM	Done
Delete an instance	apache-instance	gce.oreilly@gmail.com	Start: Aug 6, 2014 1:47:16 PM End: Aug 6, 2014 1:47:36 PM	Done
Delete a disk	metadata-test	gce.oreilly@gmail.com	Start: Aug 6, 2014 1:47:19 PM End: Aug 6, 2014 1:47:20 PM	Done
Delete a disk	my-instance	gce.oreilly@gmail.com	Start: Aug 6, 2014 1:47:19 PM End: Aug 6, 2014 1:47:20 PM	Done
Delete a disk	custom-image-reference	gce.oreilly@gmail.com	Start: Aug 6, 2014 1:47:28 PM End: Aug 6, 2014 1:47:28 PM	Done
Delete a disk	apache-instance	gce.oreilly@gmail.com	Start: Aug 6, 2014 1:47:39 PM End: Aug 6, 2014 1:47:39 PM	Done
Delete a disk	apache-server	gce.oreilly@gmail.com	Start: Aug 6, 2014 1:47:40 PM End: Aug 6, 2014 1:47:40 PM	Done
Delete a disk	cloud-datastore-test	gce.oreilly@gmail.com	Start: Aug 6, 2014 1:47:41 PM End: Aug 6, 2014 1:47:41 PM	Done
Create a disk	disk-1	gce.oreilly@gmail.com	Start: Aug 8, 2014 10:02:58 AM End: Aug 8, 2014 10:03:06 AM	Done
Create a disk	disk-1	gce.oreilly@gmail.com	Start: Aug 8, 2014 10:03:31 AM End: Aug 8, 2014 10:03:31 AM	RESOURCE_ALREADY_EXISTS

Figure 1-6. Operations tab in the Developers Console

You can click the operation to get more details about its status (see Figure 1-7). The resulting page shows the progress of the operation, the user who performed the operation, and any errors that occurred during the operation (see Figure 1-8).

Figure 1-7. Operation information

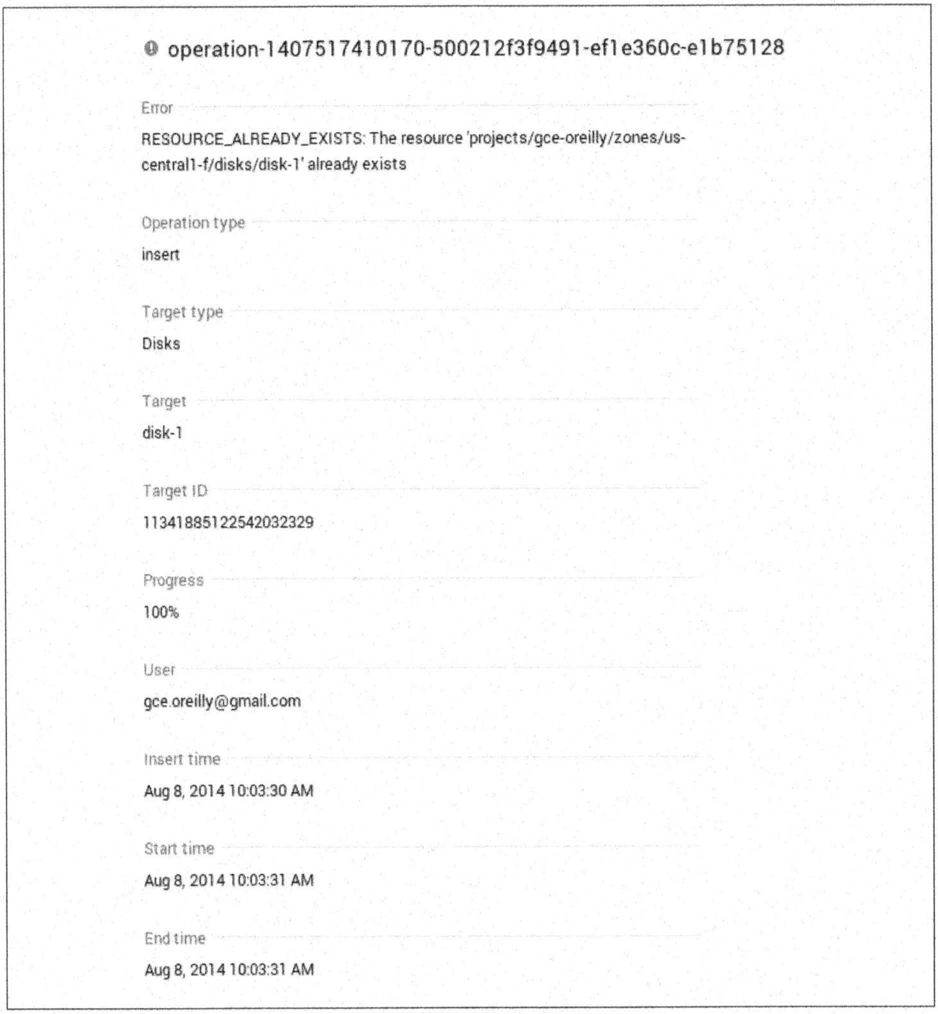

Figure 1-8. Operation information for an operation that failed

Quotas. The Quotas section provides a summary of the number of resources available for your project and the number of resources in use (see Figure 1-9).

Quotas Change request		
RESOURCE	USAGE	LIMIT
Snapshots	0	1000
Networks	3	5
Firewall rules	7	100
Images	1	100
Routes	6	100
Forwarding rules	1	50
Target pools	1	50
Health checks	1	50
Target instances	0	50
Region asia-east1		
CPUs	0	24
Total persistent disk reserved (GB)	0	5120
Static IP addresses	0	7
In-use IP addresses	0	23
SSD_TOTAL_GB	0	1024

Figure 1-9. Quotas tab in the Developers Console

The Change request link at the top of the page links to a form where you can request increased quota.

Cloud SDK

The Cloud SDK (*https://cloud.google.com/sdk/*) contains multiple tools and libraries that allow you to interact with Google Cloud Platform. For example, the Cloud SDK contains `gsutil`, a command-line tool for managing your Cloud Storage buckets and objects, and `bq`, a command-line tool for working with and querying your BigQuery datasets.

Similar to `gsutil` and `bq`, the Cloud SDK also contains a tool called `gcloud compute` that provides a command-line interface for managing your Compute Engine resources. Similar to the UI, `gcloud compute` allows you to start or stop instances, add or remove persistent disks, and create or destroy firewalls. gcloud compute is useful for learning how Compute Engine works and also for writing bash scripts to control your Compute Engine resources.

We'll use gcloud compute and gsutil throughout the remainder of this book, so let's take a look at how to download and install the Cloud SDK.

Install on Linux / Mac.   To download the Cloud SDK, run the following command from your shell or Terminal window:

```
$ curl https://sdk.cloud.google.com | bash
```

That's it! Restart your shell or Terminal. You can now use the tools provided in the Cloud SDK.

Install on Windows.   Download the Google Cloud SDK installer for Windows from here:

https://dl.google.com/dl/cloudsdk/release/GoogleCloudSDKInstaller.exe

Launch the downloaded *GoogleCloudSDKInstaller.exe* installer and follow the prompts.

When the installation finishes, open a command prompt (*cmd.exe*) or the Google Cloud SDK Shell from the Desktop or Start Menu to start using the tools provided in the Cloud SDK.

Authorize.   Once the SDK is downloaded and installed, you must go through the authorization flow in order to give the Cloud SDK access to your account. Use the gcloud auth login command to perform authorization:

```
$ gcloud auth login
```

The gcloud auth login command uses the OAuth 2.0 authorization flow to authorize your account to Google's Cloud services. You can revoke the credentials at any time using the gcloud auth revoke command, replacing <account> with the account name:

```
$ gcloud auth revoke <account>
```

Set the project ID.   After completing the authorization flow, make sure to enter the ID of your Cloud project using the following command:

```
$ gcloud config set project <project>
```

The *project ID* is equivalent to the project ID you entered when creating the project via the Developers Console. You can find the project ID in the Developers Console on the project list page under the PROJECT ID column. You will be using this project ID for exercises throughout the remainder of this book, so make sure to take note of its value.

Use gcloud compute.   Now that you have gone through the OAuth 2.0 flow and set the project ID, you can start using gcloud compute to access your Compute Engine resources. Let's start with a simple example. We'll use gcloud compute to retrieve information about our newly created project. Open a shell or Terminal window and run the following command:

```
$ gcloud compute project-info describe --format=json
```

The output will be similar to the following:

```
{
  "commonInstanceMetadata": {
    "fingerprint": "Arv4IW4Njmk=",
    "items": [
      {
        "key": "sshKeys",
        "value": "gce_oreilly..."
      }
    ],
    "kind": "compute#metadata"
  },
  "creationTimestamp": "2014-01-10T13:04:30.298-08:00",
  "description": "",
  "id": "83060252553764467278",
  "kind": "compute#project",
  "name": "gce-oreilly",
  "quotas": [
    {
      "limit": 1000.0,
      "metric": "SNAPSHOTS",
      "usage": 0.0
    },
    {
      "limit": 5.0,
      "metric": "NETWORKS",
      "usage": 3.0
    },
    {
      "limit": 100.0,
      "metric": "FIREWALLS",
      "usage": 7.0
    },
    {
      "limit": 100.0,
      "metric": "IMAGES",
      "usage": 1.0
    },
    {
```

```
      "limit": 100.0,
      "metric": "ROUTES",
      "usage": 6.0
    },
    {
      "limit": 50.0,
      "metric": "FORWARDING_RULES",
      "usage": 1.0
    },
    {
      "limit": 50.0,
      "metric": "TARGET_POOLS",
      "usage": 1.0
    },
    {
      "limit": 50.0,
      "metric": "HEALTH_CHECKS",
      "usage": 1.0
    },
    {
      "limit": 50.0,
      "metric": "TARGET_INSTANCES",
      "usage": 0.0
    }
  ],
  "selfLink": "https://www.googleapis.com/compute/v1/projects/gce-oreilly"
}
```

The output contains information about your Compute Engine project, including quotas and creation time. Because the --format flag was set to JSON, the results were printed as JSON. You can also specify a format of YAML or text.

gcloud compute has a comprehensive help library available that provides valuable information about its usage. To see the full list of available commands and their functions, run the gcloud compute command with the --help flag:

```
$ gcloud compute --help
```

We'll use gcloud compute throughout the remainder of this book to manage your Compute Engine resources, including starting and stopping instances, but first let's take a look at the Compute Engine API.

Compute Engine API

Compute Engine's API allows you to build a multitude of tools and applications to manage your Compute Engine resources. It provides an access point for integration with Cloud Management solutions, open source Cloud service libraries, and/or your own Cloud tooling libraries. In fact, both gcloud compute and the Compute Engine portion of the Developers Console are built using this API.

The Compute Engine API has a RESTful interface. HTTP requests are used to list, start, and stop instances, add firewalls and networks, and update instance metadata or tags. The base URL of the API is:

https://www.googleapis.com/compute/<version>/

A version of the API needs to be specified in the URL. As of the writing of this book, the current version is v1. The API version is subject to change with new releases. Check online for the latest version: *https://developers.google.com/compute/docs/refer ence/latest/*.

The Compute Engine API Compute Engine Resources are represented as JSON objects in the API. The keys and values of the JSON object provide information about the resource it represents. For example, the JSON object representing an instance contains fields for the machine type, zone, tags, and disks. Here's the structure of a full instance JSON object, along with the available fields and data type of each field:

```
{
  "kind": "compute#instance",
  "id": unsigned long,
  "creationTimestamp": string,
  "zone": string,
  "status": string,
  "statusMessage": string,
  "name": string,
  "description": string,
  "tags": {
    "items": [
      string
    ],
    "fingerprint": bytes
  },
  "machineType": string,
  "canIpForward": boolean,
  "networkInterfaces": [
    {
      "network": string,
      "networkIP": string,
      "name": string,
      "accessConfigs": [
        {
          "kind": "compute#accessConfig",
          "type": string,
          "name": string,
          "natIP": string
        }
      ]
    }
  ],
  "disks": [
    {
```

```
    "kind": "compute#attachedDisk",
    "index": integer,
    "type": string,
    "mode": string,
    "source": string,
    "deviceName": string,
    "boot": boolean,
    "initializeParams": {
      "diskName": string,
      "sourceImage": string,
      "diskSizeGb": long,
      "diskType": string
    },
    "autoDelete": boolean,
    "licenses": [
      string
    ]
  }
],
"metadata": {
  "kind": "compute#metadata",
  "fingerprint": bytes,
  "items": [
    {
      "key": string,
      "value": string
    }
  ]
},
"serviceAccounts": [
  {
    "email": string,
    "scopes": [
      string
    ]
  }
],
"selfLink": string,
"scheduling": {
  "onHostMaintenance": string,
  "automaticRestart": boolean
}
}
```

Using the API, your application can perform many actions on Compute Engine resources, such as inserting a new resource, listing the available resources within your project, updating a particular resource, or deleting a resource. There are also custom actions that can be performed on specific resources, such as adding a disk to an instance. These actions are performed via HTTP requests to the Compute Engine API. Each resource has its own unique URL to which HTTP requests are made to perform these actions.

There are two URL parameters to consider when making HTTP requests to interact with your Compute Engine resources. The first parameter is the project name. Because all Compute Engine resources are contained within a project, the project name must be specified in the URL. The URL syntax is as follows (substitute <project> with your project ID):

https://www.googleapis.com/compute/v1/projects/<project>

The second URL parameter is the hierarchical level (scope) at which the resource is available. As described earlier in this chapter, all Compute Engine resources are contained within one of three scopes: global, regional, and zonal. When making an HTTP request to the Compute Engine API to interact with your resources, the scope is specified in the URL. The URL syntax for global resources is as follows:

https://www.googleapis.com/compute/v1/projects/<project>/global

The URL for regional resources is as follows (substitute <region> with the name of the region in which the resource resides, for example, us-central1):

https://www.googleapis.com/compute/v1/projects/<project>/regions/<region>

The URL for zonal resources is as follows (substitute <zone> with the name of the zone in which the resource resides, for example, us-central1-a):

https://www.googleapis.com/compute/v1/projects/<project>/zones/<zone>

Let's take a look at the instance resource for an example of the types of HTTP requests that can be made using the API. Instances are a zonal resource, so the URL must be scoped according to the zone in which the instance resides or will reside. To work with instances in the zone us-central1-a owned by a project called my-compute-project, use the following URL endpoint:

https://www.googleapis.com/compute/v1/projects/my-compute-project/zones/us-central1-a/instances

To start a new instance in the project my-compute-project, issue a POST HTTP request to this URL, sending an Instance JSON resource as the body of the request. To list all instances in my-compute-project and running in zone us-central1-a, send a GET HTTP request to the same URL.

To perform actions on a specific instance, the instance name is appended to the end of the URL. For example, if we have an instance named my-instance, the URL endpoint would look as follows:

https://www.googleapis.com/compute/v1/projects/my-compute-project/zones/us-central1-a/instances/my-instance

To retrieve the JSON document representing the VM named "my-instance," send a GET HTTP request to this URL. To destroy the VM named "my-instance," send a DELETE HTTP request to the same URL.

So far, we've been using standard HTTP methods to perform actions on Compute Engine instances. Some resources have custom actions that require the addition of the method (i.e., verb) to the end of the resource URL. As an example, attaching a disk to an instance requires a custom verb called attachDisk. The URL for this action is as follows (using my-instance as our example):

https://www.googleapis.com/compute/v1/projects/my-compute-project/zones/us-central1-a/instances/my-instance/attachDisk

A POST HTTP request is made to this URL with a Disk JSON resource sent as the body of the request.

You can find a full API reference for all Compute Engine resources within the online documentation: *https://developers.google.com/compute/docs/reference/latest/*. You can also test out the API online using the Google APIs Explorer: *https://develop ers.google.com/apis-explorer/#p/compute/v1/*.

Authorization.   Authorization is required when interacting with Compute Engine resources via the API. The Compute Engine API uses OAuth 2.0 for authorization, which is the standard authorization mechanism used by most Google APIs. At its most basic level, OAuth 2.0 provides an access token to your application so it can access your or your users' Compute Engine resources. The access token is obtained via the OAuth "flow." The general steps of the flow vary according to the type of application you're building. Application types include client side (JavaScript), installed (such as an Android app or command-line interface), or server to server.

Let's take a look at the OAuth 2.0 flow for installed applications, as the majority of the samples in this book are installed apps. The basic steps for this type of OAuth flow are as follows:

1. A user accesses your application.
2. Your application redirects the user to the Google Authorization Server via a web browser, sending a variety of parameters along with the request. These parameters include:
   a. A client ID, which the application uses to identify itself to Google, and
   b. The scope(s), which indicate(s) what API and what level of access is being requested (most frequently either read or read/write).
3. The Google Authorization Server prompts the user to first log in (if not already logged in) and then asks the user to grant your application access to their Compute Engine resources.

4. When access is granted, the Google Authorization Server provides your application with an authorization code.

5. The application exchanges the authorization code for an access token by sending an HTTP request to the Google Authorization Server. Parameters for this request include:

   a. The authorization code obtained in step 4,

   b. The client ID, and

   c. The client secret, which is a secret string shared between your application and Google that proves your application is allowed to make requests on behalf of the user (make sure to keep the secret a secret!).

6. The access token acquired in step 5 is then sent as an `Authorization: Bearer` HTTP header when making Compute Engine API calls.

7. The access token is short-lived. Once expired, the user will have to go through steps 1–4 again. If long-term access is required without user intervention, a refresh token can also be retrieved from the Google Authorization Server. The refresh token lasts indefinitely (until revoked by the user) and can be used to programmatically request new access tokens from the Authorization Server.

Notice that a client ID and secret are required for requests that your application sends to the Google Authorization Server. Let's create a client ID and secret now, which you will use for the samples in this book.

Point your browser to the Developers Console URL:

http://console.developers.google.com

Select your project from the list. In the lefthand navigation, expand the APIS & AUTH section, and select Credentials from the list. The Credentials section of the Developers Console displays all client IDs and API keys that have been created for your project (see Figure 1-10).

Figure 1-10. Credentials section of the Developers Console

Create a new client ID by clicking the "Create new Client ID" button. A dialog box will open with several options that reflect the type of application you're building (see Figure 1-11).

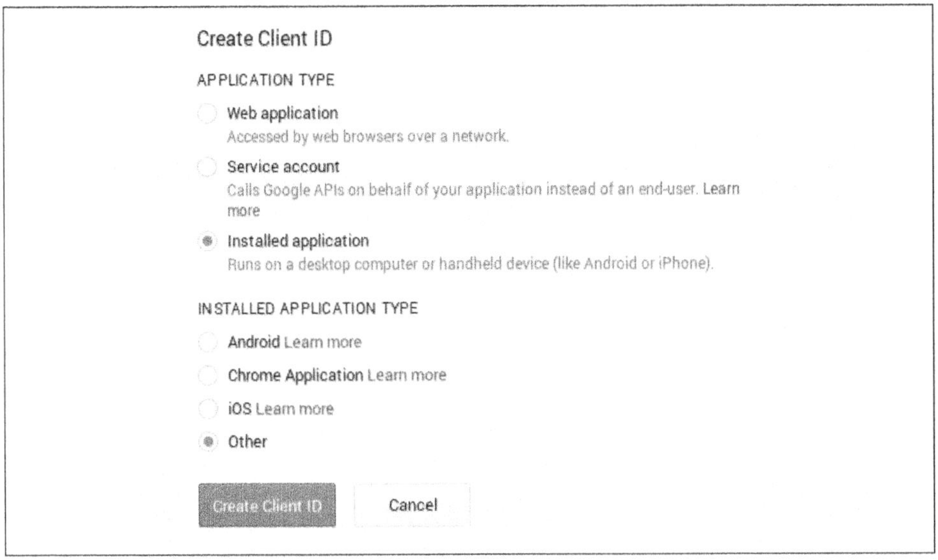

Create Client ID

APPLICATION TYPE

○ Web application
Accessed by web browsers over a network.

○ Service account
Calls Google APIs on behalf of your application instead of an end-user. Learn more

◉ Installed application
Runs on a desktop computer or handheld device (like Android or iPhone).

INSTALLED APPLICATION TYPE

○ Android Learn more

○ Chrome Application Learn more

○ iOS Learn more

◉ Other

[Create Client ID]   Cancel

Figure 1-11. Create client ID dialog box

Select "Installed application" from the list of Application Types and Other from the list of Installed Application Types. Click the Create Client ID button. A new client ID for a native application will show up in your list of OAuth Client IDs.

Because this client ID will be used in the samples throughout this book, let's download the associated JSON file. To do so, click the Download JSON button, and then rename the downloaded file to *client_secret.json*. The downloaded file contains a JSON dictionary with your client ID, secret, redirect URIs, and some other OAuth 2.0 information. The JSON dictionary is structured so that can be used directly with Google's API Client Libraries, which will be discussed in the next sections.

There's a lot more information about OAuth 2.0 that will not be covered in this book, including different OAuth 2.0 flows and service accounts. See the online documentation to learn more: *https://developers.google.com/accounts/docs/OAuth2* or check out Ryan Boyd's book *Getting Started with OAuth 2.0* (ISBN: 9781449311605, *http://shop.oreilly.com/product/0636920021810.do*).

Google API libraries. Google has developed a convenient set of libraries that simplify both the OAuth 2.0 flow and the HTTP requests to all of Google's APIs, including the Compute Engine API. The libraries are available in a variety of languages, such as Java, Python, JavaScript, and Ruby. The libraries are available from the Google APIs

Client Library page in the Compute Engine online documentation (*https://develop ers.google.com/compute/docs/api/libraries*).

My first Compute Engine application.   Let's take a look at how to use the Python Google API Client Library to make an HTTP request to the Compute Engine API to retrieve information about your project.

Python is normally natively available on Linux and Mac OS X systems, but Microsoft Windows users will need to download and install the Python interpreter (from *http://www.python.org*) before running the Python code samples throughout this book.

For the first part of this exercise, we'll review and run the code in the *ch1-1.py* file in the gce-oreilly GitHub repository (*https://github.com/GoogleCloudPlatform/gce- oreilly/blob/master/ch1-1.py*). Get a copy of this file however you like, and then make sure to copy your *client_secret.json* file to the same directory.

All the code samples in this book are available online in the GoogleCloudPlatform gce-oreilly GitHub repository: *https:// github.com/GoogleCloudPlatform/gce-oreilly*. You can download the entire repository using the URL *https://github.com/GoogleCloudPlat form/gce-oreilly/archive/master.zip*.

As mentioned earlier in this chapter, OAuth 2.0 authorization is required for your application to gain access to your user's Compute Engine resources. To run through the OAuth 2.0 flow, we start by defining the path to the *client_secret.json* file. An OAuth 2.0 flow is then created using the client secret file, a list of scopes, and a message to display if the client secret file is missing:

```
# CLIENT_SECRET is the name of a file containing the OAuth 2.0 information
# for this application, including client_id and client_secret.
CLIENT_SECRET = os.path.join(os.path.dirname(__file__), 'client_secret.json')

# Set up a Flow object to be used for authentication. PLEASE ONLY
# ADD THE SCOPES YOU NEED. For more information on using scopes please
# see <https://developers.google.com/compute/docs/api/how-tos/authorization>.
FLOW = client.flow_from_clientsecrets(
    CLIENT_SECRET,
    scope=['https://www.googleapis.com/auth/compute'],
    message=tools.message_if_missing(CLIENT_SECRET))
```

The following lines of code run through the previously defined flow and store the resulting OAuth 2.0 credentials, including the access token, in a local file called *sample.dat*:

```
# If the credentials don't exist or are invalid run through the native client
# flow. The Storage object will ensure that if successful the good
```

```
# credentials will get written back to the file.
storage = file.Storage('sample.dat')
credentials = storage.get()
if credentials is None or credentials.invalid:
  credentials = tools.run_flow(FLOW, storage, flags)
```

The credentials are used to authorize an `httplib2.Http` object. An authorized `httplib2.Http` object applies the access token to the HTTP requests as an `Authorization: Bearer` HTTP header:

```
# Create an httplib2.Http object to handle our HTTP requests and authorize it
# with our Credentials.
http = httplib2.Http()
http = credentials.authorize(http)
```

After authorization, a service object is created by passing in the name of the Google API we want to use ("compute," in our case), the version of the API (currently "v1"), and the authorized httplib2.Http instance. The service object uses the authorized httplib2.Http instance to make HTTP requests to the Compute Engine API. You use this service object to perform various actions on your Compute Engine resources:

```
# Construct the service object for the interacting with the
# Compute Engine API.
service = discovery.build('compute', 'v1', http=http)
```

Now try running the *ch1-1.py* file from a shell or Terminal window as follows:

```
$ python ch1-1.py
```

You should see a web browser pop up, prompting you to authorize this sample app to access your Compute Engine resources. Return to the shell or Terminal window. You should see, "Success! Now add code here." printed on the screen.

Congratulations! You now have a working skeleton app, which handles OAuth 2.0 authorization and provides access to the Compute Engine API.

Let's make this script do something a bit more interesting. You can start with the complete code in the gce-oreilly GitHub repository (*https://github.com/GoogleCloud Platform/gce-oreilly/blob/master/ch1-2.py*). If you prefer to do some typing, copy *ch1-1.py* and rename it as *ch1-2.py*. Open the *ch1-2.py* source file using your favorite text editor and comment out this line (by prepending the line with the Python comment character #):

```
# print 'Success! Now add code here.'
```

Insert the following code directly below the commented-out `print` statement making sure to preserve indentation consistently with the containing file:

```
PROJECT_ID = 'your-project-id'
# Build a request to get the specified project using the Compute Engine API.
request = service.projects().get(project=PROJECT_ID)

try:
  # Execute the request and store the response.
  response = request.execute()
except Exception, ex:
  print 'ERROR: ' + str(ex)
  sys.exit()

# Print the response.
print response
```

Whether you downloaded the complete code from GitHub or manually typed it, substitute your project ID for the string your-project-id. Run the sample app from a shell or Terminal window using the command:

```
$ python ch1-2.py
```

The result should look something like the following (pretty-printed here for legibility):

```
{
  u'kind': u'compute#project',
  u'description': u'',
  u'commonInstanceMetadata': {u'kind': u'compute#metadata'},
  u'quotas': [
    {u'usage': 0.0, u'metric': u'SNAPSHOTS', u'limit': 1000.0},
    {u'usage': 1.0, u'metric': u'NETWORKS', u'limit': 5.0},
    {u'usage': 2.0, u'metric': u'FIREWALLS', u'limit': 100.0},
    {u'usage': 0.0, u'metric': u'IMAGES', u'limit': 100.0},
    {u'usage': 2.0, u'metric': u'ROUTES', u'limit': 100.0},
    {u'usage': 0.0, u'metric': u'FORWARDING_RULES', u'limit': 50.0},
    {u'usage': 0.0, u'metric': u'TARGET_POOLS', u'limit': 50.0},
    {u'usage': 0.0, u'metric': u'HEALTH_CHECKS', u'limit': 50.0},
    {u'usage': 0.0, u'metric': u'TARGET_INSTANCES', u'limit': 50.0}],
  u'creationTimestamp': u'2013-10-28T10:54:02.016-07:00',
  u'id': u'8306025255376467278',
  u'selfLink': u'https://www.googleapis.com/compute/v1/projects/gce-oreilly',
  u'name': u'gce-oreilly'
}
```

Let's take a look at what the code is doing. In the following line:

```
request = service.projects().get(project=PROJECT_ID)
```

the service object generates an `apiclient.http.HttpRequest` object, which is used to make calls to the Compute Engine API. The `apiclient.http.HttpRequest` object is created by first specifying the resource we want to access (in this case, "projects"), then specifying what action to perform on that resource (in this case, "get"). We pass in any parameters required for this request (in this case, the project ID).

 To find the list of all available resources and methods, check out the Compute Engine API in the Google APIs Explorer: *https://devel opers.google.com/apis-explorer/#p/compute/v1/*. Clicking any of the methods in the list displays what parameters are available for that particular action.

Our `apiclient.http.HttpRequest` object makes the HTTP GET request to the project URL[2] using the execute method:

```
response = request.execute()
```

The response returned from the Compute Engine API consists of the Project JSON resource.

Congratulations! You now have a working Compute Engine app.

Summary

In this chapter, you set up all the components required to start working with Compute Engine: you created a Compute Engine project using the Google Developers Console and enabled billing on the project. You also learned how to manage Compute Engine's resources using the console, `gcloud compute`, and the API.

Up Next

In the next chapter, you will start working with Compute Engine's VMs.

---

2 The Compute Center API details, including resource URLs, query parameters, and JSON elements are all documented online at *https://developers.google.com/compute/docs/api/getting-started*.

## CHAPTER 2

Instances

The core capability provided by Google Compute Engine is an *instance*, also called a *virtual machine* (VM). An instance is a simulated computer, running in a partitioned environment on a real server in one of Google's data centers. From the user's point of view, an instance behaves like a dedicated physical computer, with its own operating system, storage devices, network adapters, and so on.

Virtualization is the process of mapping a virtual machine's environment and resources onto services provided by real hardware. The software managing the virtualization service is called a *hypervisor* or *virtual machine manager*. There are many popular virtualization systems in use today. Google Compute Engine uses the Linux Kernel-based Virtual Machine (KVM) software.

The KVM hypervisor runs in a standard Linux environment, which means that virtualized and nonvirtualized workloads can run side by side on the same physical hardware. This eliminates the need to manage a separate pool of resources dedicated to the Compute Engine product—the same hardware and software stack used to serve Google search, Gmail, Maps, and other Google services can also provide Compute Engine virtual machines.

In this chapter, we'll learn about Compute Engine instances and their attributes. Along the way, we'll learn how to create, access, and delete instances via three different access modes:

- The Developers Console Web UI
- The gcloud command-line tool
- The Google Python client library

In the gcloud command-line tool section, we'll include a summary of attributes you can configure and inspect when creating your own virtual machines.

Creating an Instance Using the Developers Console

Compute Engine instances can be created using any of the access mechanisms described in the previous chapter. You can use the Developers Console Web UI, which gives you a browser-based interface for creating and managing instances. The gcloud tool gives you a powerful command-line interface to manage your infrastructure. And the Compute Engine API gives you the ability to programmatically manage your computing resources.

Let's create an instance now using the Google Developers Console. Point your web browser to the following URL: *http://console.developers.google.com/*. You'll be greeted by a list of your projects, as shown in Figure 2-1.

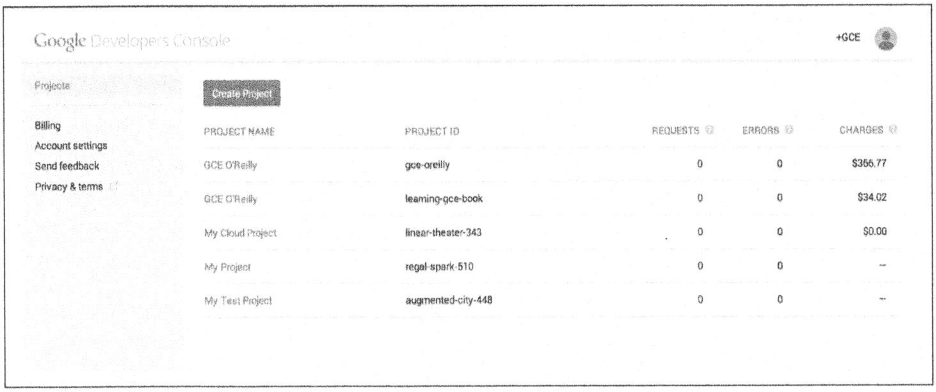

Figure 2-1. Google Developers Console—project selection

Click a project for which you've enabled Compute Engine. You'll then see a dashboard-like page, which should look similar to Figure 2-2.

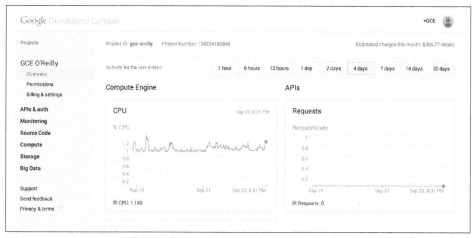

Figure 2-2. Google Developers Console—selected project

Now click the Compute->Compute Engine service, from the lefthand navigation list, to administer your virtual machines and other Compute Engine resources.

The screenshot shown in Figure 2-3 illustrates the VM Instances tab, which shows you all instances currently active in any state in your project, along with a summary of the most useful information about each instance:

Name
> The name given to the instance when it was created

Zone
> The location in which the instance is situated

Disk
> The name of the instance's boot persistent disk (we'll cover persistent disks in Chapter 3, but for now just think of this as the instance's boot drive)

Network
> The name of the virtual network associated with the instance

External IP
> The instance's externally accessible IP address

Connect
> Provides three ways to remotely log in to the instance

Later in this chapter, we'll describe these and other instance attributes in more detail.

Figure 2-3. Google Developers Console—Compute Engine Instances tab

From the Compute Engine VM Instances tab, you can press the "New instance" button to create a new virtual machine. Figure 2-4 illustrates the new instance dialog.

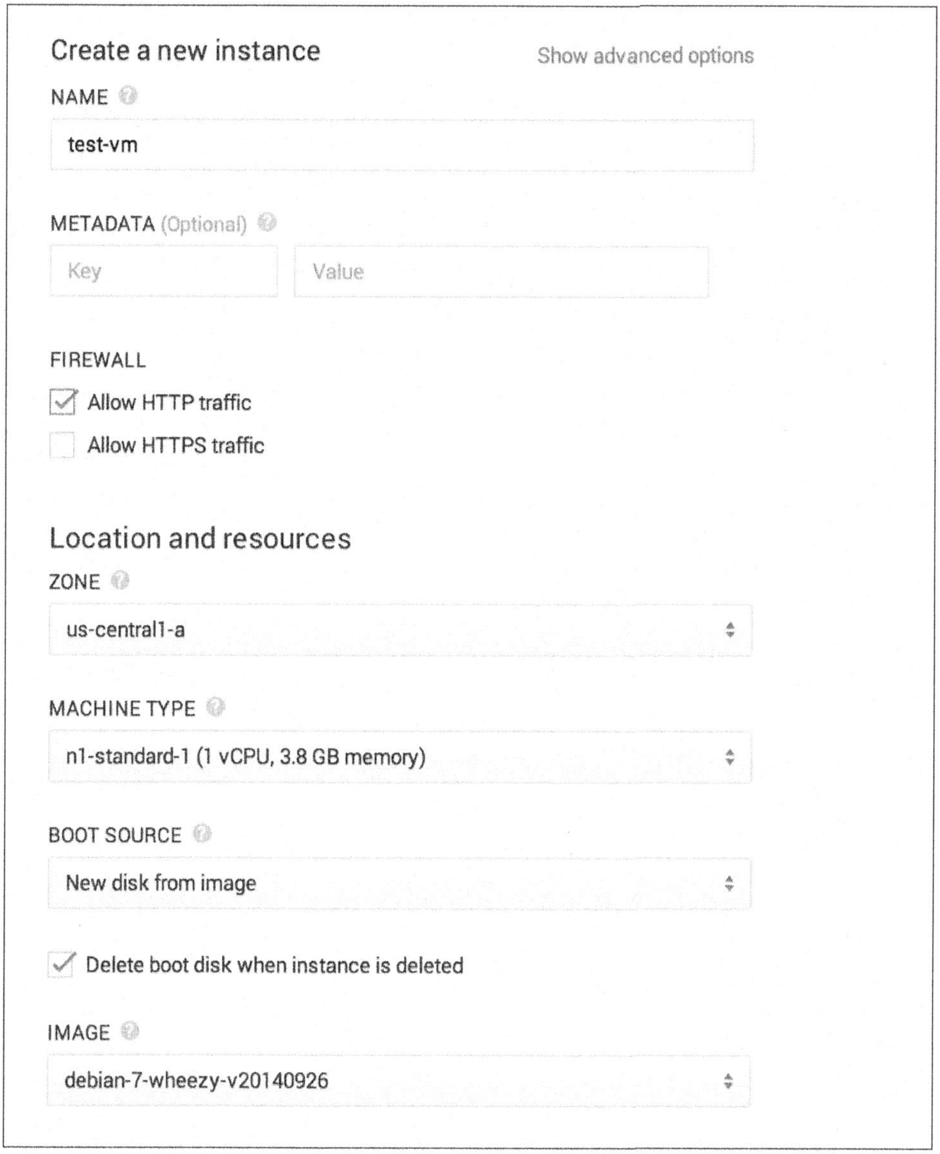

Create a new instance

Show advanced options

NAME

> test-vm

METADATA (Optional)

Key	Value

FIREWALL

☑ Allow HTTP traffic

☐ Allow HTTPS traffic

Location and resources

ZONE

> us-central1-a   ↕

MACHINE TYPE

> n1-standard-1 (1 vCPU, 3.8 GB memory)   ↕

BOOT SOURCE

> New disk from image   ↕

☑ Delete boot disk when instance is deleted

IMAGE

> debian-7-wheezy-v20140926   ↕

Figure 2-4. Google Developers Console—new instance

In Figure 2-4, we're setting the new instance name to test-vm, selecting zone us-central1-a, machine type n1-standard-1, image debian-7-wheezy-v20140926, and we're taking defaults for the remaining options.

Do you see the "Equivalent REST or command line" links underneath the Create and Cancel buttons? Try clicking on the REST button—it opens a pop-up window containing the JSON document you'd want to send via the RESTful HTTP interface to create the same instance. Now close that window and click the "command line" link. It opens a pop-up window containing the gcloud command-line syntax to achieve the same result. You can use these links to generate or cross-check the syntax required to build the equivalent request via the API or the gcloud command, respectively. We'll cover the gcloud command and API access later in this chapter.

Using the Developers Console, we have the same set of input specifications available that we have via the command line and the programmatic API, and we can override defaults for any of the instance attributes. If we now click the Create button, our instance will be created and we are returned to the VM Instances page, with an indication that our new VM is in the process of being created. Within several seconds, our VM creation will be completed and the instances summary will then include our new VM.

Accessing an Instance Using the Developers Console

To remotely log in to a Compute Engine instance from the instance summary page, click the instance you'd like to access, which takes you to a page providing a summary of the instance's attributes. Along the top of the page you should see four buttons: SSH, Reboot, Clone, and Delete, as shown in Figure 2-5.

Figure 2-5. Google Developers Console—accessing an instance

Click the SSH button to create an in-browser SSH session to your virtual machine in a new window, like the one shown in Figure 2-6.

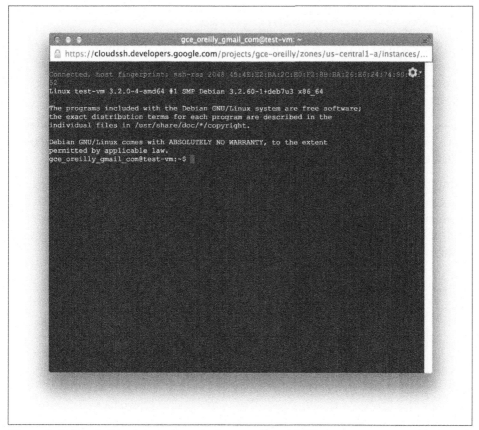

Figure 2-6. Google Developers Console-browser-based SSH access

Deleting an Instance Using the Developers Console

To delete a Compute Engine instance, from the instance summary page, click the instance you'd like to delete, which takes you to a page providing a summary of the instance's attributes. Along the top of the page, you should see four buttons: SSH, Reboot, Clone, and Delete, as shown in Figure 2-5 in the previous section.

Clicking the Delete button presents a dialog confirming you'd like to also delete the associated persistent disk (more on PDs in Chapter 3). Clicking the Delete button on that dialog launches the instance delete request, leaving you back on the instance summary page. After a few seconds, the deleted instance (and its associated boot disk, if you so requested) will disappear.

Creating an Instance Using gcloud

We've just walked through a sequence of steps that illustrated how to use the Developers Console to create, access, and delete a virtual machine. In this section, we'll use the gcloud command, which provides a command-line interface to Compute Engine resources, to create, access, and delete a virtual machine.

Choose a name for your virtual machine (I'll call mine test-vm). The name you select exists within the scope of your project, so you are free to choose any name you like, even if that name is already in use by instances in other projects.

From the computer on which you installed and configured gcloud in Chapter 1, run the command gcloud compute instances create <instance-name>. You'll be prompted for a zone, and you'll inherit a default machine type and image. We'll explain those attributes later in this section, but for now, you can follow the transcript in this example:

```
$ gcloud compute instances create test-vm
For the following instances:
 - [test-vm]
choose a zone:
 [1] asia-east1-b
 [2] asia-east1-c
 [3] asia-east1-a
 [4] europe-west1-b
 [5] europe-west1-a
 [6] us-central1-a
 [7] us-central1-f
 [8] us-central1-b
Please enter your numeric choice:  6
Created     [https://www.googleapis.com/compute/v1/projects/gce-oreilly/zones/us-
central1-a/instances/test-vm].
NAME       ZONE          MACHINE_TYPE INTERNAL_IP    EXTERNAL_IP
test-vm us-central1-a n1-standard-1 10.240.232.130 146.148.NNN.NNN
```

You can provide multiple instance names to the gcloud compute instances create command, which can be useful for creating a collection of virtual machines with one command. The bash {x..y} syntax provides a handy way to take advantage of this capability. For example, you could request the creation of 100 instances with this one command:

```
$ gcloud compute instances create vm-{1..100}\
--zone=us-central1-a
```

We've specified the desired zone to use for these instances, to avoid being prompted for that information 100 times.

Now that we've created a virtual machine, we might like to verify the Compute Engine service has a record of our new instance. We might also like to find out more information about this resource. For example, which image was used to create this instance? In which zone was this instance created? We can verify our new VM's existence and request information about its configuration data and current state using the `gcloud compute instances describe` command. Try running that command now, using your own instance name, adding your zone via the `--zone` option, and including the `--format text` option to obtain human readable output, like this:

```
$ gcloud compute instances describe test-vm --zone us-central1-a --format text
canIpForward:                                 False
creationTimestamp:                            2014-09-24T02:43:02.629-07:00
disks[0].autoDelete:                          True
disks[0].boot:                                True
disks[0].deviceName:                          persistent-disk-0
disks[0].index:                               0
disks[0].kind:                                compute#attachedDisk
disks[0].mode:                                READ_WRITE
disks[0].source:
https://www.googleapis.com/compute/v1/projects/gce-oreilly/zones/us-central1-
a/disks/test-vm
disks[0].type:                                PERSISTENT
id:                                           17946628611305723276
kind:                                         compute#instance
machineType:
https://www.googleapis.com/compute/v1/projects/gce-oreilly/zones/us-
central1-a/machineTypes/n1-standard-1
metadata.fingerprint:                         TQN1cUHvpQg=
metadata.kind:                                compute#metadata
name:                                         test-vm
networkInterfaces[0].accessConfigs[0].kind:   compute#accessConfig
networkInterfaces[0].accessConfigs[0].name:   external-nat
networkInterfaces[0].accessConfigs[0].natIP:  146.148.NNN.NNN
networkInterfaces[0].accessConfigs[0].type:   ONE_TO_ONE_NAT
networkInterfaces[0].name:                    nic0
networkInterfaces[0].network:
https://www.googleapis.com/compute/v1/projects/gce-
oreilly/global/networks/default
networkInterfaces[0].networkIP:               10.240.42.89
scheduling.automaticRestart:                  True
scheduling.onHostMaintenance:                 MIGRATE
selfLink:
https://www.googleapis.com/compute/v1/projects/gce-oreilly/zones/us-central1-
a/instances/test-vm
serviceAccounts[0].email:
134224180845@developer.gserviceaccount.com
serviceAccounts[0].scopes[0]:
https://www.googleapis.com/auth/devstorage.read_only
status:                                       RUNNING
tags.fingerprint:                             42WmSpB8rSM=
```

```
zone:
     https://www.googleapis.com/compute/v1/projects/gce-oreilly/zones/us-central1-a
```

The output of this command verifies the existence of our new virtual machine and provides lots of additional information, such as the creation time, the machine type, the image with which the instance was created, the requested zone, and the current state of the VM (RUNNING, in this example). We also see information about our virtual machine's storage and networking capabilities, which we'll discuss in later chapters.

Another way to verify your new instance is to use the `gcloud compute instances list` command. This command provides a list of all the virtual machines that exist in your project, along with a summary of their states, internal and external IP addresses, and the zones in which they reside. Try running that command now:

```
$ gcloud compute instances list
NAME        ZONE          MACHINE_TYPE  INTERNAL_IP     EXTERNAL_IP  STATUS
[..]
apache      us-central1-a n1-standard-1 10.240.213.178 [..]         RUNNING
test-vm     us-central1-a n1-standard-1 10.240.42.89   [..]         RUNNING
startup-2   us-central1-a n1-standard-1 10.240.224.180 [..]         RUNNING
[..]
```

This output shows I have several instances, including the newly created `test-vm`, all of which are in the RUNNING state, have machine type `n1-standard-1`, and reside in zone `us-central1-a`, along with each instance's internal and external IP addresses.

Instance Attributes

When we created an instance, we were given the opportunity to specify the new instance's zone. This is an example of an instance attribute, which defines a virtual machine's configuration and state. In this section, we'll explain instances attributes and how they affect virtual machine behavior.

States

At any given time, an instance will be in one (and only one) of the following states:

PROVISIONING
  Resources are being allocated and initialized to serve your VM.

STAGING
  Your chosen image and associated resources are being loaded and activated.

RUNNING
  Your virtual machine is active. Note that a VM in the RUNNING state could be booting or shutting down the guest operating system, so a state of RUNNING doesn't necessarily guarantee the operating system and application software is accessible at that instant.

STOPPING
> Your VM is in the process of shutting down. This is a transient, short-lived state.

TERMINATED
> Your VM has been shut down or failed for some reason (e.g., kernel panic or zone entered a scheduled maintenance event and your instance was not automatically migrated).

Machine types

Compute Engine provides support for several machine types. Machine types provide predefined sets of configuration options, including:

Virtual CPUs (cores)
> 1, 2, 4, 8, or 16

Virtual RAM (main memory)
> 3.75 GB per CPU (n1-standard-* machines only)

Machine types fall into several broad categories:

Standard
> A balanced combination of processing power and memory, well suited to general-purpose tasks

High memory
> Optimized for memory capacity relative to processing power

High CPU
> Optimized for processing power relative to memory capacity

Shared core
> More economical, smaller configurations

You can find the currently supported list of machine types, along with a detailed description of each, in the online Compute Engine documentation (*http://goo.gl/815PWP*) (see *http://goo.gl/815PWP*).

The gcloud compute machine-types list command can be used to display a table of the currently supported machine types and associated attributes, as shown here:

```
$ gcloud compute machine-types list
NAME              ZONE           CPUS MEMORY_GB DEPRECATED
[..]
g1-small          us-central1-a  1       1.70
n1-highmem-4      us-central1-a  4      26.00
n1-standard-2     us-central1-a  2       7.50
n1-highmem-2      us-central1-a  2      13.00
n1-standard-1     us-central1-a  1       3.75
n1-highmem-8      us-central1-a  8      52.00
n1-highcpu-2      us-central1-a  2       1.80
n1-highcpu-16     us-central1-a  16     14.40
f1-micro          us-central1-a  1       0.60
n1-standard-16    us-central1-a  16     60.00
n1-highcpu-4      us-central1-a  4       3.60
n1-highmem-16     us-central1-a  16    104.00
n1-standard-8     us-central1-a  8      30.00
n1-standard-4     us-central1-a  4      15.00
n1-highcpu-8      us-central1-a  8       7.20
[..]
```

Images

The base software for a hosted virtual machine, including the operating system and all associated system and application software (libraries, commands, etc.), is called an *image*. Several standard images are supported natively by Compute Engine. Within those categories, several versioned images are available. You can also create your own custom images, building on one of the default images (we'll cover the details of how to generate a custom image in Chapter 7).

You can list both the system provided images and your own custom images using the gcloud compute images list command, like this:

```
$ gcloud compute images list
NAME                            PROJECT        ALIAS     DEPRECATED STATUS
centos-6-v20140718              centos-cloud   centos-6             READY
centos-7-v20140903              centos-cloud   centos-7             READY
coreos-alpha-444-0-0-v20140919  coreos-cloud                       READY
coreos-beta-440-0-0-v20140918   coreos-cloud                       READY
coreos-stable-410-0-0-v20140902 coreos-cloud   coreos              READY
backports-debian-7-wheezy-[..]  debian-cloud   debian-7-[..]       READY
debian-7-wheezy-v20140828       debian-cloud   debian-7            READY
opensuse-13-1-v[..]             opensuse-cloud opensuse-13         READY
rhel-6-v20140718                rhel-cloud     rhel-6              READY
sles-11-sp3-v20140826           suse-cloud     sles-11             READY
```

The list of supported Compute Engine images is likely to change over time, so this command output should be taken as an example, rather than an authoritative source. Occasionally, you may find an image marked DEPRECATED. That means that it has been given an end-of-life date and further use is discouraged. One of the newer images should be preferred over deprecated images.

Regions and zones

Compute Engine divides the world into regions and zones. A zone corresponds to a physical data center (or a portion thereof), and a region represents a collection of zones located within a large geographic area, like the US Central region. The lowest network latency between instances is achieved by VMs communicating within a zone. VMs communicating across zones within a particular region will experience slightly higher average latency than VMs within a zone. Still higher latencies will be experienced by VMs communicating across regions.

The gcloud compute regions list command can be used to display a list of the currently supported regions along with their associated attributes:

```
$ gcloud compute regions list
NAME          CPUS         DISKS_GB  ADDRESSES  RESERVED_ADDRESSES  STATUS
asia-east1    0.00/24.00   0/5120    0/23       0/7                 UP
europe-west1  0.00/24.00   0/5120    0/23       0/7                 UP
us-central1   13.00/24.00  630/5120  14/23      1/7                 UP
```

The gcloud compute zones list command can be used to display a list of the currently supported zones along with their associated region and status:

```
$ gcloud compute zones list
NAME           REGION        STATUS NEXT_MAINTENANCE
asia-east1-b   asia-east1    UP
asia-east1-c   asia-east1    UP
asia-east1-a   asia-east1    UP
europe-west1-b europe-west1  UP
europe-west1-a europe-west1  UP
us-central1-a  us-central1   UP
us-central1-f  us-central1   UP
us-central1-b  us-central1   UP
```

Along with each zone's current status, you can see an indication of the next planned maintenance window for each zone. If a maintenance window is scheduled, you'll see the date and time here; otherwise you'll see nothing displayed, which indicates the zone is free of scheduled maintenance events.

Service account scopes

When you enable Compute Engine for your project, the Google Developers Console automatically creates a special account for you called a service account. Unlike your personal Gmail account (or your business account, if your company uses Google Apps for Business), a service account embodies an application identity, rather than a person's identity. Your application can use service account credentials to access Google Cloud Platform resources without requiring an individual's account credentials.

When your instance is created, it comes with built-in capabilities that make it easy to access Google Cloud Platform resources using your assigned service account. An example will help clarify how this works. When you create a virtual machine, you can optionally specify one or more scopes to apply to your service account. Let's create an instance without specifying any service account scope and see what happens. Using `gcloud compute instances create`, create a new virtual machine with no specific service account scope:

```
$ gcloud compute instances create serv-acct-none
```

Follow the prompts to select a zone. Once the virtual machine is ready, use the following command to log in to your new VM:

```
$ gcloud compute ssh serv-acct-none
    :
serv-acct-none$
```

The text up to and including the dollar sign is your shell prompt. It confirms the hostname of the virtual machine you're logged into (`serv-acct-none` in this example). Now, while logged into your new instance, try running the `gcloud compute instances list` command:

```
serv-acct-none$ gcloud compute instances list
ERROR: (gcloud.compute.instances.list) Some requests did not succeed:
 - Insufficient Permission
```

This command failed, just as it would if you ran it on another machine with an unauthorized account. Of course, you can complete the authorization sequence in the same way you did in Chapter 1 when you first set up the `gcloud` command, but there's a much easier way.

Create another instance, but this time add the option `--scopes compute-rw` to your command, like this:

```
$ gcloud compute instances create serv-acct-gce --scopes compute-rw
```

This tells Compute Engine to create an instance named `serv-acct-gce`, with service account scope `compute-rw` (read/write access to the Compute Engine service). As before, follow the prompt to select a preferred zone. Once the virtual machine is ready, log in to your VM using the following command:

```
$ gcloud compute ssh serv-acct-gce
    :
serv-acct-gce$
```

The shell prompt confirms you're now logged into the `serv-acct-gce` instance. Now, while logged into this instance, try running the `gcloud compute instances list` command again:

```
marccohen@serv-acct-gce:~$ gcloud compute instances list
NAME         ZONE      MACHINE_TYPE INTERNAL_IP EXTERNAL_IP  STATUS
[..]
serv-ac[..] us-ce[..] n1-standard-1 10.[..]211  146.[..]204 RUNNING
serv-ac[..] us-ce[..] n1-standard-1 10.[..]167   23.[..]123 RUNNING
[..]
```

Notice the difference: this time around, the gcloud compute instances list command worked without requiring you to execute the manual authorization process. The command worked as expected because you created this instance with a service account scope providing access to your Compute Engine project.

This feature provides a very convenient set of functionality—you can now access all Compute Engine services from any instance you create with the compute-rw scope. For example, you can create and destroy instances from an existing virtual machine. But it's even more powerful than that: by adding additional service account scopes, you can give your instances access to a wide variety of Google services.

Each service account scope has a short alias name and a full URI-formatted name. The short names are most convenient to use, so we'll use them here. Refer to the online Compute Engine documentation (*http://goo.gl/wnNGFg*) (*http://goo.gl/wnNGFg*) for more details about these scopes, including the full name for each. At the time of this writing, the following scopes are supported and may be specified via the --scopes option:

Google Cloud Platform service	Shorthand name for scope
BigQuery	bigquery
Cloud SQL	sql
Cloud SQ (admin)	sql-admin
Compute Engine (read-only)	compute-ro
Compute Engine (read-write)	compute-rw
Cloud Storage (read-only)	storage-ro
Cloud Storage (read-write)	storage-rw
Cloud Storage (full)	storage-full
Datastore	datastore
App Engine Task Queue	taskqueue

You can get a list of currently supported scopes via the gcloud compute instances create --help command.

Service account scopes can also be specified via the other mechanisms available to create instances. And you can specify any combination of supported service account scopes to give your virtual machines access to any number of Google services.

External IP address. By default, your instances are dynamically allocated an external IP address at creation time. Unless you're using a static IP address, when you re-instantiate an instance, your VM is not guaranteed to have the same external IP address it had in a former incarnation. If your project has one or more static IP addresses allocated, then you may circumvent this rule by explicitly specifying a static IP address at instance creation time. We'll cover IP address allocation and related features in Chapter 6.

Metadata. You can think of instance metadata as a distributed key/value data store built into the fabric of Compute Engine. It's a powerful mechanism for propagating configuration or status data and for synchronizing behavior throughout a cluster of related virtual machines. We'll share more information and examples of instance and project metadata usage in Chapter 7.

Tags. Tags are mnemonic names you can apply to one or more virtual machines. Doing so gives you a convenient way to address a group of machines collectively. For example, you could configure a group of virtual machines into a MapReduce cluster and give all VMs the tag "mapreduce." From that point forward, you can use the map-reduce tag to refer to that subgroup of VMs in your network configuration.

Accessing an Instance Using gcloud

Once you have a running instance, you can access it via the TCP/IP protocol suite, the key identifier, of course, being your virtual machine's IP address. Your instance has two such addresses assigned to it: one is internal, for communicating between VMs in your project, and the other address is external and is used when communicating with a VM from outside the domain of Compute Engine.

When you create a VM, you have the option to request a particular IP address allocated to your project or to have the service select one for you from a pool of available addresses. As noted earlier, in the description of external IP addresses, permanently assigned addresses are called "static" addresses, whereas automatically assigned addresses are called "ephemeral" addresses. Note that an instance with the same name may be recreated any numbers of times. Ephemeral addresses are allocated on a transient basis, so there is no guarantee that different incarnations of the same instance name will be assigned the same ephemeral IP address.

By default, if you don't specify a static IP address, your instance will receive an ephemeral address, which is fine for this exercise. You can find the ephemeral IP address allocated to your instance by inspecting the EXTERNAL_IP value in the output of the gcloud compute instances list command.

Now, let's verify that we can access our new instance. The easiest way to do that is to log in to the newly created virtual machine using SSH. By default, our instance allows unrestricted incoming access to port 22 (the SSH service) from any source on the public Internet. Thus, we can now use the SSH command (or any standard SSH client application) to log in to our VM via its external IP address. The gcloud compute ssh <instance-name> command provides a convenient wrapper for the SSH command. It automatically converts our VM's logical name into the corresponding external IP address and specifies the location of our Compute Engine private SSH key.

Note that in addition to using gcloud compute ssh to remotely access your instances, you can also use the SSH shell command or any other standard SSH client of your choice. Run the gcloud compute ssh command now to remotely log in to your new virtual machine, like this:

```
$ gcloud compute ssh test-vm --zone us-central1-a
[..]
Debian GNU/Linux comes with ABSOLUTELY NO WARRANTY, to the extent
permitted by applicable law.
Last login: Wed Sep 24 11:09:17 2014 from 74.125.NNN.NNN
test-vm$
```

Now that we've logged into an interactive shell on our virtual machine, we have complete access to all of our VM's resources. We also have access to the Linux root login via the sudo facility. By default, we cannot directly log in to the root account on our VM, but we can run any command as root like this:

```
test-vm$ sudo id
uid=0(root) gid=0(root) groups=0(root)
```

We can also access an interactive shell as root using sudo <shell>, as follows:

```
test-vm$ sudo bash
root@test-vm#
```

We need root access to install software on our virtual machine. Let's imagine we want to install the Apache web server. We can do that by running sudo apt-get update followed by sudo apt-get install apache2,[1] like this:

```
test-vm$ sudo apt-get update
[..]
test-vm$ sudo apt-get install apache2
Reading package lists... Done
Building dependency tree
Reading state information... Done
[..]
[ ok ] Starting web server: apache2.
Setting up apache2 (2.2.22-13) ...
```

---

[1] The apt-get command is not available on CentOS systems. CentOS users will want to use the analogous yum command to install Apache.

```
Setting up libswitch-perl (2.16-2) ...
[..]
```

Try pasting your new VM's external IP address into the address bar in your favorite web browser. This should fail because of a missing firewall rule, which enables connectivity between external parties on the public Internet and the Apache web server running on your instance. We'll describe firewall rules in more detail in Chapter 6, but for now we can add the missing firewall rule using the `gcloud compute firewall-rules create` command, like this:

```
test-vm$ gcloud compute firewall-rules create http --allow tcp:80
Created [https://www.googleapis.com/compute/v1/projects/gce-
oreilly/global/firewalls/http].
NAME NETWORK SRC_RANGES RULES  SRC_TAGS TARGET_TAGS
http default 0.0.0.0/0  tcp:80
```

The `--allowed=tcp:80` flag tells Compute Engine to allow all incoming connection requests via the TCP protocol and port 80 (the default port for HTTP/web service).

Now that we've explicitly allowed incoming HTTP traffic into our network, retry accessing your virtual machine by pasting the external IP address[2] into a web browser. This time it should succeed and you should see the default Apache web page, which should look something like Figure 2-7.

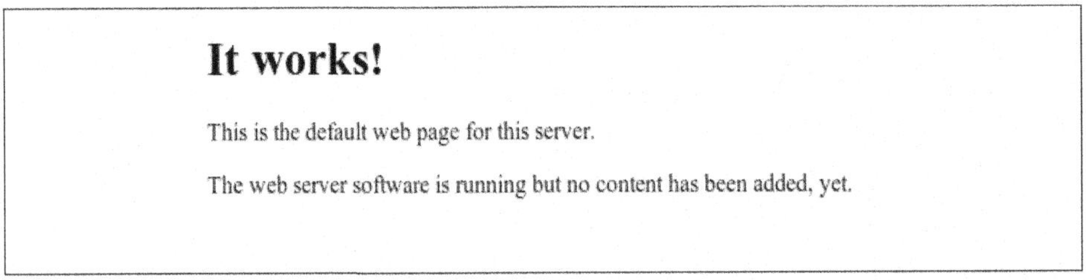

It works!

This is the default web page for this server.

The web server software is running but no content has been added, yet.

Figure 2-7. Serving a default web page from a Compute Engine Instance

Just to convince ourselves that we're really accessing our new VM, let's modify the default page served by Apache so that it displays a custom message. View the contents of the default file served by Apache, */var/www/index.html*. In that file you'll see a simple HTML document that looks something like this:

```
test-vm$ cat /var/www/index.html
<html><body><h1>It works!</h1>
<p>This is the default web page for this server.</p>
<p>The web server software is running but no content has been added, yet.</p>
</body></html>
```

---

2 As we saw earlier in this chapter, a VM's external IP address can be obtained from the instance list in the Developer's Console or the output of the `gcloud compute instances list` command.

Now use a text editor of your choice (nano is a good choice for beginners) to add the string "Hello from Google Compute Engine!" (or any other text you'd like to use for this exercise):[3]

```
$ sudo nano /var/www/index.html
```

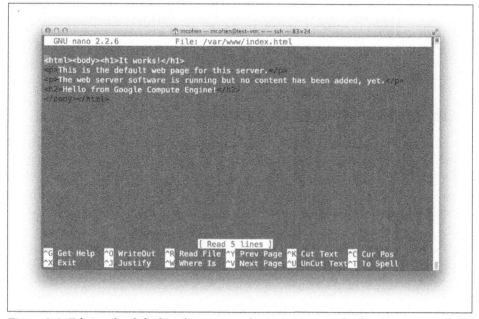

Figure 2-8. Editing the default web page stored in /var/www/index.html

As you can see, I've added a new second-level heading (`<h2>Hello from Google Com pute Engine!</h2>`) to include an additional string of text in the default page served by Apache. Save your work and then redirect your web browser to your VM's external IP address (or refresh the page you already have open to your VM's external IP address). You should see something like the page shown in Figure 2-9, indicating that Apache is now serving your customized page.

---

3 You'll want to prefix your editor command with sudo because writing this file requires root access.

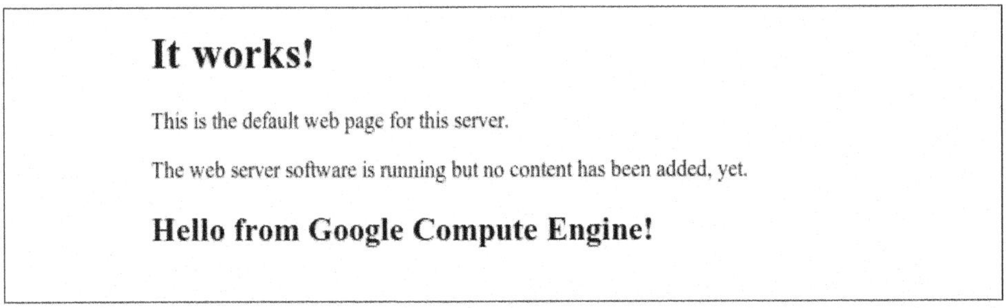

It works!

This is the default web page for this server.

The web server software is running but no content has been added, yet.

Hello from Google Compute Engine!

Figure 2-9. Serving a customized web page from a Compute Engine Instance

Deleting an Instance Using gcloud

Now that we've seen how to create an instance, log in to an instance using SSH, and install a web server, let's see how to delete an instance. Log out of your VM (using the exit or logout shell command) and, from your original computer, run the gcloud compute instances delete <instance-name> command and specify the zone in which you created your instance, like this:

```
$ gcloud compute instances delete test-vm --zone us-central1-a
The following instances will be deleted. Attached disks configured to
be auto-deleted will be deleted unless they are attached to any other
instances. Deleting a disk is irreversible and any data on the disk
will be lost.
 - [test-vm] in [us-central1-a]
Do you want to continue (Y/n)?  y
Deleted [https://www.googleapis.com/compute/v1/projects/gce-oreilly/zones/us-
central1-a/instances/test-vm].
```

At this point, your virtual machine no longer exists. Any attempt to connect to that instance via SSH, a web browser, or any other mode of access will fail because the resource no longer exists. You can, of course, recreate the instance by creating a new instance with the same name, machine type, zone, image, etc.; however, the resulting instance will be a completely new incarnation of the previous virtual machine.

Creating an Instance Programmatically

Compute Engine provides two layers of APIs: a RESTful web services API and client libraries for a number of popular programming languages. In this section, we'll cover how to create a Compute Engine instance using the Google Python client library; however, the concepts here apply equally well to any of the client libraries supported by Google.

In a sense, the RESTful web service API is the lowest common denominator of all access paths. The gcloud command, the Developers Console, and the language-specific client libraries are all implemented as layers on top of the web-services API.

Thus, the RESTful API dictates the functionality offered by all other access methods. The RESTful API and client libraries are a great choice if you need to do complex, repetitive, or automated tasks. A common example of such a use case would be creating and maintaining a large cluster of related instances.

We'll now use the Google Python client library to create a new instance, similar to the ones we created in previous sections using gcloud and the Developers Console. Following the instructions in the "My first Compute Engine application" on page 21 section of Chapter 1, obtain a copy of the *ch2-1.py* file from the gce-oreilly GitHub repository (*https://github.com/GoogleCloudPlatform/gce-oreilly/raw/master/ch2-1.py*). Make sure you have a valid *client_secret.json* file in the same directory.

Edit the contents of *ch2-1.py* to substitute your project ID for the string your-project-id. Under the covers, this code is formulating and sending an HTTP POST request to the instance resource URI.[4] An instance resource dictionary, encoded in JSON, is being sent as the request body.

Before we can run *ch2-1.py*, we need to install the Google Python client library on our test-vm instance, which, in turn, requires us to install pip, a Python package-management utility. We do this with the following command sequence:

```
test-vm$ wget https://bootstrap.pypa.io/get-pip.py
[..]
test-vm$ sudo python get-pip.py
Downloading/unpacking pip
  Downloading pip-1.5.6-py2.py3-none-any.whl (1.0MB): 1.0MB downloaded
Downloading/unpacking setuptools
  Downloading setuptools-6.0.1-py2.py3-none-any.whl (533kB): 533kB downloaded
Installing collected packages: pip, setuptools
Successfully installed pip setuptools
Cleaning up...
test-vm$ pip install --upgrade google-api-python-client
[..]
```

The following example shows the code you downloaded. You can tune any configuration settings (e.g., zone, image, machine type, etc.) to suit your needs:

```
"""Retrieve project information using the Compute Engine API.
Usage:
  $ python ch2-1.py
You can also get help on all the command-line flags the program understands
by running:
  $ python ch2-1.py --help
"""

import argparse
```

---

4 The Compute Engine API details, including resource URIs, query parameters, and JSON elements are all documented online at *https://developers.google.com/compute/docs/api/getting-started*.

```
import httplib2
import os
import sys

from apiclient import discovery
from oauth2client import file
from oauth2client import client
from oauth2client import tools

# Parser for command-line arguments.
parser = argparse.ArgumentParser(
    description=__doc__,
    formatter_class=argparse.RawDescriptionHelpFormatter,
    parents=[tools.argparser])

# CLIENT_SECRET is the name of a file containing the OAuth 2.0 information
# for this application, including client_id and client_secret.
CLIENT_SECRET = os.path.join(os.path.dirname(__file__), 'client_secret.json')

# Set up a Flow object to be used for authentication. PLEASE ONLY
# ADD THE SCOPES YOU NEED. For more information on using scopes
# see <https://developers.google.com/compute/docs/api/how-tos/authorization>.
FLOW = client.flow_from_clientsecrets(
    CLIENT_SECRET,
    scope=['https://www.googleapis.com/auth/compute'],
    message=tools.message_if_missing(CLIENT_SECRET))

def main(argv):
  # Parse the command-line flags.
  flags = parser.parse_args(argv[1:])

  # If the credentials don't exist or are invalid run through the native
  # client flow. The Storage object will ensure that if successful
  # the good credentials will get written back to the file.
  storage = file.Storage('sample.dat')
  credentials = storage.get()
  if credentials is None or credentials.invalid:
    credentials = tools.run_flow(FLOW, storage, flags)

  # Create an httplib2.Http object to handle our HTTP requests and authorize it
  # with our good Credentials.
  http = httplib2.Http()
  http = credentials.authorize(http)

  # Construct the service object for the interacting with the Compute Engine
  # API.
  service = discovery.build('compute', 'v1', http=http)

  # Set project, zone, and other constants.
  URL_PREFIX = 'https://www.googleapis.com/compute'
  API_VERSION = 'v1'
  PROJECT_ID = 'your-project-id'
```

```
PROJECT_URL = '%s/%s/projects/%s' % (URL_PREFIX, API_VERSION, PROJECT_ID)
INSTANCE_NAME = 'test-vm'
ZONE = 'us-central1-a'
MACHINE_TYPE = 'n1-standard-1'
IMAGE_PROJECT_ID = 'debian-cloud'
IMAGE_PROJECT_URL = '%s/%s/projects/%s' % (
    URL_PREFIX, API_VERSION, IMAGE_PROJECT_ID)
IMAGE_NAME = 'debian-7-wheezy-v20140807'

BODY = {
  'name': INSTANCE_NAME,
  'tags': {
    'items': ['frontend']
  },
  'machineType': '%s/zones/%s/machineTypes/%s' % (
      PROJECT_URL, ZONE, MACHINE_TYPE),
  'disks': [{
    'boot': True,
    'type': 'PERSISTENT',
    'mode': 'READ_WRITE',
    'zone': '%s/zones/%s' % (PROJECT_URL, ZONE),
    'initializeParams': {
      'sourceImage':     '%s/global/images/%s'    %    (IMAGE_PROJECT_URL,
IMAGE_NAME)
    },
  }],
  'networkInterfaces': [{
    'accessConfigs': [{
      'name': 'External NAT',
      'type': 'ONE_TO_ONE_NAT'
    }],
    'network': PROJECT_URL + '/global/networks/default'
  }],
  'scheduling': {
    'automaticRestart': True,
    'onHostMaintenance': 'MIGRATE'
  },
  'serviceAccounts': [{
    'email': 'default',
    'scopes': [
      'https://www.googleapis.com/auth/compute',
      'https://www.googleapis.com/auth/devstorage.full_control'
    ]
  }],
}

# Build and execute instance insert request.
request = service.instances().insert(
    project=PROJECT_ID, zone=ZONE, body=BODY)
try:
  response = request.execute()
except Exception, ex:
```

```
      print 'ERROR: ' + str(ex)
      sys.exit()

    # Instance creation is asynchronous so now wait for a DONE status.
    op_name = response['name']
    operations = service.zoneOperations()
    while True:
      request = operations.get(
          project=PROJECT_ID, zone=ZONE, operation=op_name)
      try:
        response = request.execute()
      except Exception, ex:
        print 'ERROR: ' + str(ex)
        sys.exit()
      if 'error' in response:
        print 'ERROR: ' + str(response['error'])
        sys.exit()
      status = response['status']
      if status == 'DONE':
        print 'Instance created.'
        break
      else:
        print 'Waiting for operation to complete. Status: ' + status

if __name__ == '__main__':
  main(sys.argv)
```

Here we see some similar boilerplate to the code we used in Chapter 1 to initialize the client library and perform authentication. In this particular example, we've added a block of configuration variables (in all uppercase, e.g., INSTANCE_NAME, ZONE, MACHINE_TYPE, etc.) along with a JSON document (BODY) which uses the configuration variables to specify our instance-creation request. We then issue a client API request (service.instances().insert()) referencing our project ID, desired zone, and the JSON document containing details of our instance-creation request. Because our request is asynchronous, we then enter a polling loop, repeatedly checking the results of our request for status DONE, which tells us our request has completed.

After inserting your project ID and tuning the configuration variables to your liking, you can run this app using the python ch2-1.py command. The result should look like the following transcript:

```
$ python ch2-1.py
Waiting for operation to complete. Status: PENDING
[..]
Waiting for operation to complete. Status: RUNNING
[..]
Waiting for operation to complete. Status: RUNNING
Instance created.
```

If you now check the Developers Console or run the `gcloud compute instances list` command, you should see your new instance, along with a summary of the attributes you assigned.

Creating an Instance Using a Service Account

Earlier in this chapter we showed how much easier it is to use the `gcloud` command on a VM with a service account defined (it just worked—there was no need to do the "OAuth dance"). A similar benefit accrues when we access the Compute Engine API. In this section, we're going to show how the code in the previous section gets correspondingly simpler when we take advantage of service accounts.

Log in to the VM you just created in the previous section, using the `gcloud compute ssh` command:

```
$ gcloud compute ssh test-vm --zone us-central1-a
[..]
test-vm$
```

Following the instructions in the "My first Compute Engine application" on page 21 section of Chapter 1, obtain a copy of the *ch2-2.py* file from the *gce-oreilly* GitHub repository (*https://github.com/GoogleCloudPlatform/gce-oreilly/raw/master/ch2-2.py*). Make sure you have a valid *client_secret.json* file in the same directory.

Just as we did in the previous example, edit the contents of *ch2-2.py* to substitute your project ID for the string `your-project-id`.

Using the `diff ch2-1.py ch2-2.py` command, take a look at the differences between ch2-1.py and ch2-2.py.

We've changed the instance name (to avoid trying to create a VM with the same name as the one on which we're running this exercise). We've added a new import to gain access to the `AppAssertionCredentials` method, which gives us easy access to our service account's OAuth credentials:

```
from oauth2client.gce import AppAssertionCredentials
```

Most significantly, we've replaced several lines of code dedicated to managing our client OAuth2 credentials with one simple line of code:

```
credentials =
    AppAssertionCredentials(['https://www.googleapis.com/auth/compute'])
```

Perhaps even more useful, we no longer need to worry about populating and managing a *client_secret.json* file containing sensitive authentication data.

After inserting your project ID and tuning the configuration variables to your liking, you can run this app using the `python ch2-2.py` command. The result is the following transcript (which should look very much like the output from the previous, non-service account, example):

```
$ python ch2-2.py
Waiting for operation to complete. Status: PENDING
[..]
Waiting for operation to complete. Status: RUNNING
[..]
Waiting for operation to complete. Status: RUNNING
Instance created.
```

If you now check the Developers Console or run the `gcloud compute instances list` command, you should see your new instance, along with a summary of the attributes you assigned.

The simplicity and brevity of this program show the tangible benefits obtained by using service accounts to authenticate applications running on a Compute Engine virtual machine.

Selecting an Access Mode

So how can you determine which access mode—the Developers Console, the `gcloud` command, or the Compute Engine API—to use? The Developers Console provides an intuitive, menu-driven user interface, so if you're completing a one-off task that doesn't need to be automated, the Developers Console is probably the easiest and quickest path to success. If you're trying to automate a moderately simple operations task or capture a reproducible procedure, the `gcloud` tool may be your best bet, because it can be embedded in shell scripts, shared via email and other mechanisms, and generally used to capture and automate simple repetitive tasks. But if you're trying to do something complicated, highly repetitive, or custom, you should consider using a programming language to harness the full power of the Compute Engine API.

Cleaning Up

Before moving on to the next chapter, let's delete the VM we created in this chapter, using the `gcloud compute instances delete` command, like this:

```
$ gcloud compute instances delete test-vm --zone us-central1-a
The following instances will be deleted. Attached disks configured to
be auto-deleted will be deleted unless they are attached to any other
instances. Deleting a disk is irreversible and any data on the disk
will be lost.
 - [test-vm] in [us-central1-a]
Do you want to continue (Y/n)?  y
Deleted [https://www.googleapis.com/compute/v1/projects/gce-
oreilly/zones/us-central1-a/instances/test-vm].
```

Summary

In this chapter, we learned all about Compute Engine instances, also known as virtual machines. We learned how to create instances, how to log in to them, and how to delete them using our three main access modes: the Developers Console web UI, the gcloud command-line tool, and the Compute Engine programmatic API. We also explained all the attributes associated with instances and showed how service accounts simplify the authentication logic required to access Google services from a VM.

Up Next

Now that we've learned about instances and created a few of our own using three different access modes, in the next chapters, we'll explore the mechanisms built into Compute Engine for storing persistent data.

## CHAPTER 3

Storage: Persistent Disk

Compute Engine provides a rich array of storage mechanisms, which we'll describe in detail in this and the next two chapters. Along the way, we'll learn how to use each mechanism via our three main access methods: the Developers Console Web UI, the gcloud command-line tool, and the Compute Engine API.

Compute Engine Storage Options at a Glance

Compute Engine supports numerous storage options. Persistent disk (PD) is the primary mechanism available for block storage and is the method of choice for storing filesystem data. Virtual machines boot from persistent disks and also use PDs to store supplementary (i.e., nonboot) filesystems or raw data. This chapter describes persistent disks in depth.

Persistent disks are local storage devices. They are available from Compute Engine virtual machines only. The other storage options we'll cover in this book are available both within a VM and outside of Compute Engine as well. Google Cloud Storage, which provides an Internet-wide, high capacity, highly scalable binary object store, is described in Chapter 4. Cloud SQL and Cloud Datastore (both described in Chapter 5), provide managed MySQL database instances, and a highly scalable global NoSQL database in the cloud, respectively.

Table 3-1 provides a summary of the storage mechanisms available to Compute Engine users, along with several key attributes of each.

Table 3-1. Overview of storage options

Option[1]	Data model	Managed	Storage scope	Access scope	Encrypted	Redundant	Max size
Persistent disk	Block device	Yes	Zone	GCE	Yes	Yes	3/10 TB[2]/disk
Cloud Storage	BLOB store/ HTTP	Yes	Global	General	Yes	Yes	5 TB/blob
Cloud SQL	Relational database	Yes	Global	General	Yes	Yes	500 GB / database
Cloud Datastore	Key/value store	Yes	Global	General	No	Yes	unlimited

The columns in Table 3.1 are interpreted as follows:

- The "Data model" column indicates how the storage mechanism appears to the end user or programmer. For example, persistent disks appear as a block device (normally accessed via a local filesystem), and thus are directly accessible by any software that operates on a Linux or Windows filesystem. Cloud Storage provides a mechanism to store and retrieve binary large object (BLOBs) via a purpose-built API as well as via HTTP requests.

- "Managed" indicates whether Google is responsible for monitoring, operating, and ensuring integrity and availability of the storage service.

- "Storage scope" indicates whether data stored by a given mechanism is limited to a Compute Engine zone or region, or is available across any geographic location (global).

- "Access scope" indicates whether a storage mechanism is limited to use within the context of Compute Engine or provides a standalone storage service that can be used inside or outside the scope of Compute Engine.

- "Encrypted" indicates whether data stored by a given mechanism is automatically encrypted at rest.

- The "Redundant" column tells whether the underlying storage mechanism is multiply replicated and, hence, has no single point of failure and resulting high availability.

- "Max size" indicates the maximum size of an instance of that storage type.

In this chapter, we'll examine persistent disks and learn how to use them via multiple access methods.

---

1 Pricing is not included in this table because it is subject to change. The latest pricing details are available online at *https://cloud.google.com/*.

2 The f1-micro and g1-small machine types are limited to 3 TB per disk. For all other machine types, the limit is 10 TB per disk.

Persistent Disk

Persistent disks (PDs) are network-attached, block storage devices that provide consistently high throughput and low latency for most usage scenarios. The data stored on a persistent disk is decoupled from the lifetime of any particular virtual machine. An instance can write to a persistent disk, the instance can be deleted, and the data on the persistent disk will continue to be retained indefinitely (until the PD is deleted). A new instance can mount that persistent disk and pick up where the deleted instance left off.

Persistent disk data is stored redundantly within a zone, so in addition to providing persistence, they also provide high availability and durability. Persistent disks can be arbitrarily sized (up to certain limits), can be mounted by multiple VMs (in read-only mode), and can have their contents saved and restored via the snapshot feature, which we'll describe later.

Compute Engine offers two types of persistent disks:

Standard
Traditional magnetic disk drives

Solid-state drive (SSD)
Electronic data storage

Standard PDs offer higher capacity and are ideally suited to large block sequential I/O. SSD PDs are ideal for random access I/O with lower capacity needs.

Persistent disks have three primary use cases:

Stateful root/boot drive
Provides a persistent root device for booting VMs into a predefined state quickly and repeatedly

User-managed data volume
Supplemental, persistent, high performance storage (e.g., for SQL data, NoSQL data, HDFS, or a file server)

Read-only shared volume
High performance distribution of static content

Persistent disks can be mounted read/write or read-only. In the read/write case, the disk must be dedicated exclusively to one particular virtual machine at a time. In the read-only case, access to a single persistent disk may be shared across any number of virtual machines in the same zone in which the persistent disk resides; however, in that case, all attached VMs have read-only access—there can be no writers in that scenario. This provides a way to efficiently distribute static data to many instances within a zone. It's also worth noting that boot persistent disks must be mounted read/

write and therefore, a PD used as a boot drive cannot be shared across multiple virtual machines.

Persistent disks are defined within a particular zone, which is specified at disk creation time, and they may be used only in the zone in which they are created. This means that you cannot create a disk in zone A and attach it to an instance in zone B. The disk and the instance that use the disk must be in the same zone. Fortunately, Compute Engine offers a powerful feature called *persistent disk snapshots*, which enable saving and restoring the contents of a persistent disk within and across zones and regions. We'll provide more information about snapshots later in this chapter.

Persistent Disk Performance

Persistent disks are designed such that their performance scales proportionally with their capacity. Each PD has associated software-defined throughput and bandwidth limitations. Higher-capacity disks have increasingly larger limits, which means that they can sustain higher performance levels than smaller disks. So the choice of an optimal disk size for a given application is a function of both the required capacity and the required performance targets.

Virtual machines also have I/O limitations. In practice, the actual performance obtained for a given disk and VM combination will be the minimum of the performance limits imposed by each. Thus, the capacity of both resource types must be taken into account to ensure that the required performance level for a given application will be obtainable.

See the Compute Engine online documentation[3] for the most up-to-date information about persistent disk and VM I/O performance.

Create a Persistent Disk Using Developers Console

In Chapter 2, we created a new instance, using an automatically created persistent disk as the root device. In this section, we'll use the Developers Console to achieve the same net result in two steps: we'll create a bootable persistent disk, and then we'll create a virtual machine using our newly created disk as its boot device.

We start by navigating to the Developers Console (*http://console.develop ers.google.com/*). Select the project you want to work with, then select the Disks tab (under the Compute Engine service) from the lefthand navigation panel. Click the New Disk button to see the new disk creation dialog, which is shown in Figure 3-1.

---

3 *https://cloud.google.com/compute/docs/disks*

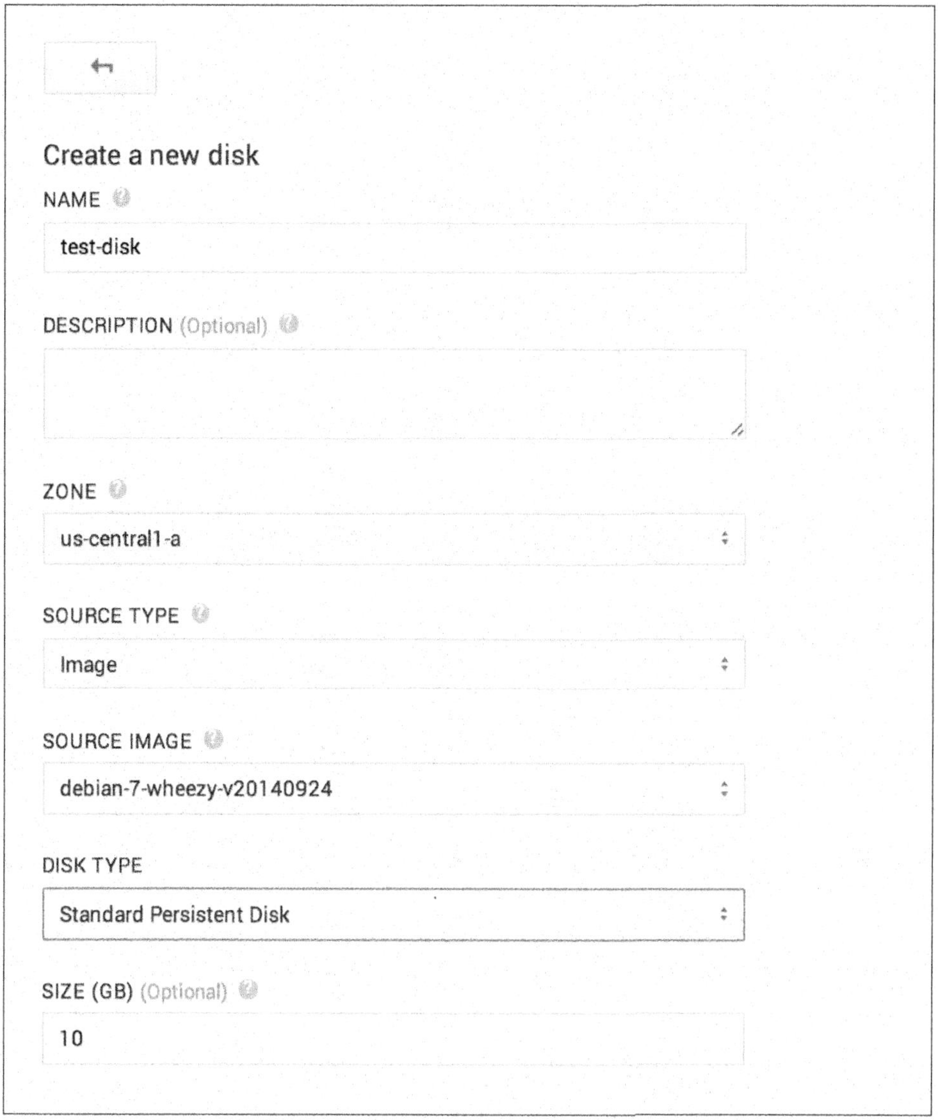

Figure 3-1. New persistent disk creation dialog

We've named our new disk `test-disk`, we're creating it in zone `us-central1-a`, we've taken the default 10 GB of space, and we'd like the disk to be populated using the `debian-7-wheezy-v20140924` image. Including an image makes the disk bootable. Notice the DISK TYPE option, which gives us the opportunity to select between a standard PD or the newer SSD PD. Click the Create button, and in a few moments, a new resource appears in our list of persistent disks.

Now let's create a new instance via the Developers Console, using our new persistent disk as the root device. To do this, we simply select the VM Instances tab, click the New Instance button, give your instance a name (I used `test-instance`), select a zone that matches the zone where you created your bootable PD, and select "Existing disk" from the BOOT SOURCE menu, along with the your new disk's name (`test-disk`, in my example) from the SOURCE DISK menu.

For convenience, make sure the "Delete boot disk when instance is deleted" checkbox is checked. This ensures your boot disk will be automatically deleted by the Compute Engine service if and when you delete the associated instance. If you want your disk to remain available after deleting your instance, simply uncheck that box. A completed version of this dialog is shown in Figure 3-2.

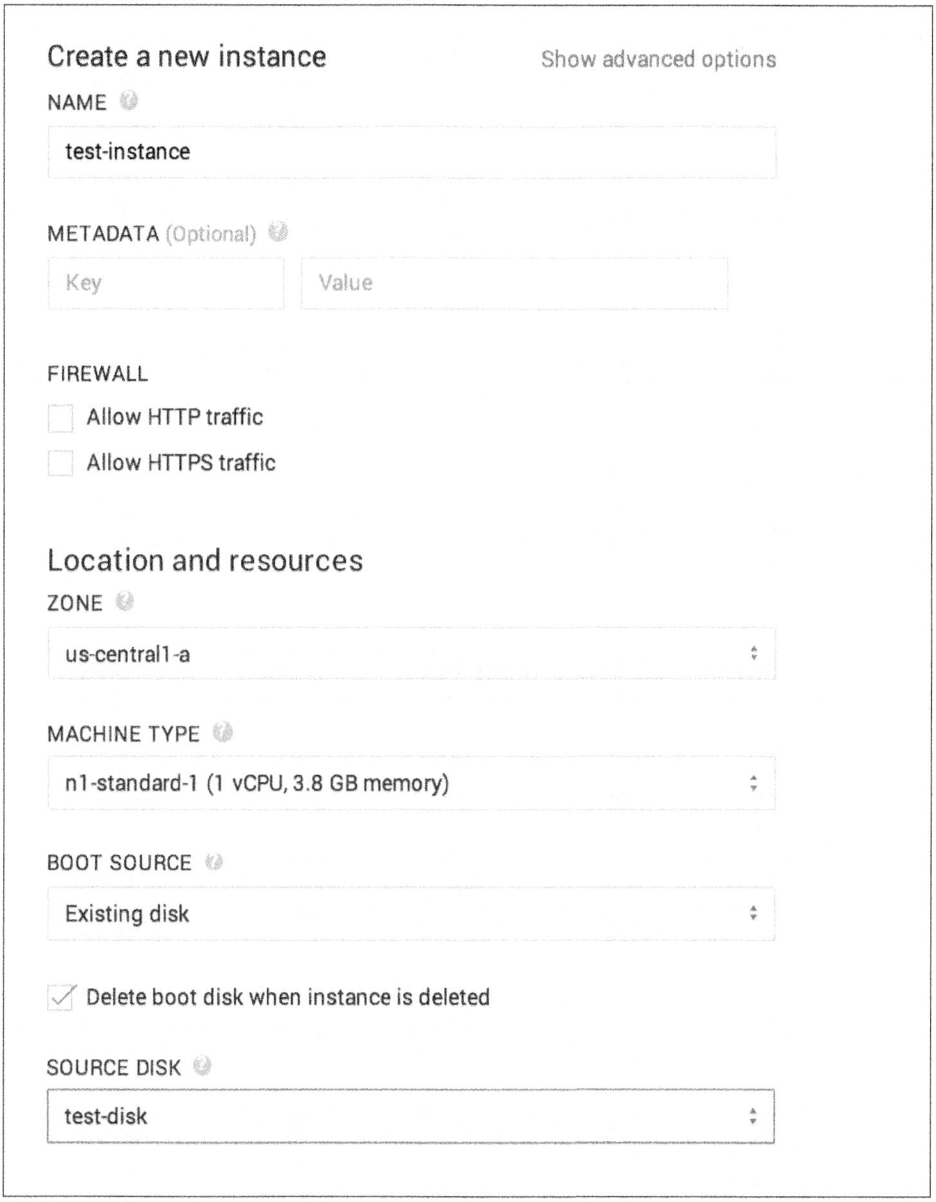

Create a new instance

Show advanced options

NAME ⊚

> test-instance

METADATA (Optional) ⊚

Key	Value

FIREWALL

☐ Allow HTTP traffic

☐ Allow HTTPS traffic

Location and resources

ZONE ⊚

> us-central1-a ⇕

MACHINE TYPE ⊚

> n1-standard-1 (1 vCPU, 3.8 GB memory) ⇕

BOOT SOURCE ⊚

> Existing disk ⇕

☑ Delete boot disk when instance is deleted

SOURCE DISK ⊚

> test-disk ⇕

Figure 3-2. New instance-creation dialog using existing persistent disk

Next, we click the Create button, and shortly thereafter, a VM shows up in our instance list with the name of the new VM and its boot persistent disk.

Create a Persistent Disk Using gcloud

Let's start by exercising a typical use case: creating a new virtual machine with its root device stored on a persistent disk. We can do that in one of two ways:

One-step creation
> Create an instance with a root persistent disk.

Two-step creation
> Create a persistent disk, then create an instance using the newly created persistent disk as its root device.

One-step creation

First, let's exercise the one-step method, using the gcloud command:

```
$ gcloud compute instances create test-vm
For the following instances:
 - [test-vm]
choose a zone:
 [1] asia-east1-b
 [2] asia-east1-c
 [3] asia-east1-a
 [4] europe-west1-b
 [5] europe-west1-a
 [6] us-central1-a
 [7] us-central1-f
 [8] us-central1-b
Please enter your numeric choice:  6
Created    [https://www.googleapis.com/compute/v1/projects/gce-oreilly/zones/us-
central1-a/instances/test-vm].
NAME    ZONE          MACHINE_TYPE INTERNAL_IP EXTERNAL_IP   STATUS
test-vm us-central1-a n1-standard-1 10.240.62.24 146.148.52.42 RUNNING
```

The single command just shown caused two separate requests to be executed in sequence:

1. A bootable persistent disk was created and populated with our selected (in this case, default) image. We never explicitly specified a name for this disk. The disk name was automatically generated for us to match the associated instance name, so the resulting disk in this example is named test-vm. We can see our new disk using the gcloud compute disks list command.
2. A new instance named test-vm was created, which uses the new test-vm persistent disk as its root storage device.

Let's log in to the new instance and examine our storage configuration:

```
$ gcloud compute ssh test-vm --zone us-central1-a
[..]
Debian GNU/Linux comes with ABSOLUTELY NO WARRANTY, to the extent
```

```
                                   permitted by applicable law.
test-vm$ df -k
Filesystem                            1K-blocks    Used Available Use% Mounted on
rootfs                                10188088  488120   9159400   6% /
udev                                     10240       0     10240   0% /dev
tmpfs                                   380128     100    380028   1% /run
/dev/disk/by-uuid/19a8da7a-7ae4..     10188088  488120   9159400   6% /
tmpfs                                     5120       0      5120   0% /run/lock
tmpf                                    760240       0    760240   0% /run/shm
```

The df command summarizes the space available and in use by all mounted filesystems (-k requests space units expressed in kilobytes). This output shows us that the root device contains 10,188,088 1K blocks of total storage space, which is the default size used by the gcloud command for a persistent disk used as a root filesystem. Of that 10 GB, we're already using 488,120 blocks, which amounts to roughly 6% of the total disk capacity on the root device. This reveals how much of our root persistent disk is used by this particular image, before we've stored a single byte of our own.

Let's verify the persistence of this PD by leaving a fingerprint on the root drive, re-creating the VM, and verifying that the fingerprint still exists and can be seen on the new VM. Our fingerprint will be the installation of a new package (we'll use apache2 for this example). Let's first verify the apache2 package is not already installed on our VM:

```
test-vm$ dpkg --get-selections | grep apache2
test-vm$
```

The empty response indicates the package is not installed. Let's now install it using the apt-get update and apt-get install commands (which must be run as root, so we use sudo):

```
test-vm$ sudo apt-get update
[..]
test-vm$ sudo apt-get install apache2
Reading package lists... Done
Building dependency tree
Reading state information... Done
[..]
Setting up apache2-mpm-worker (2.2.22-13) ...
[ ok ] Starting web server: apache2.
```

Now let's verify the apache2 package has been installed:

```
test-vm$ dpkg --get-selections | grep apache
apache2                               install
apache2-mpm-worker                    install
apache2-utils                         install
apache2.2-bin                         install
apache2.2-common                      install
```

As you can see, the package (and some related dependencies) are now reported by dpkg as installed on our virtual machine. We're now going to delete the virtual machine, create a new instance with the same name reusing our persistent disk as the root device, log in, and verify the apache2 packages are still installed.

We now log out of our ssh session and, from the computer we used to create test-vm, we delete the instance using the gcloud compute instances delete command (note the use of the --keep-disks boot option to avoid auto-deleting our boot PD):

```
$ gcloud compute instances delete test-vm --zone us-central1-a --keep-disks boot
The following instances will be deleted. Attached disks configured to
be auto-deleted will be deleted unless they are attached to any other
instances. Deleting a disk is irreversible and any data on the disk
will be lost.
 - [test-vm] in [us-central1-a]
Do you want to continue (Y/n)?  y
Updated [https://www.googleapis.com/compute/v1/projects/gce-oreilly/zones/us-
central1-a/instances/test-vm].
Deleted [https://www.googleapis.com/compute/v1/projects/gce-oreilly/zones/us-
central1-a/instances/test-vm].
```

The test-vm instance is now deleted, but the test-vm persistent disk continues to exist independently of the instance with which it was previously associated. We can verify this using the gcloud compute instances list and gcloud compute disks list commands:

```
$ gcloud compute instances list
NAME     ZONE    MACHINE_TYPE INTERNAL_IP EXTERNAL_IP STATUS
[..] # no occurrence of test-vm
$ gcloud compute disks list
NAME                ZONE         SIZE_GB TYPE        STATUS
test-vm             us-central1-a 10      pd-standard READY
[..]
```

The output of the previous commands show the test-vm instance no longer exists, as expected, but our test-vm disk continues to be alive and well. Let's now create a new instance, using the --disk name=test-vm boot=yes option to request our existing persistent disk be used as the root drive for the recreated test-vm instance. Once that finishes, we'll see if we can find our fingerprint (apache2 packages installed). Note that we also specify the zone in which our PD resides and a service account scope granting our VM access to Compute Engine services—we'll take advantage of the service account scope later in this chapter:

```
$ gcloud compute instances create test-vm --zone us-central1-a \
  --disk name=test-vm boot=yes --scopes compute-rw
Created [https://www.googleapis.com/compute/v1/projects/gce-oreilly/zones/us-
central1-a/instances/test-vm].
NAME     ZONE          MACHINE_TYPE INTERNAL_IP    EXTERNAL_IP    STATUS
test-vm us-central1-a n1-standard-1 10.240.228.154 146.148.52.42 RUNNING
```

Now, let's log in to the new VM and look for the fingerprint:

```
$ gcloud compute ssh test-vm --zone us-central1-a
[..]
Debian GNU/Linux comes with ABSOLUTELY NO WARRANTY, to the extent
permitted by applicable law.
Last login: Fri Sep 26 08:56:05 2014 from 90.197.156.23
test-vm$ dpkg --get-selections | grep apache
apache2                                 install
apache2-mpm-worker                      install
apache2-utils                           install
apache2.2-bin                           install
apache2.2-common                        install
```

Sure enough, there's our Apache2 installation. Despite deleting and recreating our instance, by making the root device persistent, we were able to pick up where we left off without having to retrace our steps. Being able to recover previously stored data is a significant advantage when building resilient systems.

Two-step creation

In the previous section, we could have created the persistent disk separately using the gcloud compute disks create command and then used it as a boot drive for a new instance. Let's try that now, specifying a source image to make the created disk bootable, like this:

```
$ gcloud compute disks create boot-disk --zone us-central1-a --image debian-7
Created [https://www.googleapis.com/compute/v1/projects/gce-oreilly/zones/us-
central1-a/disks/boot-disk].
NAME      ZONE          SIZE_GB TYPE        STATUS
boot-disk us-central1-a 10      pd-standard READY
```

In this example, we've named our disk boot-disk, but we could use any name we like so long as we don't already have another disk in our project with the same name. Because persistent disks are affiliated with a particular zone, we specified a zone in which to locate this disk. We also specified an image to make this PD bootable with a particular initial software installation.

Next, we create a new instance, called test-vm-2, using gcloud compute instances create, and referencing the bootable disk we just created, like this:

```
$ gcloud compute instances create test-vm-2 --zone us-central1-a \
  --disk name=boot-disk boot=yes
Created [https://www.googleapis.com/compute/v1/projects/gce-oreilly/zones/us-
central1-a/instances/test-vm-2].
NAME      ZONE          MACHINE_TYPE  INTERNAL_IP   EXTERNAL_IP    STATUS
test-vm-2 us-central1-a n1-standard-1 10.240.92.30  146.148.44.211 RUNNING
```

Now we have a running instance that uses a bootable persistent disk created separately.

Attaching/Detaching a PD to/from a Running VM

In addition to booting a VM with a persistent disk, as we've just done, we can also dynamically attach and detach a persistent disk to/from a running instance. Let's try that now. We'll create a new, nonbootable persistent disk and attach it as a data drive to one of our running instances. First, we create the new persistent disk. We'll call it data-disk to signify that it's intended as a data (i.e., not a boot) drive:

```
$ gcloud compute disks create data-disk --zone us-central1-a
Created [https://www.googleapis.com/compute/v1/projects/gce-oreilly/zones/us-
central1-a/disks/data-disk].
NAME      ZONE          SIZE_GB TYPE        STATUS
data-disk us-central1-a 500     pd-standard READY
```

Notice two things about this example: we didn't specify a source image, because we don't want this disk to be bootable, and we specified the same zone we used when creating the virtual machine to which we want to attach this disk.

Now let's log in to the test-vm instance we created previously in this chapter and examine its filesystem inventory:

```
$ gcloud compute ssh test-vm --zone us-central1-a
[..]
Debian GNU/Linux comes with ABSOLUTELY NO WARRANTY, to the extent
permitted by applicable law.
test-vm$ df -k
Filesystem                      1K-blocks    Used Available Use% Mounted on
rootfs                           10188088  488120   9159400   6% /
udev                                10240       0     10240   0% /dev
tmpfs                              380128     100    380028   1% /run
/dev/disk/by-uuid/19a8da7a-7ae4.. 10188088  488120   9159400   6% /
tmpfs                                5120       0      5120   0% /run/lock
tmpf                               760240       0    760240   0% /run/shm
```

This output shows a 10 GB root file system and no user mounted file systems. Next, let's dynamically attach our data-disk PD to our running instance, using the gcloud compute instances attach-disk command (we can run this command right from the test-vm instance because it was created with compute-rw service account scope):

```
test-vm$ gcloud compute instances attach-disk test-vm \
        --disk data-disk --zone us-central1-a
Updated [https://www.googleapis.com/compute/v1/projects/gce-oreilly/zones/us-
central1-a/instances/test-vm].
```

Note that we didn't have to run the gcloud compute instances attach-disk command from the instance to which we're attaching the disk—that just happened to be a convenient place to run the command but we could just as easily have attached the disk to our VM by running the command from any computer attached to the Internet.

The attach disk request seems to have succeeded, so let's verify that we can access the attached disk:

```
test-vm$ df -k
Filesystem                          1K-blocks    Used Available Use% Mounted on
rootfs                               10188088  625128   9022392   7% /
udev                                    10240       0     10240   0% /dev
tmpfs                                  380128     108    380020   1% /run
/dev/disk/by-uuid/19a8da7a-7ae4..    10188088  625128   9022392   7% /
tmpfs                                    5120       0      5120   0% /run/lock
tmpfs                                  760240       0    760240   0% /run/shm
```

This seems like a failed test because we don't see evidence of the attached persistent disk. The reason we don't see the newly attached device is because, although the persistent disk is now logically attached to the virtual machine, we need to format the disk contents and mount it to a filesystem on our VM before we can use it.

Let's do that by creating a mount point (we'll use */mnt/pd0*, in this example) like this:

```
test-vm$ sudo mkdir -p /mnt/pd0
```

Next, let's find out the device path where your data_disk is attached by running this command:

```
test-vm$ ls -l /dev/disk/by-id/google-*
lrwxrwxrwx 1 root root  9 Sep 26 09:19 /dev/disk/by-id/google-persistent-
disk-0 -> ../../sda
[..]
lrwxrwxrwx 1 root root  9 Sep 26 10:39 /dev/disk/by-id/google-persistent-
disk-1 -> ../../sdb
```

The first PD shown (google-persistent-disk-0) is our boot drive. The second PD (google-persistent-disk-1) is our attached data_disk. It's attached to device */dev/sdb*, so let's now use the safe_format_and_mount command to format our disk and mount this device to our mount point (*/mnt/pd0*) like this:

```
test-vm$ sudo /usr/share/google/safe_format_and_mount -m \
         "mkfs.ext4 -F" /dev/sdb /mnt/pd0
[..]
```

Now let's run df -k again and see if we have a working filesystem:

```
test-vm$ df -k
Filesystem                          1K-blocks    Used Available Use% Mounted on
rootfs                               10188088  626248   9021272   7% /
udev                                    10240       0     10240   0% /dev
tmpfs                                  380128     108    380020   1% /run
/dev/disk/by-uuid/19a8da7a-7ae4..    10188088  626248   9021272   7% /
tmpfs                                    5120       0      5120   0% /run/lock
tmpfs                                  760240       0    760240   0% /run/shm
/dev/sdb                            515930552   71448 489628320   1% /mnt/pd0
```

As you can see, the last line shows us a new 500 GB filesystem, using device */dev/sdb* and mounted on */mnt/pd0*. This is our persistent disk, which we've dynamically attached to a running virtual machine as a data drive. We're now free to use it by reading and writing into the */mnt/pd0* directory tree.

Now for a similar test to the one we did with the root persistent disk, let's leave a fingerprint on our data disk, then detach it from the running instance, and then re-attach it and verify that the fingerprint persists. We'll produce the fingerprint this time by simply creating a new directory on the persistent disk, in the */mnt/pd0* directory, as follows:

```
test-vm$ cd /mnt/pd0
test-vm:/mnt/pd0$ ls
lost+found
test-vm:/mnt/pd0$ sudo mkdir we_were_here
test-vm:/mnt/pd0$ ls
lost+found  we_were_here
```

In preparation for a detach operation, we need to unmount the persistent disk (we first change out of the */mnt/pd0* directory tree to avoid a device busy error):

```
test-vm:/mnt/pd0$ cd /
test-vm$ sudo umount /mnt/pd0
```

The df -k command now shows us that the data drive is no longer available:

```
test-vm$ df -k
Filesystem                         1K-blocks   Used Available Use% Mounted on
rootfs                             10188088 626248   9021272   7% /
udev                                  10240      0     10240   0% /dev
tmpfs                                380128    108    380020   1% /run
/dev/disk/by-uuid/19a8da7a-7ae4..  10188088 626248   9021272   7% /
tmpfs                                  5120      0      5120   0% /run/lock
tmpfs                                760240      0    760240   0% /run/shm
```

Now we detach the persistent disk using the gcloud compute instances detach-disk command, as follows (again, we can run this command right from the test-vm instance because it was created with compute-rw service account scope):

```
test-vm$ gcloud compute instances detach-disk test-vm --disk data-disk --zone
us-central1-a
Updated [https://www.googleapis.com/compute/v1/projects/gce-oreilly/zones/us-
central1-a/instances/test-vm].
```

Listing our attached persistent disks shows that PD1 (our data-disk device) is indeed detached and no longer available:

```
test-vm$ ls -l /dev/disk/by-id/google-*
lrwxrwxrwx 1 root root  9 Sep 26 09:19 /dev/disk/by-id/google-persistent-
disk-0 -> ../../sda
[..]
```

Let's now reattach the device:

```
test-vm$ gcloud compute instances attach-disk test-vm \
        --disk data-disk --zone us-central1-a
Updated [https://www.googleapis.com/compute/v1/projects/gce-oreilly/zones/us-
central1-a/instances/test-vm].
```

Next, we remount the filesystem using the same tool we used before, safe_for
mat_and_mount. This command is smart enough to know this persistent disk is
already formatted, so there's no need to reformat it (in fact, it would be undesirable to
do so, because that would obliterate the current disk contents):

```
test-vm$ sudo /usr/share/google/safe_format_and_mount -m \
        "mkfs.ext4 -F" /dev/sdb /mnt/pd0
safe_format_and_mount: Running: fsck.ext4 -a /dev/sdb
safe_format_and_mount: /dev/sdb: clean, 12/32768000 files, 2107225/131072000
blocks
safe_format_and_mount: Running: mount -o discard,defaults /dev/sdb /mnt/pd0
```

Now if we run the df -k command once more, we see the filesystem associated with
our data drive is back:

```
test-vm$ df -k
Filesystem                         1K-blocks     Used Available Use% Mounted on
rootfs                             10188088   626360   9021160   7% /
udev                                  10240        0     10240   0% /dev
tmpfs                                380128      108    380020   1% /run
/dev/disk/by-uuid/19a8da7a-7ae4..  10188088   626360   9021160   7% /
tmpfs                                  5120        0      5120   0% /run/lock
tmpfs                                760240        0    760240   0% /run/shm
/dev/sdb                          515930552    71452 489628316   1% /mnt/pd0
```

This mount succeeded and, once again, we see our 500 GB persistent disk mounted
at /mnt/pd0. In addition, we see that the fingerprint we created before detaching and
reattaching the disk is still there:

```
test-vm$ ls /mnt/pd0
lost+found  we_were_here
```

And with that, we've reattached a persistent disk to a running instance. Now let's
examine how to work with the Compute Engine API to manage persistent disks programmatically.

Create a Persistent Disk Programmatically

Simple management tasks can be handled easily using the Developers Console web
UI. Moderately-sized or somewhat repetitive tasks lend themselves well to the gcloud
command-line tool. But the most demanding tasks call for a programmatic interface,
where complex resource-management tasks can be mediated by software. In Chapter 2, we programmatically created an instance with an associated persistent disk as
the boot device in one request. In this section, we'll do the same thing in two steps:

we'll create a bootable persistent disk and then we'll create an instance using the newly created disk as its boot device. We'll use a helpful feature built into the Google Developers Console to generate the required code.

Figure 3-3 shows a screenshot of the New Disk creation dialog, where we've entered a disk named `new-disk`, zone `us-central1-a`, source type `Image`, and source image `debian-7-wheezy-v20140924`.

Note the "Equivalent REST or command line" text just below the Create button. Don't actually submit the Create Disk request. Instead, click the REST link. The Cloud Console generates a pop-up window (Figure 3-4) containing a JSON document with details of the disk creation request for use via the Compute Engine API. Copy and paste this text into a file for safekeeping.

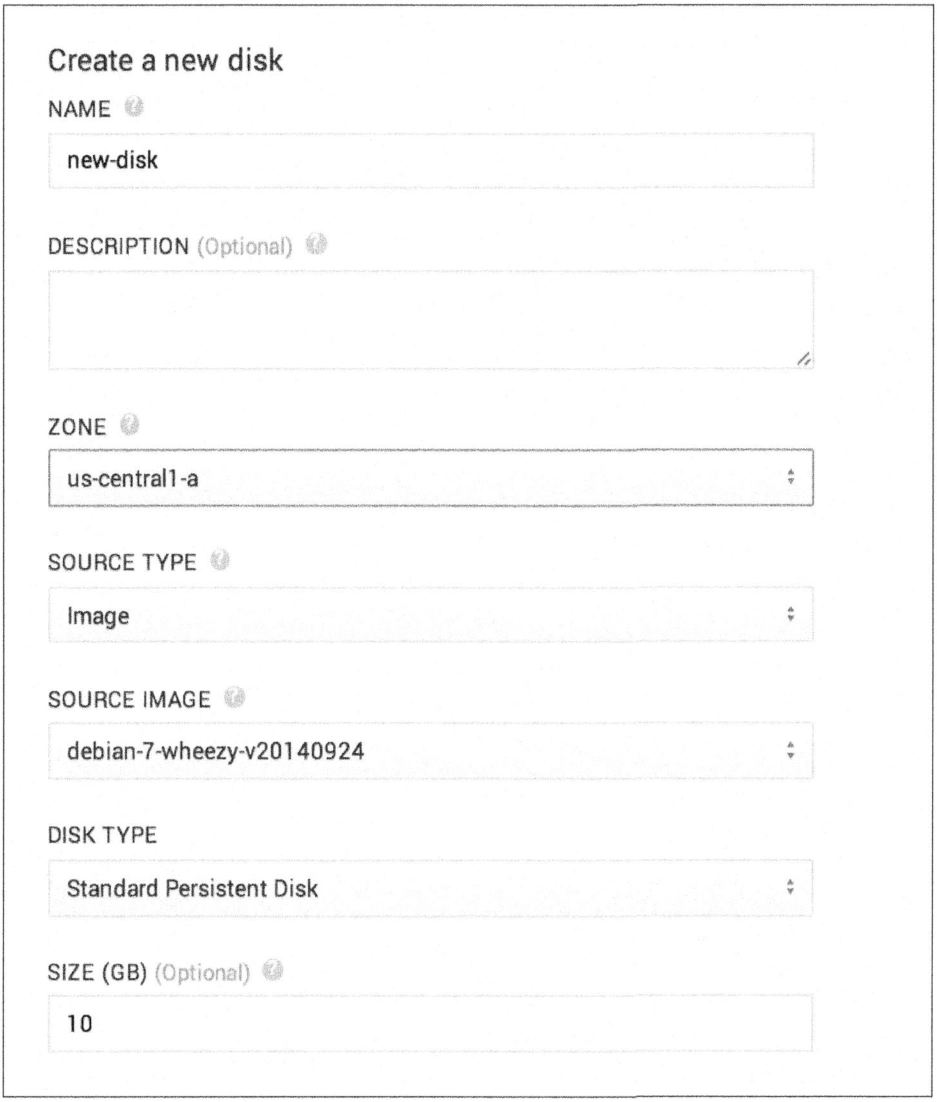

Figure 3-3. Cloud Console new disk creation

```
Equivalent REST request

This is the REST request with the parameters you have selected.

POST https://www.googleapis.com/compute/v1/projects/gce-oreilly/zones/us-central1-a/disks'
{
  "name": "new-disk",
  "zone": "https://www.googleapis.com/compute/v1/projects/gce-oreilly/zones/us-central1-a'
  "type": "https://www.googleapis.com/compute/v1/projects/gce-oreilly/zones/us-central1-a,
  "sizeGb": "10"
}
```

☐ Line wrapping

Close   REST API reference
```

*Figure 3-4. Equivalent REST for new disk creation*

Repeat this process with the new instance dialog. Choose the same zone you selected for the persistent disk for which you just captured the JSON document. Select "Existing disk" for the Boot Source, and choose any existing disk for the Source Disk (we'll replace this disk name with the name of the disk we're about to create programmatically) and take the rest of the defaults. Don't actually submit the Create Instance request. Instead, click the REST link to see the JSON document specifying the details of this instance creation request for use via the Compute Engine API. Copy and paste this text into the same file you used earlier to save the disk-creation request.

Starting with the Python program we wrote in Chapter 2 (*ch2-1.py*), let's replace the definition of BODY to two different bodies, BODY1 and BODY2 (to capture the data associated with the two separate requests we need to submit). We construct these two
```

request bodies by copying and pasting fragments of the JSON document generated by
the Developers Console:

```
# JSON doc capturing details of persistent disk creation request.
BODY1 = {
  "name": "new-disk",
  "zone": "https://www.googleapis.com/compute/v1/projects/gce-oreilly/zones/us-
central1-a",
  "type": "https://www.googleapis.com/compute/v1/projects/gce-oreilly/zones/us-
central1-a/diskTypes/pd-standard",
  "sizeGb": "10"
}
# JSON doc capturing details of instance creation request,
# referencing newly created persistent disk as boot device.
BODY2 = {
  "disks": [
    {
      "type": "PERSISTENT",
      "boot": True,
      "mode": "READ_WRITE",
      "deviceName": "new-disk",
      "zone": "https://www.googleapis.com/compute/v1/projects/gce-oreilly/zones/us-
central1-a",
      "source": "https://www.googleapis.com/compute/v1/projects/gce-oreilly/zones/us-
central1-a/disks/new-disk",
      "autoDelete": True
    }
  ],
  "networkInterfaces": [
    {
      "network": "https://www.googleapis.com/compute/v1/projects/gce-
oreilly/global/networks/default",
      "accessConfigs": [
        {
          "name": "External NAT",
          "type": "ONE_TO_ONE_NAT"
        }
      ]
    }
  ],
  "metadata": {
    "items": []
  },
  "tags": {
    "items": []
  },
  "zone": "https://www.googleapis.com/compute/v1/projects/gce-oreilly/zones/us-
central1-a",
  "canIpForward": False,
  "scheduling": {
    "automaticRestart": True,
    "onHostMaintenance": "MIGRATE"
```

```
    },
    "machineType": "https://www.googleapis.com/compute/v1/projects/gce-oreilly/zones/us-
central1-a/machineTypes/n1-standard-1",
    "name": "new-instance",
    "serviceAccounts": [
      {
        "email": "default",
        "scopes": [
          "https://www.googleapis.com/auth/devstorage.read_only"
        ]
      }
    ]
  }
```

Next, we modify our previous request logic, which launched and waited for a single instance creation request to launch and wait for completion of the two separate requests. We do this by refactoring the code that waits for an asynchronous result into the following function that we can call repeatedly:

```python
def wait_for_result(obj_type, response):
  # Wait for response to asynch operation.
  print 'waiting for', obj_type
  op_name = response["name"]
  operations = service.zoneOperations()
  while True:
    request = operations.get(project=PROJECT_ID, zone=ZONE,
                operation=op_name)
    try:
      response = request.execute()
    except Exception, ex:
      print "ERROR: " + str(ex)
      sys.exit()
    if "error" in response:
      print "ERROR: " + str(response["error"])
      sys.exit()
    status = response["status"]
    if status == "DONE":
      print obj_type + " created."
      break
```

Finally, we modify the main logic in our program to loop over the two requests (disk creation and instance creation), using our new `wait_for_result` function to sequentially wait for the asynchronous results. Here's the new code:

```python
requests = (('Disk', service.disks, BODY1),
            ('Instance', service.instances, BODY2))
# Build and execute two requests in sequence.
for (type, method, body) in requests:
  request = method().insert(project=PROJECT_ID, zone=ZONE, body=body)
  try:
    response = request.execute(http)
  except Exception, ex:
```

```
        print "ERROR: " + str(ex)
        sys.exit()
    wait_for_result(type, response)
```

The completed version of the Chapter 3 program can be found in the *ch3-1.py* file, which can be obtained from the *gce-oreilly* GitHub repository (*https://github.com/ GoogleCloudPlatform/gce-oreilly/raw/master/ch3-1.py*). Make sure you have a valid *client_secret.json* file in the same directory.

Now run the Chapter 3 code using a similar command to the one we used in Chapter 2. Where previously we saw a one-step instance creation, this time we see two steps completing successfully:

```
$ python ch3-1.py
Waiting for Disk creation.
Disk created.
Waiting for Instance creation.
Instance created.
```

If you check the Developers Console or run the gcloud compute disks list and gcloud compute instances lists commands, you should see your new persistent disk and your new instance, along with a summary of the attributes you assigned to each.

Persistent Disk Snapshots

Snapshots are another important feature available with persistent disks. As the name suggests, snapshots provide a way to record the state of a persistent disk as it existed at a given point in time. A method is also available to perform the inverse operation— to reload the contents of a persistent disk from a previously recorded snapshot. In other words, snapshots provide a fast load-and-store mechanism for persistent disks.

Persistent disk snapshots are geo-replicated and, hence, offer very high availability. The principal use cases for snapshots are:

- Disaster recovery to back up and restore disk contents
- Data archiving/backup, for incremental content storage over time
- Data migration, for moving information between zones or regions
- Data cloning, for fast copy of disk contents

Snapshots can be taken while a persistent disk is mounted by one or more virtual machines. In fact, taking a snapshot of a mounted disk does not impact the performance of the associated virtual machine's access to the disk, but you do need to consider data consistency.

The steps required to safely take a snapshot are straightforward:

1. Flush data and freeze the application (this step is application specific). Note that some advanced applications, like MySQL, have built-in journaling support and can recover lost write buffers that are never flushed to disk. In that case, you can afford to skip the application freeze step, but you may pay for that convenience in real-time performance cost when loading the snapshot because the application may require some additional time to recover missing data from its transaction log.

2. Run the `sudo sync` command to flush operating system caching of written data.

3. Flush and freeze the filesystem (use `fsfreeze` for ext3/ext4). Note that you cannot freeze the boot filesystem, so for that device, you will skip this step.

4. Take a snapshot (using Google Developers Console, `gcloud`, or the Compute Engine API) and wait until the resulting operation reaches the state `READY` or `UPLOADING`.[4]

5. Unfreeze the filesystem (use `fsfreeze -u` for ext3/ext4).

6. Unfreeze the application.

 It's critical that you use a journaling filesystem to store data on a persistent disk. Anything less runs the risk of data corruption and data loss, due to the possibility of buffered writes not making it to the disk in the event of an unexpected outage.

Compute Engine persistent disk snapshots are differential, which means that only the first snapshot taken of a given disk is a complete copy of all the data stored on that disk. Each subsequent snapshot is incremental (i.e., it captures only the disk blocks that have been added or changed since the last snapshot). Persistent disk snapshots have global scope, which means they exist outside the scope of any particular Compute Engine zone or region.

Like all Compute Engine capabilities, you can use any of the three supported modes of access to record a snapshot from an existing persistent disk, to create a new persistent disk from an existing snapshot, and to create a new instance using a boot persistent disk whose contents are initialized from a snapshot.

---

4 `READY` means the snapshot is completed. `UPLOADING` means the snapshot has been recorded and is in the process of being copied to Google Cloud Storage. In both of those states, it's safe to unfreeze the filesystem and the application in the mounting virtual machine(s).

Although persistent disks have zonal scope (and, hence, their usage is limited to a single zone and their replication is limited to multiple copies within a zone), snapshots are stored in Google Cloud Storage (which we'll cover in the next chapter) and have global scope. This is powerful because it means one global snapshot can be used to initialize disks in any zone or region. This gives us a mechanism to create new VMs with identical disk contents (i.e., to clone VMs) from one global snapshot into any region or zone we like. It also gives us the ability to migrate persistent disks from one zone to another, based on the following simple algorithm:

1. Take a snapshot of persistent disk A in zone X.
2. Create a new persistent disk B in zone Y based on the snapshot taken in step 1.

Snapshots are also quite useful for backing up persistent disks. You can periodically take a snapshot of a persistent disk, using any of the available access methods, and the disk contents will be safely stored away in geo-replicated, durable storage. If, for any reason, your persistent disk data becomes unusable (e.g., if an application-layer problem causes your VM to overwrite valuable data), you'll have the option to restore your persistent disk as of the time of your last completed snapshot.

Another interesting use of snapshots is in support of cross-zone static data distribution. Imagine a persistent disk with data that you'd like to share on a read-only basis across multiple zones. The multiple VM read-only mounting of a single disk works fine within a zone; but because persistent disks have zonal scope, that single disk cannot be mounted across zones. Snapshots provide a way to easily and efficiently distribute the static data to a disk in each zone, where it can be multiply mounted read-only by many instances. The following algorithm summarizes the process:

1. Create a persistent disk, attach it to a virtual machine, and populate it with the desired data.
2. Take a snapshot.
3. Clone the disk by creating additional disks in different zones using the snapshot from step 2 as the initial disk contents.
4. In each zone of interest, mount the per-zone disk read-only by the desired number of local instances.

With this approach, you can share vast amounts of static data with thousands of servers spread across any number of zones. If one disk doesn't provide sufficient capacity, you can use multiple seed volumes, snapshots, and disk clones, thereby arbitrarily expanding the capacity of this arrangement.

Summary

This chapter presented an overview of Compute Engine storage options. We learned about Compute Engine persistent disks and how to create and use PDs in a variety of configurations, using our three main access modes.

Up Next

Now that we've learned about the persistent disk mechanism built into Compute Engine, we'll explore another important and very powerful storage mechanism available both inside and outside of virtual machines: Google Cloud Storage.

## CHAPTER 4

Storage: Cloud Storage

Google Cloud Storage provides the ability to store binary large objects (a.k.a. BLOBs) in the cloud. You can read or write BLOBs from anywhere on the Internet, subject to access control that you can define, including from any Compute Engine instance, no matter which zone it is in. Your BLOBs are also stored in a durable, available, and secure way, and are served by a massively scalable distributed infrastructure.

This makes Cloud Storage ideal for two key scenarios:

- Storing and retrieving unstructured data from any Compute Engine instance in any zone
- Storing and retrieving unstructured data from both inside and outside Compute Engine (e.g., for sharing data with your customers)

A particularly important special case of the second scenario is importing or exporting large quantities of data into and out of Google's Cloud Platform.

It is important to understand the difference between durability and availability when it comes to storage. Roughly speaking, durability is defined by the probability that an object will not be permanently and irrevocably lost, whereas availability is defined by the probability that an object can be retrieved at a particular point in time. Cloud Storage provides a service-level agreement (SLA) that clearly specifies what level of availability the customer should expect and what sort of compensation the customer will receive if that SLA is not met. Cloud Storage offers multiple classes of storage, at different prices, with different SLAs. However, in all the current offerings, the data is stored in a highly durable way, which means that even if you can't access your data *right now*, it is not lost forever. It will become available again at some point in the (not too distant) future. Google does not provide an estimate of durability. In practice, with multiple copies of your data stored in multiple data centers, the probability of losing every copy of your data is extremely low, making the theoretical durability incredibly high.

Understanding BLOB Storage

BLOB has become a common industry term for a file of any type. While formats such as ASCII or Unicode are not generally considered binary files, they are made up of ones and zeros just like JPEG images, MPEG movies, Linux-executable files, or any other type of file. Cloud Storage is considered a BLOB Storage system because it treats all files as unstructured binary data.

Similarly, there's no particular reason why a BLOB needs to be particularly large. Cloud Storage is perfectly happy to store an object that has zero bytes of content. BLOBs in Cloud Storage can be up to 5 TB in size.

At this point, you might be saying to yourself, "A BLOB sounds a whole lot like a file to me." And you would be exactly correct. However, one reason the industry has taken to referring to this style of storage as a "BLOB store" instead of "filesystem," and thus calling the contents "BLOBs" or "objects" instead of "files" is because the word "filesystem" implies a great deal of functionality that so-called "BLOB stores" typically do not provide. Not providing certain filesystem features offers some useful scalability tradeoffs. After we've taken a tour of Cloud Storage, we'll return to this topic and examine it in more detail; but for now, just keep in mind that while Cloud Storage may look and feel a whole lot like a filesystem, particularly when viewed through the lens of some higher-level tools (e.g., gsutil, Cloud Console), in the end, it's not a traditional filesystem, and if you expect it to behave exactly like the filesystems you are accustomed to, you may get some surprises. For example, Cloud Storage does not have directories, in the traditional sense.

The Cloud Storage documentation refers to an individual piece of data stored in Cloud Storage as an "object," not as a "BLOB," and throughout this book, we will use the term "object" as well.

Getting Started

Go to *http://cloud.google.com/console* and select the project you created in the "Creating a Compute Engine Project" section in Chapter 1. In the lefthand navigation bar, click Storage > Cloud Storage > Storage browser. Assuming you have not used this project to access Cloud Storage before, you should see a welcome message, as shown in Figure 4-1.

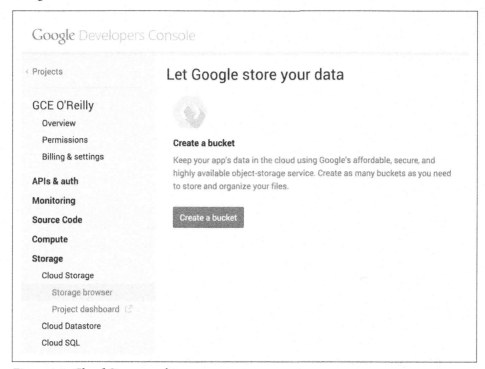

Figure 4-1. Cloud Storage welcome screen

 If you have not yet completed the steps from the "Creating a Compute Engine Project" on page 2 in Chapter 1, you may be prompted to enter billing information.

As the UI suggests, your first act should be to create a new bucket. A bucket is a container for objects. Press the "Create a bucket" button, and enter a name for your new bucket. Normally, bucket names may contain only lowercase letters, dashes, and underscores. Also, bucket names must be globally unique across the entire Cloud Storage service, so if you choose something obvious, like "test," there's a good chance you'll get an error, because someone else already created a bucket with that name.

As mentioned earlier, Cloud Storage does not support the concept of directories in the traditional sense. While a bucket is a container for objects, similar to how a directory is a container for files, you cannot nest buckets within buckets, the way you can nest subdirectories into parent directories in a hierarchy like most filesystems provide.

If you've created a bucket, then congratulations! Your project is set up to use Cloud Storage. You can use the Storage browser in the Cloud Console to create and delete buckets, upload objects, download objects, delete objects, and adjust object permissions and metadata. If you're only working with a handful of objects, this is probably the quickest and easiest way to do what you need. However, just as with Compute Engine, there are several ways to use Cloud Storage, including an API and a command-line tool, gsutil, which we examine next.

Introducing gsutil

In earlier chapters, you have been using the gcloud compute command to interact with Compute Engine. gsutil is the equivalent command for Cloud Storage. Let's create a Compute Engine instance called test-vm so we can take gsutil for a spin. Note the use of the --scopes flag, which was introduced in Chapter 2:

```
$ gcloud compute instances create test-vm \
    --zone us-central1-a --scopes storage-full
[..]
```

Now we can ssh into your new instance to take gsutil for a spin:

```
$ gcloud compute ssh test-vm --zone us-central1-a
[..]
```

The gsutil ls command gives you a list of your buckets, and we can see the bucket we created using the Cloud Console Web UI in the previous section. Note that because of the global bucket namespace, your bucket name will be different than the bucket name shown in this sample output:

```
test-vm$ gsutil ls
gs://gce-oreilly-example/
```

gsutil uses a URI syntax to allow the user to express, "This is a local file" (e.g., file://path/to/local/file), versus, "This is an object in Google Cloud Storage" (e.g., gs://bucket/object), versus, "This is an object in another cloud storage system" (e.g., s3://bucket/object). If you don't specify a scheme on the URI, gsutil assumes you mean a local file.

Now let's create our first object. Be sure to use your bucket name with these commands, not the bucket name shown in this example:

```
test-vm$ echo 'Hello Cloud Storage!' > hello
test-vm$ gsutil cp hello gs://gce-oreilly-example
Copying file://hello [Content-Type=application/octet-stream]...
test-vm$ gsutil ls gs://gce-oreilly-example
gs://gce-oreilly-example/hello
test-vm$ gsutil cat gs://gce-oreilly-example/hello
Hello Cloud Storage!
```

You have now stored and retrieved an object in Cloud Storage. If you go back to the Cloud Console Web UI page you were using earlier and click your bucket name, you should now see the hello object there.

There's a fair bit going on here, so let's break it down. First of all, you'll notice that you did not need to install gsutil. The images provided by Compute Engine already have a version of gsutil installed and ready to go.

> There are many occasions where you'll want to use gsutil outside of a Compute Engine instance. For example, perhaps you have files on your development workstation that you want to upload to a Cloud Storage bucket, so you can then operate on that data from Compute Engine. Fortunately, if you followed the instructions in Chapter 1 to install the Cloud SDK, you already have a copy of gsutil installed on your workstation.

Next, you'll notice that you didn't need to provide any credentials to gsutil: no OAuth flow, no editing configuration files. Somehow, it obtained appropriate credentials to act on Cloud Storage. As we discussed in Chapter 2, this particular piece of magic is enabled via the --scopes flag that you passed to gcloud compute when you asked it to create the instance. What you did with that flag is tell Compute Engine that you want programs running on this instance to be able to use the service account that was automatically created when you created your project. The storage-full part of that flag tells it what services you want those programs to be able to use (in this case, Cloud Storage). Finally, gsutil understands that it is running in a Compute Engine instance configured this way and automatically acts as the project's service account, because that's obviously what you intended if you created the instance using the --scopes flag.

This is why you were able to ssh into your freshly created Compute Engine instance and immediately issue the gsutil ls command and see a list of the buckets owned by the project that owns the Compute Engine instance. If you signed into a different instance owned by a different project, you would see that project's buckets instead.

gsutil is a very powerful tool that exposes every significant feature provided by Cloud Storage. Because this book is about Compute Engine and not Cloud Storage, there's a lot we don't have space to cover. However, spending some quality time with gsutil's extensive built-in help is highly recommended. The gsutil help command is your starting point.

 One of the many useful features of gsutil is that it can transparently work with local files (e.g., */tmp/my-local-file*), objects in Cloud Storage (e.g., *gs://my-bucket/my-object*), or objects in Amazon's S3 service (e.g., *s3://my-s3-bucket/my-s3-object*). This means the following gsutil command is legal and does exactly what you might expect (copy all the objects in an S3 bucket to a Cloud Storage bucket):

```
$ gsutil cp s3://my-s3-bucket/* gs://my-gcs-bucket
```

If the bucket is large, you'll probably want to use the -m (multithreaded) command-line switch as well. -l (log) and -n (noclobber) are also very handy for this sort of operation, as is the gsutil rsync command. gsutil help can tell you more about those options and commands.

Using Cloud Storage from Your Code

As useful as the Cloud Console and gsutil can be, there may come a time when you need to perform some operations on your objects or buckets in the context of a larger program. Shelling out to gsutil is always an option, but may not always be the best option. Fortunately, Cloud Storage provides a full featured API that your programs can use to interact directly with your objects and buckets. In fact, it provides two APIs: an XML-oriented one and a JSON-oriented one.

The two APIs provide almost all the same functionality, but with different styles. If you're starting from scratch, the JSON API is probably the one you want to use and is the one we will demonstrate here. It is consistent in style and structure with other Google APIs such as Google Maps, Google+, and Google Analytics. This makes it possible for Google to provide helpful client libraries in many different languages and useful tools such as the Google Plugin for Eclipse. The consistency between Google APIs makes is easier for a developer who is familiar with one Google API to be immediately productive with a different Google API.

The XML API, not coincidentally, closely resembles Amazon's S3 REST API, making it easy for developers to add support for Cloud Storage to existing tools, libraries, and other code that was originally written for use with S3. If you have some existing code that works with S3 and you want to migrate to Cloud Storage, the XML API makes that easier.

Before writing any code, you need to install the Google APIs Client Library for Python. These Python libraries make it easier to work with many different Google APIs, not just Cloud Storage. pip is a great tool for installing Python packages and is available via apt-get on Debian-based Compute Engine instances. ssh into the test-vm instance you created earlier and run these commands:

```
test-vm$ sudo apt-get update
[..]
test-vm$ sudo apt-get install python-pip
[..]
test-vm$ sudo pip install --upgrade google-api-python-client
Downloading/unpacking google-api-python-client
[..]
Successfully installed google-api-python-client httplib2
Cleaning up...
```

The following command downloads a simple Python program that demonstrates how to access an object in Cloud Storage:

```
test-vm$ gsutil cp gs://gce-oreilly/hello_cloud_storage.py .
Copying gs://gce-oreilly/hello_cloud_storage.py...
```

Here is the content of *hello_cloud_storage.py*:

```python
import httplib2
from apiclient.discovery import build
from oauth2client import gce

# These two lines take care of all the often tricky authorization
# steps by getting us an Http object that automatically adds the
# appropriate Authorization: header to our requests, using the
# service account associated with the project that owns the Compute
# Engine instance on which this program is running. Note that for
# this to work, the --scopes=storage-full flag must be specified to
# gcloud compute when the instance was created.
credentials = gce.AppAssertionCredentials(
    scope='https://www.googleapis.com/auth/devstorage.read_write')
http = credentials.authorize(httplib2.Http())

# The Google APIs library dynamically builds a Python object that
# understands the operations provided by Cloud Storage. Every API
# has a name and a version (in this case, 'storage' and 'v1').
# Depending on when you are reading this, you may find there is a
# newer version of the 'storage' API available.
storage = build('storage', 'v1')
```

```
# Google APIs expose collections, which typically expose methods that
# are common across many APIs, such as list(), or get(). In the case
# of Cloud Storage, the get() method on the objects collection gets
# an object's metadata, and the get_media() method gets an object's
# data.
request = storage.objects().get_media(
    bucket='gce-oreilly', object='hello')

# Also note that get_media(), and other methods, do not perform the
# action directly. They instead return an HttpRequest object that can
# be used to perform the action. This is important, because it gives
# us the opportunity to authorize our request by passing in the Http
# object we created earlier that knows about our service account.
print request.execute(http=http)

# The previous call to get_media() fetched the object's data. This
# call to get() will fetch the object's metadata. The Google API
# libraries conveniently take care of converting the response from
# the JSON used on the network to a Python dictionary, which we can
# iterate over to print the object's metadata to the console.
request = storage.objects().get(bucket='gce-oreilly', object='hello')
metadata = request.execute(http=http)
for key, value in metadata.iteritems():
  print key + "=" + str(value)
```

When you run this through the Python interpreter, you should see the contents of
gs://gce-oreilly/hello (in URI parlance) and the metadata associated with the
object:

```
test-vm$ python hello_cloud_storage.py
Hello Cloud Storage!
kind=storage#object
contentType=application/octet-stream
name=hello
etag=CLDgk+KZhrwCEAI=
generation=1389995772670000
md5Hash=ocbFPgjShy+EHAb+0DpjJg==
bucket=gce-oreilly
[..]
size=21
```

While dumping the contents and metadata of a single object to the console is obviously the simplest possible Cloud Storage programming task, this nonetheless demonstrates several key points. First, Compute Engine makes it easy to use Cloud
Storage via the built-in service account support. Second, using the Cloud Storage
JSON API means you do not need to laboriously assemble correctly formatted custom HTTP requests. The Google APIs client library understands the operations available and how to formulate the appropriate requests. Third, the Google APIs library
handles translating JSON responses into convenient native Python dictionaries.

Configuring Access Control

Up to this point, we have seen how to create buckets and objects and read their contents using the Cloud Console Web UI, gsutil, and your own custom Python code. We have always been acting either as ourselves as an owner of our project, or as the automatically created project service account, which is also a member of the project. Unsurprisingly, owners and members of the project have, by default, the appropriate access rights to create buckets owned by that project, and create and read objects in those buckets. Where access control gets interesting, and where Cloud Storage gets particularly useful, is when you want to give specific rights to people or service accounts that are not part of your project. This is also where we will start to see some of the significant differences between Cloud Storage and traditional filesystems.

Every object in Cloud Storage has an access control list (ACL). You can use gsutil acl get to see the ACL applied to an object.

 What's an ACL? An ACL is a list of people or groups that you're granting permission to perform specific operations on an object. ACLs are more explicit and flexible than the permission bits you may be accustomed to working with on UNIX-style filesystems, which only allow you to specify permissions for the file's "owner," "group," and "everyone else," because you are not limited to granting permissions only to a single individual (the owner) and a single group.

If you are not already logged into your test-vm, use the gcutil ssh command to do so and try the following example (using your bucket name instead of the one shown here, of course):

```
test-vm$ gsutil acl get gs://gce-oreilly-example/hello
[
  {
    "entity": "project-owners-1342[..]",
    "projectTeam": {
      "projectNumber": "1342[..]",
      "team": "owners"
    },
    "role": "OWNER"
  },
  {
    "entity": "project-editors-1342[..]",
    "projectTeam": {
      "projectNumber": "1342[..]",
      "team": "editors"
    },
    "role": "OWNER"
  },
```

```
{
  "entity": "project-viewers-1342[..]",
  "projectTeam": {
    "projectNumber": "1342[..]",
    "team": "viewers"
  },
  "role": "READER"
},
{
  "entity": "user-00b4[..]145f",
  "entityId": "00b4[..]145f",
  "role": "OWNER"
}
]
```

How to read this? Notice that "entities" are being assigned "roles." In this particular case, the first three entities are groups that correspond to the various team members of your project whom you've added with "Is Owner," or "Can Edit," or "Can View" permissions. This is what Cloud Storage calls a `project-private` "canned" ACL. There are other so-called canned ACLs that are useful for common scenarios. The `project-private` canned ACL is a reasonable default ACL for many situations, giving the project team members reasonable default rights, while making sure that no one outside the project can access the object. You can apply a different canned ACL via `gsutil`. For example, if you want to make the object completely private to yourself, the `private` canned ACL will do the trick:

```
test-vm$ gsutil acl set private gs://gce-oreilly-example/hello
Setting ACL on gs://gce-oreilly-example/hello...
test-vm$ gsutil acl get gs://gce-oreilly-example/hello
[
  {
    "entity": "user-00b4[..]145f",
    "entityId": "00b4[..]145f",
    "role": "OWNER"
  }
]
```

You're now the only one in the world who can access this particular object. You have the right to modify the ACL because you are the OWNER of the object. Similarly, if you want to share your object with everyone, you can use the `public-read` canned ACL:

```
test-vm$ gsutil acl set public-read gs://gce-oreilly-example/hello
Setting ACL on gs://gce-oreilly-example/hello...
test-vm$ gsutil acl get gs://gce-oreilly-example/hello
[
  {
    "entity": "user-00b4[..]145f",
    "entityId": "00b4[..]145f",
    "role": "OWNER"
  },
  {
```

```
    "entity": "allUsers",
    "role": "READER"
  }
]
```

You can now see that the entity allUsers has READER role for this object. Objects that give allUsers the READER role do not require authentication to be accessed. This means that anyone in the world can navigate a web browser to *http://storage.googleapis.com/gce-oreilly-example/hello*, and will be able to fetch the object. If you want this to work the way most users would expect, you may want to set an appropriate Content-Type (a.k.a. MIME type) on your object, so the browser will know what to do with it. If you do not set the Content-Type, Cloud Storage uses the default of binary/octet-stream. Most browsers will interpret binary/octet-stream as a file to be downloaded and ask users where they want to save the file. If your object contains HTML data, this is probably not the behavior you want. gsutil helps you out by looking at the extension of the local filename and inferring what type it should be. For example, if you upload *hello.txt*, gsutil will automatically apply a Content-Type of text/plain. You can set the Content-Type (and a few other useful headers) on Cloud Storage objects via the gsutil setmeta command.

> You are not allowed to set arbitrary headers on your objects. See gsutil help metadata for the current list of allowed headers.

Another thing you might want to do is share an object with a particular person, or group of people, who are not part of the project team. For example, you may wish to share an object with a set of your customers or end users. The most efficient way to do this is to first create a Google group, add the individuals to that group, and grant that group permission to the object.

You can create a new Google group by going to *http://groups.google.com* and clicking Create Group. Because you're using this group to manage access to resources, you'll want to make sure that people can't add themselves to it without your permission. The group settings for this example are shown in Figure 4-2. Note that "Only invited users" is selected for who can join the group.

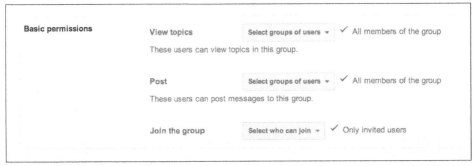

Figure 4-2. Example Google Group settings

Now that we have a group, we can grant it read permission to the object. First we restore the private canned ACL, then we use the gsutil acl ch (change ACL) command to selectively add a read permission for the group:

```
test-vm$ gsutil acl set private gs://gce-oreilly-example/hello
Setting ACL on gs://gce-oreilly-example/hello...
test-vm$ gsutil acl ch -g gce-oreilly-example@googlegroups.com:r \
        gs://gce-oreilly-example/hello
Updated ACL on gs://gce-oreilly-example/hello
test-vm$ gsutil acl get gs://gce-oreilly-example/hello
[
  {
    "entity": "user-00b4[..]145f",
    "entityId": "00b4[..]145f",
    "role": "OWNER"
  },
  {
    "email": "gce-oreilly-example@googlegroups.com",
    "entity": "group-gce-oreilly-example@googlegroups.com",
    "role": "READER"
  }
]
```

The group now has read access to the object. Just to reiterate, while you can add individual users to an object's ACL, it's a best practice to only add groups, so that when people join and leave teams, you can simply add or remove them from the group, instead of having to update the ACL on potentially millions of objects.

Understanding ACLs

So far we have only been looking at object ACLs. And you'll also notice that we've only seen two roles: OWNER and READER. That's because those are the only two roles that an object can have, and they are concentric (i.e., OWNER implies READER). The meaning of READER is pretty self-explanatory—it means you're allowed to fetch the content of the object. OWNER means that, in addition to being able to fetch the object, you also have the right to modify the ACL.

You're probably wondering where the WRITER role for objects is. This is one of the differences between a BLOB storage system and a traditional filesystem. If you think about what WRITER means in a filesystem, it means you can open the file and modify its contents. There is no such operation in Cloud Storage, as objects in Cloud Storage are immutable. Once an object is written to Cloud Storage, you can't append more data to it, or change just a few bytes in the middle of it. You can only delete the object or overwrite it with a completely new object. Thus, there is no WRITER role for objects to determine who has permission to perform a write operation, because it is impossible to perform a write operation on an object.

Instead, the WRITER role exists at the bucket level in Cloud Storage. Having the WRITER role on a bucket means that you are allowed to create, delete, or overwrite objects in that bucket.

The overwrite operation in Cloud Storage is atomic and strongly consistent. Putting this in terms of gsutil operations, if you run:

```
gsutil cp hello.html gs://mybucket/hello.html
```

to copy a new version of *hello.html* to your bucket, overwriting the version of *hello.html* that's already there, no clients will ever see a partially written *hello.html*. Before the gsutil command completes, they will see the old version, and after the gsutil command completes, they will see the new version, and at no time will they see a "Not Found" error or partially written data.

It's also important to understand that having the READER role on a bucket does not give you the right to read the content of the objects in the bucket. That privilege is granted by having the READER role on the object itself, as already discussed. Instead, having the READER role on the bucket gives you the right to get a list of the objects contained in that bucket.

Finally, the OWNER role on a bucket gives you the right to modify the ACL on the bucket and also to modify something called the "default object ACL," which we will discuss in the next section.

In this book, we use the ACL terminology from the Cloud Storage JSON API, which assigns "roles" with "entities." If you're using the Cloud Storage XML API, you'll be assigning "permissions" to "scopes," but the functionality is the same.

Using Default Object ACLs

The default object ACL is a very useful feature of Cloud Storage, and is worth under-standing well. In the case that the `project-private` canned ACL is the ACL you want for any object you add to a bucket, the default behavior demonstrated earlier is exactly what you want. But let's say you instead want to make all the objects in the bucket have an ACL that gives a specific group READ permission?

Associating a custom default object ACL with the bucket solves this problem in a clean and convenient way. What you're telling Cloud Storage with a default object ACL is "Please apply this ACL to every object that is written to this bucket, unless the ACL is explicitly overridden." In fact, every bucket has a default object ACL, and the "default" default object ACL is of course, `project-private`, which is why the first object we created had the `project-private` ACL. Now let's change the default object ACL on our test bucket to a custom default object ACL that provides READ access to a specific group:

```
test-vm$ gsutil defacl get gs://gce-oreilly-example
[
  {
    "entity": "project-owners-1342[..]",
    "projectTeam": {
      "projectNumber": "1342[..]",
      "team": "owners"
    },
    "role": "OWNER"
  },
  {
    "entity": "project-editors-1342[..]",
    "projectTeam": {
      "projectNumber": "1342[..]",
      "team": "editors"
    },
    "role": "OWNER"
  },
  {
    "entity": "project-viewers-1342[..]",
    "projectTeam": {
      "projectNumber": "1342[..]",
      "team": "viewers"
    },
    "role": "READER"
  }
]
test-vm$ gsutil defacl ch -g gce-oreilly-example@googlegroups.com:r \
        gs://gce-oreilly-example
Updated default ACL on gs://gce-oreilly-example/
test-vm$ gsutil defacl get gs://gce-oreilly-example
[
```

```
{
  "entity": "project-owners-1342[..]",
  "projectTeam": {
    "projectNumber": "1342[..]",
    "team": "owners"
  },
  "role": "OWNER"
},
{
  "entity": "project-editors-1342[..]",
  "projectTeam": {
    "projectNumber": "1342[..]",
    "team": "editors"
  },
  "role": "OWNER"
},
{
  "entity": "project-viewers-1342[..]",
  "projectTeam": {
    "projectNumber": "1342[..]",
    "team": "viewers"
  },
  "role": "READER"
},
{
  "email": "gce-oreilly-example@googlegroups.com",
  "entity": "group-gce-oreilly-example@googlegroups.com",
  "role": "READER"
}
]
```

We can use gsutil's `defacl get`, `defacl set`, and `defacl ch` commands to view and modify the bucket's default object ACL exactly like we've been using `acl get`, `acl set`, and `acl ch` to view and modify object and bucket ACLs. This sequence of commands also demonstrates that the "default" default object ACL is indeed `project-private`, and then shows how it can be modified. It is interesting to notice that the updated default object ACL does not mention the object's owner like we saw when we ran a similar sequence of commands on the `hello` object. This is because we don't know, in advance, who will create a particular object, and therefore don't know who the owner of that object will be. The owner of an object always has the `OWNER` role on an object, and the default object ACL specifies which permissions should be added in addition to the `OWNER` role.

The default object ACL on the bucket is only applied to newly created objects. To see this in action, first we ensure that the existing `hello` object is project-private:

```
test-vm$ gsutil acl set project-private gs://gce-oreilly-example/hello
Setting ACL on gs://gce-oreilly-example/hello...
```

Now we can create a second object and see that the default object ACL is applied to it:

```
test-vm$ gsutil cp hello gs://gce-oreilly-example/hello2
Copying file://hello [Content-Type=application/octet-stream]...
test-vm$ gsutil acl get gs://gce-oreilly-example/hello2
[
  {
    "entity": "project-owners-1342[..]",
    "projectTeam": {
      "projectNumber": "1342[..]",
      "team": "owners"
    },
    "role": "OWNER"
  },
  {
    "entity": "project-editors-1342[..]",
    "projectTeam": {
      "projectNumber": "1342[..]",
      "team": "editors"
    },
    "role": "OWNER"
  },
  {
    "entity": "project-viewers-1342[..]",
    "projectTeam": {
      "projectNumber": "1342[..]",
      "team": "viewers"
    },
    "role": "READER"
  },
  {
    "email": "gce-oreilly-example@googlegroups.com",
    "entity": "group-gce-oreilly-example@googlegroups.com",
    "role": "READER"
  },
  {
    "entity": "user-00b4[..]145f",
    "entityId": "00b4[..]145f",
    "role": "OWNER"
  }
]
```

Note how the default object ACL has been expanded to include an owner, and that owner has been given full control of the new object.

We can confirm that changing the default object ACL on the bucket does not modify any existing object ACLs by examining the old hello object:

```
test-vm$ gsutil acl get gs://gce-oreilly-example/hello
[
  {
    "entity": "user-00b4[..]145f",
    "entityId": "00b4[..]145f",
    "role": "OWNER"
  },
```

```
{
  "entity": "project-owners-1342[..]",
  "projectTeam": {
    "projectNumber": "1342[..]",
    "team": "owners"
  },
  "role": "OWNER"
},
{
  "entity": "project-editors-1342[..]",
  "projectTeam": {
    "projectNumber": "1342[..]",
    "team": "editors"
  },
  "role": "OWNER"
},
{
  "entity": "project-viewers-1342[..]",
  "projectTeam": {
    "projectNumber": "1342[..]",
    "team": "viewers"
  },
  "role": "READER"
}
]
```

It is very important to carefully consider the structure of your ACLs during development of your application. If you do not, you may find yourself in a situation where you need to update millions of object ACLs, individually, which can be inconvenient at best.

Understanding Object Immutability

As was mentioned a bit earlier, all objects in Cloud Storage are immutable. This means they cannot be changed. You can *overwrite* an existing object with a new one, but unlike what you may be accustomed to in a traditional filesystem, you cannot "open" an object, "seek" to an arbitrary offset in the object, "write" a series of bytes, and "close" the file. If you want to overwrite an object, you have to upload a new object, from the first byte to the last byte.

Cloud Storage does allow you to compose existing objects into new objects, which can be used to simulate a very limited form of "writing" to the middle or end of an existing object. Search the Cloud Storage documentation for "composite objects" for more details.

A corollary to the fact that all Cloud Storage objects are immutable is that you cannot read a partially written object. An object doesn't exist in Cloud Storage until you have uploaded the last byte and received a 200 OK response from the service.

Understanding Strong Consistency

Cloud Storage provides a strong "read after write" consistency guarantee when you finish writing an object. This means that if you write an object and get a 200 OK response, you can be sure that anyone, anywhere in the world who is authorized to read that object will be able to do so and will see the data you just finished writing (not some previous version you may have just overwritten). This stands in contrast to some cloud storage systems where one user could write an object, receive a 200 OK response, and then another user who attempts to read that object, perhaps from a different location, could receive a 404 "Not Found" response, or worse, read a previous, out-of-date, version of that object.

However, there are two caveats to the strong consistency of Cloud Storage. First, it does not apply to listing the contents of a bucket, or listing the buckets that belong to a project. Putting this in gsutil terms, if you gsutil cp an object into a bucket, it may take a few seconds or longer for that object to appear in the results of a gsutil ls <bucket> command, but if you know the name of the object, you are guaranteed to be able to gsutil stat that object. Similarly, when you create a bucket, it may take some time before it shows up in the results of gsutil ls.

The second caveat is that the statements on strong consistency do not apply if you allow your object to be cached using normal HTTP caching mechanisms. If you've allowed your object to be cached, which also implies it is publicly readable, then you may receive an out-of-date cached copy of an object instead of the one you just wrote, or you may still receive a copy of the object from a cache after it has been deleted from Cloud Storage. This is expected HTTP behavior. For more details, look up the Cache-Control header, both in the Cloud Storage documentation and in the HTTP specifications.

Summary

In this chapter, we learned that Cloud Storage is a BLOB storage system, and what exactly that means. Then we saw how to use Cloud Storage to create buckets and objects via the Cloud Console UI, the gsutil command-line tool, and via your own Python code using the Cloud Storage JSON API. We discussed the Cloud Storage ACL model in detail, and touched on the concepts of object immutability and strong consistency.

Up Next

Now that we've learned about the relatively unstructured storage mechanisms available to Compute Engine, namely Persistent Disk and Cloud Storage, we'll explore the more structured storage mechanisms of Cloud SQL and Cloud Datastore.

## CHAPTER 5

Storage: Cloud SQL and Cloud Datastore

The Google Cloud Platform offers two additional storage methods that are very useful for applications running on Compute Engine virtual machines, as well as for applications running outside of Compute Engine. Cloud SQL provides a managed MySQL service, and Cloud Datastore provides a highly scalable, managed NoSQL database in the cloud. We'll describe both of these services in detail in this chapter and show how to use each mechanism via our three main access methods.

Cloud SQL

Google Cloud SQL offers a cloud-hosted incarnation of the popular MySQL relational database-management system. Unlike traditional MySQL deployments, which can require significant administration skills to back up, replicate, and administer databases, this service is fully managed. Google takes care of updating the MySQL software version, replicating your stored data, and backing up your databases.

Google Cloud SQL originated as an App Engine feature, but it's since been extended to provide a general hosted relational database service for any application, anywhere. In this section, we'll walk through the steps to create a Cloud SQL relational database, and we'll access that database from a Compute Engine instance.

As with other Google Cloud services, Cloud SQL can be accessed in several ways: the Google Developers Console web UI, a command-line tool (`gcloud sql`), or the native MySQL wire protocol. There are also standard drivers available to access MySQL from just about any language, which should work well with Cloud SQL. As we work through the following tutorial steps, we'll illustrate each mode of access.

Getting Started

Point your web browser to the following URL: *http://console.developers.google.com/*. You'll be greeted by a list of your projects, as shown in Figure 5-1.

Figure 5-1. Google Developers Console—project selection

Click a project for which you've enabled Cloud SQL and you'll see a dashboard-like page. Now click the Storage->Cloud SQL service from the lefthand navigation list, to administer your Cloud SQL instances.

 If you have not yet completed the steps from the ""Creating a Compute Engine Project" on page 2" section of Chapter 1, you may be prompted to enter billing information.

Assuming this project has not yet used Cloud SQL, you should see a screen similar to that shown in Figure 5-2.

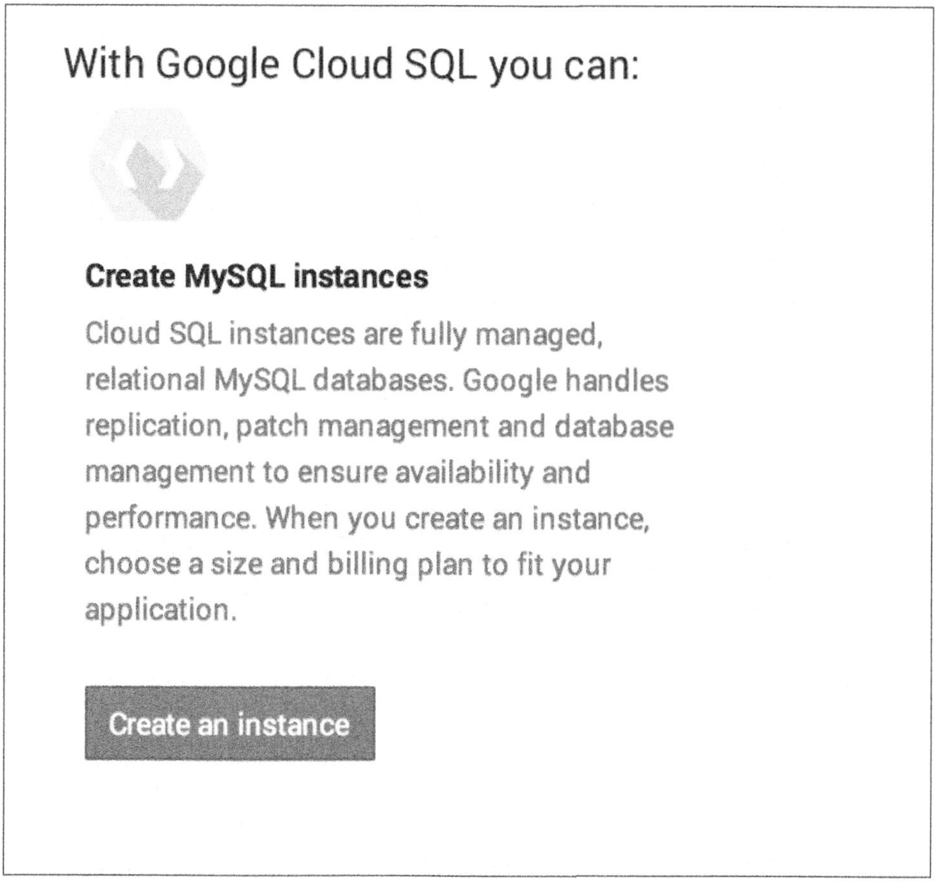

With Google Cloud SQL you can:

Create MySQL instances

Cloud SQL instances are fully managed,
relational MySQL databases. Google handles
replication, patch management and database
management to ensure availability and
performance. When you create an instance,
choose a size and billing plan to fit your
application.

Create an instance

Figure 5-2. Cloud SQL welcome screen

As the UI suggests, your first act should be to create a new Cloud SQL instance.
Clicking the "Create an instance" button presents the dialog shown in Figure 5-3.

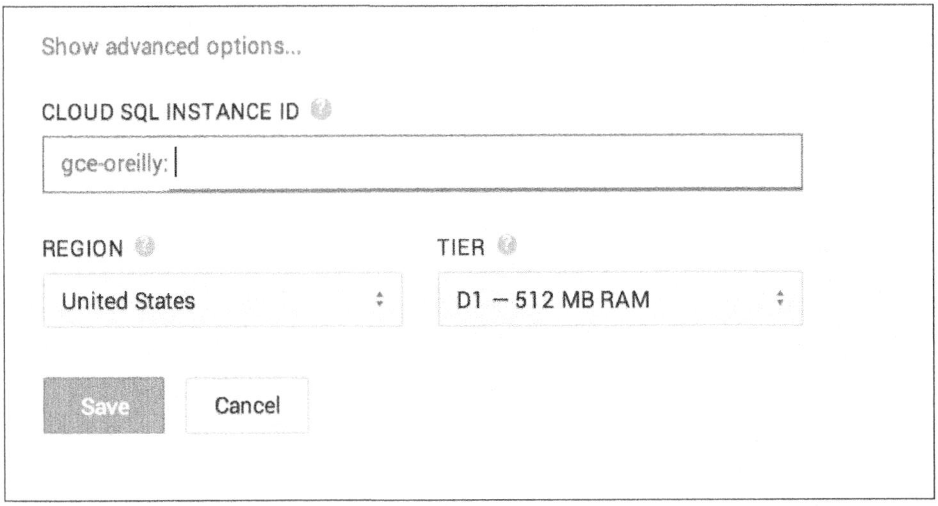

Figure 5-3. Cloud SQL instance-creation dialog

You will notice the following choices:

Instance name
> This can be any unique name within your project that contains only lowercase letters, digits, and hyphens.

Region
> Desired location for your instance. Currently supported choices are the US, Europe, and Asia (this option dictates location, not availability—the generated database instance is globally available, regardless of the selected region).

Tier
> One of several predefined price/performance levels.

You may also click the "Show advanced options" link to reveal several additional configuration choices, including:

Database version
> Version of MySQL software you'd like to use on your instances.

Billing plan
> Per-use (pay as you go) versus package (per-day) charging.

Preferred location
> Allows you to request that your databases be located in a particular Compute Engine zone, or that they stay close to the locations where an associated App Engine app is dispatched.

Backups
> Desired time of day at which you would like backups scheduled.

Activation policy
> Whether you would like your instance always active and ready to serve requests or activated on demand.

Filesystem replication
> Asynchronous replication results in faster write response times with slightly less durability, whereas synchronous replication provides the highest level of durability with slightly slower write response times.

IPv4 address
> Allocates a fixed IP address for your Cloud SQL instance.

Authorized networks
> This is a network whitelist. It allows you to enumerate a list of network addresses that are granted access to your databases.

Authorized App Engine applications
> List of App Engine application names that are permitted to access this instance directly. Authorized applications must reside in the same region as the associated instance and the Cloud SQL database will be located as close as possible to the first application listed.

MySQL flags
> These are configuration settings you can apply to your database server.

Enter instance name `cloud-sql-test`, specify your desired region and tier, take the default settings for the remaining options, and click the Save button to create your instance. The resulting page should look like the screen image shown in Figure 5-4.

Figure 5-4. Cloud SQL instance summary page

After a few minutes, the status "Being created" should change to Runnable. Clicking the hyperlinked instance ID on the instance summary page yields details about your instance parameters, as shown in Figure 5-5.

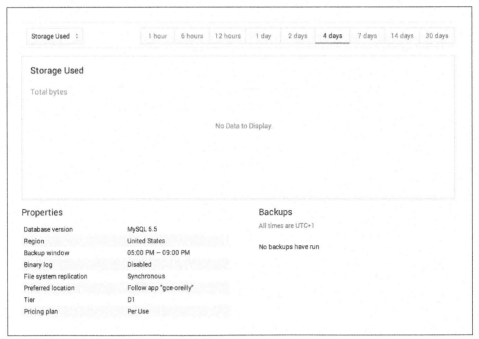

Figure 5-5. Cloud SQL instance details page

You will also see on the top of this page buttons that provide the ability to edit your settings, import data into your instance, export data from your instance, restart your instance, and delete your instance.

For security reasons, it's a good idea to restrict access to your new instance's root login. From the Cloud SQL instance details page, select the ACCESS CONTROL tab and set a root password for your instance, as shown in Figure 5-6.

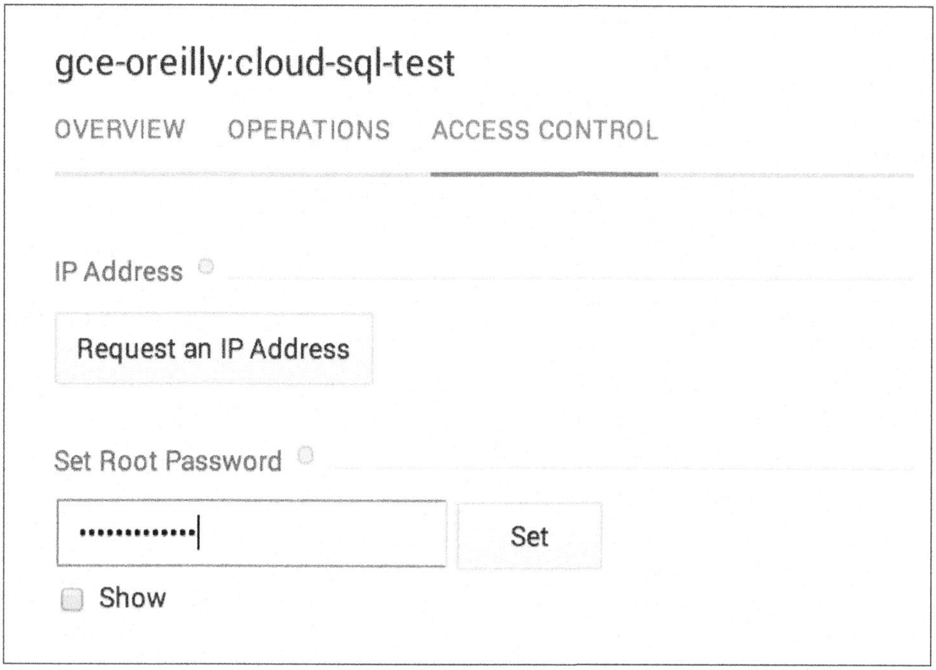

Figure 5-6. Setting root password for a Cloud SQL instance

Creating Databases and Tables

Now that we have a Cloud SQL instance, it can be accessed like any other standard MySQL database.[1] In this section, we'll create a database on our Cloud SQL instance, and store and retrieve some data to/from this database. Cloud SQL supports the standard MySQL client/server protocol so you can administer your databases and tables using any commercial or open source tool designed to work with that protocol, of which there are many choices. Because this is a book about Compute Engine, we'll install some open source software on a Compute Engine virtual machine and use that as our platform for manipulating a Cloud SQL database.

Following the examples from Chapter 2, create a virtual machine using any of the supported methods. For this exercise, let's call this VM cloud-sql-test. For example, you could use the gcloud compute instances create command to create your VM like this:

```
$ gcloud compute instances create cloud-sql-test --zone us-central1-a
Created [https://www.googleapis.com/compute/v1/projects/gce-oreilly/zones/us-central1-
a/instances/cloud-sql-test].
```

---

[1] There are lots of great resources available for learning how to use MySQL (see *http://oreilly.com/mysql/*).

```
NAME        ZONE    MACHINE_TYPE INTERNAL_IP EXTERNAL_IP STATUS
cloud-[..] us-[..] n1-[..]1     [..]        [..]        RUNNING
```

Note your new instance's external IP address for the next step.

Next, we'll grant access to your MySQL instance from your new virtual machine. Do this by returning to the Cloud SQL instance details page, ACCESS CONTROL tab (this should be where you left off when you added a root password).

In the "Authorized Networks" section, click the "Add Authorized Network" button and enter your cloud-sql-test virtual machine's external IP address in the "SUB-NET" text box, as shown in Figure 5-7.

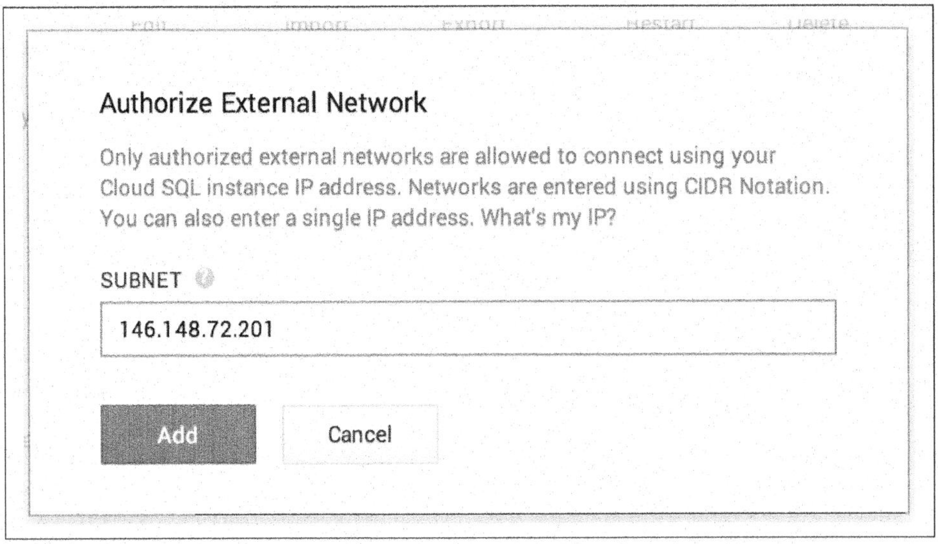

Authorize External Network

Only authorized external networks are allowed to connect using your Cloud SQL instance IP address. Networks are entered using CIDR Notation. You can also enter a single IP address. What's my IP?

SUBNET

146.148.72.201

Add   Cancel

Figure 5-7. Authorizing a VM's IP address for access to a cloud SQL instance

Click the Add button to complete the authorization. In the IP Address section, use the Request an IP Address button to allocate an address for your Cloud SQL instance. The Access Control tab should now show an IP address assigned to your Cloud SQL instance and an authorized network associated with your Compute Engine virtual machine.

Next, log in to your new VM using the gcloud compute ssh cloud-sql-test command and run the following two commands to refresh your local package repository and install an open source MySQL client, respectively:

```
$ gcloud compute ssh cloud-sql-test --zone us-central1-a
[..]
cloud-sql-test$ sudo apt-get update
[..]
cloud-sql-test$ sudo apt-get install mysql-client
[..]
```

Before trying our newly installed `mysql` client, let's download a copy of a file from the book GitHub repository, which we'll use later, by running this command:

```
cloud-sql-test$ wget https://github.com/GoogleCloudPlatform/gce-
oreilly/raw/master/ch5/beatles.sql
[..]
cloud-sql-test:$ ls
beatles.sql
```

Now we're ready to run our `mysql` client. Enter the following command, substituting your Cloud SQL instance IP address and your root password:

```
cloud-sql-test$ mysql --host=173.194.NNN.NNN --user=root \
                      --password=your-root-password
Welcome to the MySQL monitor.  Commands end with ; or \g.
Your MySQL connection id is 6
Server version: 5.5.38 (Google)
Copyright (c) 2000, 2014, Oracle and/or its affiliates. All rights reserved.
Oracle is a registered trademark of Oracle Corporation and/or its
affiliates. Other names may be trademarks of their respective
owners.
Type 'help;' or '\h' for help. Type '\c' to clear the current input
statement.
mysql>
```

The `mysql>` prompt is an interactive shell providing access to subcommands for creating, managing, and querying databases. Let's now use the MySQL shell to create and use a new database:

```
mysql> create database beatles;
Query OK, 1 row affected (0.23 sec)
mysql> use beatles;
Database changed
```

We now have a database called `beatles`. Now let's use the SQL shell to create a table of singles with columns for each song name, year of release in the US, and peak chart position:

```
mysql> create table singles (title varchar(50), year int, peak int);
Query OK, 0 rows affected (0.42 sec)
```

Next, we insert the data values into our new table:

```
mysql> insert into singles values
  ('My Bonnie', 1961, 26),
  ('Love Me Do', 1962, 1),
  [..]
  ('Free as a Bird', 1995, 6),
  ('Real Love', 1996, 11);
Query OK, 44 rows affected (0.10 sec)
Records: 44  Duplicates: 0  Warnings: 0
```

Rather than manually typing 44 rows of data, you can edit a SQL command in a text file and then use the source command to redirect input from a file. We have stored a copy of this command in the *beatles.sql* file we downloaded earlier. Now you can run that file using the source command, like this:

```
mysql> source beatles.sql
Query OK, 44 rows affected (0.15 sec)
Records: 44  Duplicates: 0  Warnings: 0
```

This is equivalent to entering the insert command and associated data interactively.

Next, let's run a SQL query to verify the data values we just entered:

```
mysql> select * from singles;
+--------------------------------+------------+-------------+
| title                          | year       | peak        |
+--------------------------------+------------+-------------+
| My Bonnie                      |       1961 |          26 |
| Love Me Do                     |       1962 |           1 |
[..]
| Free as a Bird                 |       1995 |           6 |
| Real Love                      |       1996 |          11 |
+--------------------------------+------------+-------------+
44 rows in set (0.08 sec)
```

Running SQL Queries

Now that we've set up our database and loaded information into a table, let's imagine we want to ask the following three questions:

- How many singles did The Beatles release in the US?

- How many number-one singles did The Beatles release in the US? And what were the titles of those top sellers?

- In which year did The Beatles release the most US singles and the most number one singles?

We'll answer each of those questions using SQL queries submitted via the mysql command-line tool.

To determine the total number of singles released by The Beatles in the US, we simply need to count the number of rows in the "singles" table. We can do this by running the following query via the SQL shell:

```
mysql> use beatles;
0 row(s) affected.
mysql> select count(*) from singles;
+----------------------+
| count(*)             |
+----------------------+
```

```
|                        44 |
+-----------------------+
1 row in set (0.06 sec)
```

This query tells us The Beatles released 44 singles in the US.

For our next query, we'll count the number of singles released in the US that rose to the top position on the charts. This is easy to do by extending the query with a "where" clause, like this:

```
mysql> select count(*) from singles where peak = 1;
+-----------------------+
| count(*)              |
+-----------------------+
|                    19 |
+-----------------------+
1 row in set (0.07 sec)
```

This query reveals 19 singles rose to the top position of the charts. If we wanted to identify those top-selling singles, we need only replace count(*) with *, like this:

```
mysql> select * from singles where peak = 1;
+--------------------------+------------+------------+
| title                    | year       | peak       |
+--------------------------+------------+------------+
| Love Me Do               |       1962 |          1 |
| She Loves You            |       1963 |          1 |
| I Want to Hold Your Hand |       1963 |          1 |
| Can't Buy Me Love        |       1964 |          1 |
| A Hard Day's Night       |       1964 |          1 |
| I Feel Fine              |       1964 |          1 |
| Eight Days a Week        |       1965 |          1 |
| Ticket to Ride           |       1965 |          1 |
| Help                     |       1965 |          1 |
| Yesterday                |       1965 |          1 |
| We Can Work It Out       |       1965 |          1 |
| Paperback Writer         |       1966 |          1 |
| Penny Lane               |       1967 |          1 |
| All You Need Is Love     |       1967 |          1 |
| Hello Goodbye            |       1967 |          1 |
| Hey Jude                 |       1968 |          1 |
| Get Back                 |       1969 |          1 |
| Let It Be                |       1970 |          1 |
| The Long and Winding Road |      1970 |          1 |
+--------------------------+------------+------------+
19 rows in set (0.07 sec)
```

Finally, let's determine the year in which The Beatles released the most singles in the US:

```
sql> select year, count(*) as releases from singles group by year/
order by count(*) desc limit 1;
+-------------+----------------------+
| year        | releases             |
+-------------+----------------------+
|        1964 |                   12 |
+-------------+----------------------+
1 row in set (0.07 sec)
```

This shows us that 1964 was a very productive year for The Beatles, as they released 12 singles into the U.S. market, the most of any year in their career. If we limit the query to include only number-one hits and remove the limit clause to display all results (not just the top result), we get:

```
mysql> select year, count(*) as hits from singles where peak = "1" group by year/
order by count(*) desc;
+-------------+----------------------+
| year        | hits                 |
+-------------+----------------------+
|        1965 |                    5 |
|        1964 |                    3 |
|        1967 |                    3 |
|        1963 |                    2 |
|        1970 |                    2 |
|        1962 |                    1 |
|        1966 |                    1 |
|        1968 |                    1 |
|        1969 |                    1 |
+-------------+----------------------+
9 rows in set (0.08 sec)
```

This query shows us that 1965 was the year in which The Beatles enjoyed their most chart toppers (5), along with the number of top hits for all the other years in which they released singles in the States.

Cloud Datastore

Google App Engine developers have long enjoyed a unique and powerful storage mechanism called the Datastore, which supports millions of App Engine applications, trillions of operations per month, and petabytes of data. The App Engine Datastore is a NoSQL/nonrelational database that provides many valuable features:

Scalable
    The service auto-scales effortlessly from the smallest to the largest query rates and data sizes.

Durable and available
    Data is synchronously replicated to multiple copies stored in geographically distributed regions.

Strong consistency
> Data written is immediately available to fully qualified reads and ancestor queries.

ACID
> Conventional database transaction semantics are supported.

Flexible
> The structure of your data can change incrementally over time, without needing to reformat existing data.

Google Query Language (GQL)
> A near-SQL query language is provided.

Fully managed
> The service is hosted, monitored, and managed by Google.

All of those benefits are now available to users outside of App Engine, including Compute Engine virtual machines. As with Cloud SQL, the Cloud Datastore is accessible from VMs and is fully managed, so it takes care of things like automatic failover, replication, and distribution. It also has excellent performance, availability, and durability characteristics. This is a great choice for a NoSQL database, because Google does all the heavy lifting for you.

Let's step through the process of enabling the Cloud Datastore service for your project, and then exercise the service in the following ways:

- Create an entity.
- Retrieve the entity we stored.
- Run a query matching a property of the entity you just created.

We'll carry out these steps using a combination of the Developers Console and some programs we'll write together and run on a Compute Engine virtual machine.

Getting Started

From the Developers Console (*http://console.developers.google.com/*) (*http://console.developers.google.com/*), select a project for which you've enabled Cloud Datastore and click Storage->Cloud Datastore->Dashboard, from the lefthand navigation list.

 If you have not yet completed the steps from the ""Creating a Compute Engine Project" on page 2" section of Chapter 1, you may be prompted to enter billing information.

You should see a screen similar to that shown in Figure 5-8.

Figure 5-8. Cloud Datastore dashboard page

This dashboard provides a summary overview of your Cloud Datastore entities and associated properties, but in this case, we're just getting started so we see a simple welcome screen.

Creating and Viewing Entities via the Developers Console

Data objects in the App Engine Datastore are called *entities*. An entity has one or more named *properties*, each of which can have a value. We'll reuse the Beatles song data from the previous section and create one entity per song.

As the UI suggests, your first act should be to create a new Cloud Datastore entity. Click the Create Entity button, which presents the dialog shown in Figure 5-9.

Figure 5-9. Cloud Datastore entity-creation dialog

We'll create a Namespace called "Beatles" and fill in a new Kind named "song". The combination of Namespace, Kind, and ID form the key, which uniquely identifies each entity. Below the line where we specify our key, we click the "Add property" button to define our entity's properties. In Figure 5-10, we've filled in the Namespace and Kind fields and created properties for the first song's title, year of release, and peak chart position. Each property has a name, a type, a field indicating whether that property should be indexed for fast query retrieval, and a value.

Figure 5-10. Cloud Datastore entity-creation dialog ready to submit

When you're satisfied with your input, click the "Create entity" button, which results in a confirmation message and the appearance of a new entity displayed on the Cloud Datastore summary page, as shown in Figure 5-11.

Figure 5-11. New song entity created in Cloud Datastore

You can confirm the new entity's properties by clicking the hyperlinked ID field, which displays a page summarizing entity details and providing the ability to edit the entity properties, as shown in Figure 5-12.

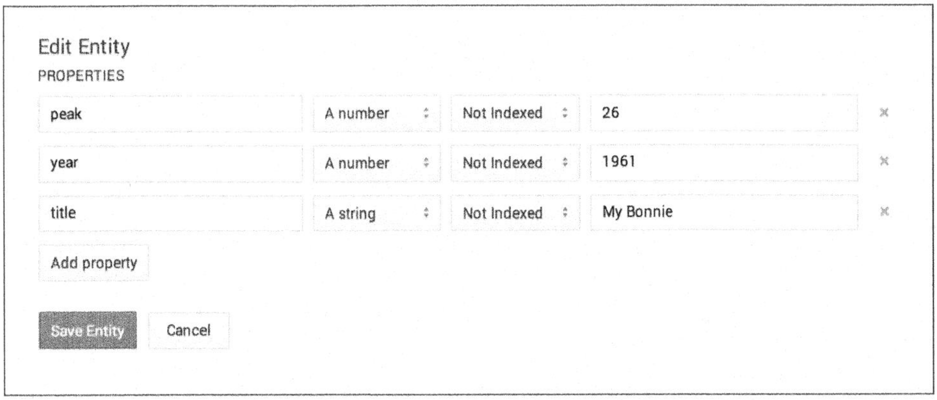

Figure 5-12. Cloud Datastore entity details page

Creating and Retrieving Entities Programmatically from a VM

Now let's write a program that uses the Datastore API to create additional entities for the other Beatles songs in our list. Although we could run this program anywhere, we'll do this exercise from a virtual machine to show how well Compute Engine and Cloud Datastore work together.

Following the examples from Chapter 2, create a virtual machine using any of the supported methods. For this exercise, let's call this VM `datastore-test`. Make sure to provide the `compute`, `datastore`, and `userinfo.email` service account scopes so that we'll be able to interact with the Compute Engine and Cloud Datastore services from this VM using our service account. For example, you could use the `gcloud com pute instances create` command to create your VM like this:

```
$ gcloud compute instances create datastore-test --zone us-central1-a \
  --scopes compute-rw datastore userinfo-email
Created [https://www.googleapis.com/compute/v1/projects/gce-oreilly/zones/us-central1-
a/instances/datastore-test].
NAME       ZONE     MACHINE_TYPE  INTERNAL_IP EXTERNAL_IP     STATUS
datas[..]t us-[..]a n1-standard-1 10.240[..] 107.178.NNN.NNN RUNNING
```

Next, let's log in to the VM we just created using the `gcloud compute ssh` command:

```
$ gcloud compute ssh datastore-test --zone us-central1-a
[..]
datastore-test$
```

We're going to write a Python program to access our Datastore entities. In order to install the Datastore client library package, we need to install pip, a Python package management utility, and the Google Python client library, as follows:

```
datastore-test$ wget https://bootstrap.pypa.io/get-pip.py
[..]
datastore-test$ sudo python get-pip.py
```

```
Downloading/unpacking pip
  Downloading pip-1.5.6-py2.py3-none-any.whl (1.0MB): 1.0MB downloaded
Downloading/unpacking setuptools
  Downloading setuptools-6.0.1-py2.py3-none-any.whl (533kB): 533kB downloaded
Installing collected packages: pip, setuptools
Successfully installed pip setuptools
Cleaning up...
datastore-test$ pip install --upgrade google-api-python-client
[..]
```

Next, download the *ch5-1.py* program from the book's GitHub repo, substitute your project ID for your-project-id, and run the resulting program using the following command sequence:

```
datastore-test$ wget https://github.com/GoogleCloudPlatform/gce-
oreilly/raw/master/ch5/ch5-1.py
[..]
datastore-test$ vi ch5-1.py  # Edit your project id in place of your-project-
id
datastore-test$ python ch5-1.py
```

Here's the relevant code from *ch5-1.py*:

```python
import argparse
import httplib2
import os
import sys

from apiclient import discovery
from oauth2client import file
from oauth2client import client
from oauth2client import tools
from oauth2client.gce import AppAssertionCredentials

# Set project, zone, and other constants.
API_NAME = 'datastore'
API_VERSION = 'v1beta2'
PROJECT_ID = 'your-project-id'
DATA = (
  ('My Bonnie', 1961, 26),
[..]
  ('Real Love', 1996, 11)
)

def commit(datastore, title, year, peak):
  body = {
    'mode': 'NON_TRANSACTIONAL',
    'mutation': {
      'insertAutoId': [
        {
          'key': {
            'partitionId': { 'namespace': 'Beatles' },
            'path': [ { 'kind': 'song' } ]
```

```
            },
          'properties': {
            'peak': { 'integerValue': peak },
            'year': { 'integerValue': year },
            'title': { 'stringValue': title }
          }
        }
      ]
    }
  }
  try:
    req = datastore.commit(datasetId=PROJECT_ID, body=body)
    resp = req.execute()
  except Exception, ex:
    print 'ERROR: ' + str(ex)
    sys.exit()

def main(argv):
  # Parse the command-line flags.
  flags = parser.parse_args(argv[1:])

  # Obtain service account credentials from virtual machine environement.
  credentials =
    AppAssertionCredentials(['https://www.googleapis.com/auth/datastore'])

  # Create an httplib2.Http object to handle our HTTP requests and authorize it
  # with our good Credentials.
  http = httplib2.Http()
  http = credentials.authorize(http)

  # Construct the service object for interacting with the Compute Engine API.
  service = discovery.build(API_NAME, API_VERSION, http=http)

  for (title, year, peak) in DATA:
    commit(service.datasets(), title, year, peak)

if __name__ == '__main__':
  main(sys.argv)
```

Now that we've inserted all of our songs into the Cloud Datastore, let's revisit the developer's console to verify that the changes we just made are now displayed there. As we can see in Figure 5-13, we now find the expected new entities, with peak, title, and year corresponding to the songs we've just added, on the Cloud Datastore summary page.

song Entities Delete			
NAME/ID	peak	title	year
Id=4795020674596864	1	Penny Lane	1967
Id=5069036098420736	17	Matchbox	1964
Id=5076495651307520	1	Help	1965
Id=5096363633147904	2	Do You Want to Know a Secret	1964
Id=5105650963054592	8	The Ballad of John and Yoko	1969
Id=5109799364691616	2	Twist and Shout	1964
Id=5144752345317376	1	A Hard Day's Night	1964
Id=5147289865682944	1	Let It Be	1970
Id=5153049148391424	1	Hey Jude	1968
Id=5167132077719552	1	Yesterday	1965
Id=5169618595348480	88	Why	1964

Figure 5-13. Cloud Datastore summary page showing newly inserted entities

Now that we've seen how to use the Cloud Datastore, let's take a look at one more storage option. Because Compute Engine provides virtual servers that can host just about any application, you are also free to deploy just about any open source or commercial database software of your own choosing.

Bring Your Own Database

In the past several years, we've seen the emergence of a plethora of powerful open source database-management systems and NoSQL storage systems, such as MySQL, Cassandra, PostgresSQL, MongoDB, Redis, CouchDB, and Riak.

Since Compute Engine provides access to generic virtual machines, you are free to use any of those storage systems in the Google Compute Engine environment. These options provide the ability to manage your own distributed database service in the cloud.

The disadvantage of using one of these options versus one of the managed storage options discussed earlier in this chapter is that you also take on the burden of autoscaling, backup, replication, availability, disaster recovery, security, and many other challenges inherent in deploying distributed storage systems. Nevertheless, this option is available for customers who require more complete and/or more fine-grained control over their storage services.

A great example of how to set up one such open source distributed database-management system is available in the *Cassandra on Compute Engine* GitHub repo[2] provided and maintained by Eric Johnson. This repo illustrates how to set up the Cassandra distributed database on a cluster of Compute Engine virtual machines. There are many other GitHub repos and resources on the Web explaining how to install other distributed storage systems in the Compute Engine environment.

Summary

In this chapter, we learned about two additional storage mechanisms, Cloud SQL and Cloud Datastore. We saw examples illustrating how to access and manipulate resources in both services, using multiple access methods.

Up Next

Now that we've learned about the various storage mechanisms available inside and outside of Compute Engine, we'll explore Compute Engine's comprehensive and powerful networking features.

---

2 *https://github.com/GoogleCloudPlatform/compute-cassandra-python*

## CHAPTER 6

Networking

Fast, responsive networking has been a critical component of Google's success. Studies have shown that, for a high-volume web business, as little as 100 milliseconds of delay in responding to web requests can have a measurable negative impact on revenue.[1] Google's average response time for over 100 billion search queries per month is roughly a quarter of a second, or 250 milliseconds. In addition to the search functionality everyone knows about, Google is constantly moving tremendous quantities of data within and across its worldwide data centers.

Compute Engine is designed to take full advantage of Google's networking resources and engineering know-how. As a result, whether you're transferring data between Compute Engine virtual machines, between VMs and other Google Cloud Platform services, or between VMs and the outside world, it's possible to attain remarkably strong and consistent network performance. In addition to performance, Google Compute Engine offers an impressive array of security, high availability, and configuration options.

In previous chapters, we've created virtual machines, persistent disks, and other resources but we haven't yet described the network environment in which those resources exist. That will be the focus of this chapter.

A Short Networking Primer

Internet Protocol (IP) gurus can safely skip this section. However, those who may be a bit vague on what TCP/IP is, or exactly what a firewall does, may find this section helpful. It won't turn anyone into a networking expert, but hopefully it will provide

---

1 Eric Schurman and Jake Brutlag. "The user and business impact of server delays, additional bytes, and HTTP chunking in web search." In Velocity Web Performance and Operations Conference. 2009.

what you need to know to understand the networking features available in Google Compute Engine.

Network Addresses and Routing

At its most basic, networking is about one computer sending a message to another computer. In the IP world, these messages are called *packets*. Sometimes it can be useful to think about computer networking via a physical analogy. You can think of network packets as postcards and the network itself as the postal service. Most people understand, at least at a high level, how the postal service is able to take a postcard addressed to a friend and deliver it to her.

First I write her *mailing address* on the postcard, something like: 1234 1st St., Hometown, USA, 99999. The postal service understands this mailing address and is able to translate it into a unique physical mailbox that happens to be sitting outside my friend's home, and take the necessary actions to cause my postcard to appear in her mailbox at some point in the future.

Similarly, for one computer to ask the network to deliver a packet to another computer, it needs to provide a *network address*. And since we're talking about the Internet Protocol (IP), these network addresses are called IP addresses. You may have seen these before. They are just 32-bit numbers, but they are generally written out in dotted quad notation like so: 169.254.0.1, where each number gives us one octet (8 bits) of the 32-bit number.

 Version 4 of the Internet Protocol (IPv4) uses 32-bit addresses as discussed here and is the version of IP you will generally encounter. Version 6 of the Internet Protocol (IPv6) is however gaining adoption and uses 128-bit addresses and a different notation. We do not discuss IPv6 further here.

In order for the network to deliver our addressed packet to the correct destination computer, it needs to understand the IP address similar to how the postal service understands a mailing address. For example, if the destination mailing address is in the same postal code, then the letter probably never leaves my neighborhood. But if the destination mailing address is in a different postal code, then the postal service has to select some sort of long-haul mechanism to get it there.

Network routing is surprisingly similar. If you're trying to send a packet from IP 169.254.0.1 to 169.254.0.2, then it is likely that these two computers are right next door to each other from a network perspective, and the routing will be extremely simple, probably just a single hop from the source computer to the destination computer. On the other hand, if you're sending a packet from IP 198.168.0.1 to 8.8.4.4, then you're probably looking at many hops across some long-haul networks.

The other thing you usually write on a postcard is a name. This is because there may be more than one person living at a particular mailing address. There's an analog for this in the networking world as well. There may be more than one process on a computer which wants to use the network. If all we have is an IP address, we can get our packet to the right computer, but when it arrives, there would be no way to decide which process is the correct recipient. This is solved by the use of a network port. A network port is just a 16-bit number, either assigned to, or selected by, the process using the network, and it allows the networking part of the operating system to deliver the network packet to the correct process. Network ports are usually written as a single number after the IP address, separated by a colon, like this: `8.8.4.4:53`

Some ports are called "well known." This means that the users of the Internet have all agreed (via the Internet Assigned Numbers Authority) to reserve certain ports for certain uses. This example showed network port 53, which is reserved for use by the Domain Name System, which we will touch on shortly.

Transport Control Protocol (TCP)

TCP is short for the Transmission Control Protocol, which is the protocol you will most likely be using for anything you do on Compute Engine. It is technically a layer on top of the Internet Protocol (IP), but they are so often used together that people often talk about the combination "TCP/IP" as the "Internet Protocol," even though that's not technically correct.

In the previous section, we likened IP packets to postcards in the postal service. Similar to how the postal service sets limits to the size and shape of a postcard, networking protocols set an upper limit to how many bytes can be sent in a single IP packet. Now let's consider how you might send the content of a book to someone if the only way you could communicate with that person was via postcards. The instructions might look something like the following:

1. Open the book to the first page.
2. Copy the letters you see onto a postcard; remember the last letter copied.
3. Mail the postcard.
4. If not done, go to step 2, starting from first uncopied letter.

However, there are some complications. There's no guarantee that the postal service will deliver the postcards in exactly the order you send them. So you probably want to number each postcard as well, so the receiver knows what order to copy the postcards into her copy of the book.

Another complication is that the postal service might occasionally lose a few postcards. The receiver can notice when this happens by looking carefully at the numbers on the postcards and looking for gaps. For example, if the receiver sees postcards numbered 10, 11, 12, 14, 15, 16, then it's a pretty good bet that postcard 13 was lost in transit. In this case, the receiver can send a postcard back to the sender that says, "Hey, postcard 13 never arrived; can you send it again?"

TCP also provides the notion of a "connection." In our postcard analogy, you could attempt to establish a connection by sending a postcard with a note like, "Hey, I have some stuff I want to send to this address; is anyone there?" If there's a recipient at that address that is willing to receive the content, she could reply with a postcard that says, "Sure, I'm here; go right ahead!"

There are a few more wrinkles to it, but in spirit, this is what TCP does for you. You can ask it to establish a connection to a particular port on another computer, and then you can hand it more data than can fit in a single IP packet. TCP will ensure that all the data arrives at the destination in the proper order by chopping it up into individually numbered IP packets and doing all the bookkeeping required to resend any packets which may be lost in transit. TCP also has mechanisms to notice if packets are not getting through for an extended period of time and notifying you of a "broken" connection.

The Domain Name System (DNS)

Earlier we introduced the concept of network addresses, which for IPv4 look like 74.125.192.132. However, there are at least two good reasons why users shouldn't be exposed directly to network addresses. First, they are hard to remember. It's much easier to ask users to remember storage.googleapis.com than it is to ask users to remember 74.125.192.132. Second, when computers and networks are upgraded over time, they are often assigned new network addresses. Even if we trained users to remember IP addresses, the correct IP address to use would change over time.

This is similar to the situation that the telephone company has with phone numbers. Phone numbers are simply the network addresses of the telephone network. Although it may be hard for some younger readers to believe, back in the dark ages before ubiquitous cell phones, when you moved from one house to another, you were assigned a new phone number. Because remembering telephone numbers is hard, and because the right telephone number to reach a particular person could change over time, the telephone company would publish a large book periodically listing everyone's name, address, and phone number.

Similarly, there's a "phone book" for the Internet, called the Domain Name System (DNS). This is what translates a friendly looking address such as storage.googleapis.com into an IP address that can be used to reach a particular computer.

The dig utility can be used to query DNS. dig is not installed by default on Google Compute Engine instances, but can be easily obtained via apt-get on Debian-based images:

```
test-vm$ sudo apt-get install dnsutils
[..]
test-vm$ dig storage.googleapis.com
[..]
;; QUESTION SECTION:
;storage.googleapis.com.    IN A
;; ANSWER SECTION:
storage.googleapis.com. 3393  IN CNAME storage-ugc.l.googleusercontent.com.
storage-ugc.l.googleusercontent.com. 93 IN A 74.125.192.132
[..]
```

Here we see that the domain name `storage.googleapis.com` eventually translates to the IP address `74.125.192.132`. In this particular example, there's a middle step, called a CNAME, or Canonical Name, where `storage.googleapis.com` is an alias for `storage-ugc.l.googleusercontent.com`, which is the "canonical" name for the IP address `74.125.192.132`.

In the preceding example, the Domain Name System does indeed look much like a phone book. You have a name, and you use the "book" to find a corresponding number. However, the implementation of the Domain Name System is not nearly as simple as the phone book is for the telephone network. In the telephone network, you have one company, the local phone company, that both operates the telephone network and provides the lookup service, and it has complete information regarding the mapping between a name and address and the corresponding telephone number. On the Internet, there is a hierarchy of both commercial and noncommercial entities that can assign domain names, and then there is a widely distributed network of computers that provide lookup services.

At the root of the Domain Name System is an organization known as the Internet Corporation for Assigned Names and Numbers, or ICANN. However, you can't go to ICANN and register a domain name. That responsibility is delegated by ICANN to many different Domain Name Registrars. For example, the responsibility for the registration of any domain name that ends with .com (e.g., gce-oreilly.com) is delegated to VeriSign. However, you can't go to VeriSign to register a new .com domain, because it is essentially a "wholesaler" of .com domains. To actually register a new .com domain name, you must go to a "retail" domain name registrar, of which there are many. These registrars generally provide user-friendly ways to sign up for a new domain name, provide email and telephone support service, allow you to pay with a credit card, provide convenient web administration apps to update your data, and do other things that end users need to effectively manage their domain names.

The last part of a domain name (e.g., .com) is known as the top-level domain (TLD). TLDs such as .com, .net, and .org are known as generic top-level domains (gTLDs). For a long time, there were very few gTLDs. However, quite recently ICANN began accepting applications for, and granting, new gTLDs. There are also TLDs based on country code, such as .us for the United States. The authority for these country code

TLDs (ccTLDs) generally rests with the government of the respective countries, which set the rules for who can register domains under these ccTLDs, and the rules will vary from country to country. Typically the governments will contract with a third party to actually operate the domain registry, and often those third parties are in a "wholesale" position similar to VeriSign's position for the .com domain.

Hypertext Transfer Protocol (HTTP)

We have now discussed almost all the pieces required to understand what is happening when you type a web address, such as *http://storage.googleapis.com/gce-oreilly/ hello*, into a web browser. First, your browser will consult DNS to translate the domain `storage.googleapis.com` into an IP address such as `74.125.192.132`. Then, the web browser will establish a TCP connection to `74.125.192.132:80`. TCP port 80 is the default "well known" port for the Hypertext Transfer Protocol (HTTP). Once a connection is established, the web browser will send a `GET` message to the server, asking for a particular resource. The server will then (hopefully) reply with an `OK` message and the requested content. The exact format of the `GET` request and `OK` responses are defined by the HTTP specification.

`curl` is a command-line tool, available by default on Debian-based Compute Engine instances, that you can use to issue simple `GET` requests to see this in action. For example, we can use `curl` to `GET` the example object:

```
test-vm$ curl http://storage.googleapis.com/gce-oreilly/hello
Hello Cloud Storage!
```

Using the `-v` option requests that `curl` output more than just the body of the response, which allows us to see some of the details of HTTP in action:

```
test-vm$ curl -v http://storage.googleapis.com/gce-oreilly/hello
* About to connect() to storage.googleapis.com port 80 (#0)
*   Trying 74.125.142.132...
* connected
* Connected to storage.googleapis.com (74.125.142.132) port 80 (#0)
> GET /gce-oreilly/hello HTTP/1.1
> User-Agent: curl/7.26.0
> Host: storage.googleapis.com
> Accept: */*
>
[..]
< HTTP/1.1 200 OK
< Expires: Fri, 17 Jan 2014 23:47:47 GMT
< Date: Fri, 17 Jan 2014 22:47:47 GMT
< Cache-Control: public, max-age=3600
< Last-Modified: Fri, 17 Jan 2014 21:56:12 GMT
[..]
< Content-Type: application/octet-stream
[..]
Hello Cloud Storage!
```

```
* Connection #0 to host storage.googleapis.com left intact
* Closing connection #0
```

Here we can see that `curl` is doing exactly what we described earlier. It used DNS to translate `storage.googleapis.com` into `74.125.142.132`. Then it established a TCP connection to port 80 of that address. Then it sent a `GET` message for the resource `/gce-oreilly/hello`, and finally received the `200 OK` response, along with the content `Hello Cloud Storage!`

You can see in the example output that there are some additional lines in both the request and response that look like `Name: Value`. These are called headers, and they convey additional information about the request or response. For example, the request contains the header `Accept: */*` which tells the server that the client is willing to accept the response in any format the server wants to provide it. Similarly in the response, we see the header `Content-Type: application/octet-stream`, which is the server telling the client that the body of the response is just a series of unstructured bytes. The browser may choose to behave differently depending on the `Content-Type`. For example, usually a web browser will offer to save the content to disk if it is of type `application/octet-stream`, but will format and display in the browser window content of type `text/html`.

Load Balancing

There are some mailing addresses that receive an unusually large volume of mail—more mail than a normal, ordinary residential mailbox could ever hold, or a single person could ever read. This type of mail is usually addressed to a post office box (e.g., Really Big Company, P.O. Box 1234, Big City, USA 99999). The company may employ a variety of techniques to deal with such a large volume of mail, ranging from a team of people to specialized mail-processing machines. But one thing is pretty much assured in these high volume scenarios—there will be more than one human at the destination, any one of whom is ready and able to deal with the letter you sent.

The analog for the "P.O. box" in computer networks is called a load balanced address. Packets that are addressed to a load-balanced IP address go to special, distributed, and redundant hardware that can handle a high volume of IP traffic. However, that special hardware is able to handle such a high volume because it doesn't actually do much with each packet. Instead, it is configured to distribute, or *load balance* that traffic across a number of more ordinary computers, each of which can actually process the packets, similar to how the person who opens a P.O. box doesn't actually read all the mail, but instead simply delivers it quickly, efficiently, and hopefully somewhat evenly to a larger number of people who do read and act on the mail.

Most of the letters that flow through a P.O. box are not related to each other, so each letter can be sent to any of the people processing them. The situation with a load balancer is often different. For example, if the packets are part of an HTTP conversation between a web browser and a web server, then they are part of an ongoing TCP connection, and all of those packets must be sent to the same destination computer.

In this way, a load balancer is able to provide the illusion that it is a single super powerful web server with a single IP address, when in fact it is parceling out each of the incoming HTTP requests to one of many normal web servers. This is called load *balancing* because the load balancer makes an effort to distribute the work somewhat evenly across the servers to avoid some being idle while others are overloaded.

Firewalls

There are some tricks that computer networks can do that we can't easily model via analogy to the postal service. One is the firewall. This colorful name comes from the notion that the firewall is there to keep dangerous things out, like the firewall that separates the rather heat-sensitive occupants of a passenger car from the dangerous hot burning things in the engine compartment. Keeping the bad stuff out of a computer network is easy, of course—simply block all network traffic, and nothing bad can ever reach you. Of course, that's not particularly useful either—you can achieve the same effect by simply unplugging the computer from the network. The tricky part is letting only some things through the firewall. For example, the physical firewall in your car has carefully engineered holes in it to let useful things like the cable that connects the throttle pedal to the engine through. Similarly, network firewalls are carefully configured to let only certain types of network traffic through. This traffic is not necessarily safe (just like fire could still come through the throttle cable hole in your car's firewall) but hopefully the risk is minimized and reasonably well understood, and it's far safer than letting everything through.

Default Networking

Before we dig into how to configure networking in Google Compute Engine, it's useful to understand what we get by default. Every project gets its own virtual private cloud. As far as your instances are concerned, the network they are attached to is only accessible to other instances from that same project. To see this in action, let's create a couple of instances:

```
$ gcloud compute instances create vm-1 vm-2 --zone us-central1-a
[..]
NAME  ZONE          MACHINE_TYPE  INTERNAL_IP     EXTERNAL_IP    STATUS
vm-1  us-central1-a n1-standard-1 10.240.117.104  146.148.XX.XX  RUNNING
vm-2  us-central1-a n1-standard-1 10.240.66.220   146.148.YY.YY  RUNNING
```

The first thing to notice is that Compute Engine, by default, assigns each instance two IP addresses, one internal, one external. Notice that the internal network address starts with 10. This is a special IP address that is used for private networks (i.e., networks that are controlled by a single organization and are not directly connected to the global Internet). Each Compute Engine project has its very own private network to which its Compute Engine instances are attached by default. Only Compute Engine instances in that project can use that network.

Indeed, if we ssh into vm-1, we find we can ping vm-2 via the internal address:

```
$ gcloud compute ssh vm-1 --zone us-central1-a
[..]
vm-1$ ping -c 1 10.240.66.220
PING 10.240.66.220 (10.240.66.220) 56(84) bytes of data.
64 bytes from 10.240.66.220: icmp_req=1 ttl=64 time=0.854 ms
--- 10.240.66.220 ping statistics ---
1 packets transmitted, 1 received, 0% packet loss, time 0ms
rtt min/avg/max/mdev = 0.854/0.854/0.854/0.000 ms
```

 If you're unfamiliar with network troubleshooting, ping is a very useful command-line tool that's available on most operating systems. It sends Internet Control Message Protocol (ICMP) "Echo Request" packets and listens for the "Echo Response" packets. This is a great way to confirm that one computer can talk to another computer and also has the benefit of telling you how far away they are from each other, in terms of network latency.

Furthermore, we find that the name vm-2 conveniently resolves to the same IP address:

```
vm-1$ ping -c 1 vm-2
PING vm-2.c.gce-oreilly.internal (10.240.66.220) 56(84) bytes of data.
64 bytes from vm-2.c.gce-oreilly.internal (10.240.66.220):
   icmp_req=1 ttl=64 time=0.806 ms
  --- vm-2.c.gce-oreilly.internal ping statistics ---
1 packets transmitted, 1 received, 0% packet loss, time 0ms
rtt min/avg/max/mdev = 0.806/0.806/0.806/0.000 ms
```

 Compute Engine instances are configured by default to use their metadata server to resolve DNS queries. The metadata server knows the names of all the instances on the private network and resolves DNS queries to these names, such as vm-2 in the preceding example, to the internal address of those instances. That's why in the previous example, ping -c 1 vm-2 worked. If you tried the same command from a computer that wasn't a Compute Engine instance from that project, the name vm-2 would probably not resolve to an IP address, and ping would say "unknown host." DNS queries that don't match an instance name on the private network are forwarded to Google's public DNS servers. The metadata server is useful for much more than just DNS however. See Chapter 7 for more information on the metadata server.

What else can we do by default? If you examine the output of the `gcloud compute ssh` command we used earlier, you will see the external address was used in an `ssh` command. But you may recall from Chapter 2 that we were not able to connect to an Apache server on a Compute Engine instance from the outside world without additional steps.

Unlike the internal address, the external address can be used to access VMs remotely. The external address assigned to the VMs in these examples could be assigned to different VMs in the future. To avoid the confusion that could be caused by readers following these examples verbatim and attempting to access VMs that are not their own, the last one or two octets of external addresses in this book have been replaced with NN, which is simply a placeholder for the actual octets of the external address actually assigned to the reader's VM. In some cases, the last octet may be replaced with something like XX, YY, or ZZ to show that they are different, without using a literal number.

You can examine the properties of the default network with the `gcloud compute networks` command:

```
$ gcloud compute networks list
NAME     IPV4_RANGE      GATEWAY_IPV4
default 10.240.0.0/16 10.240.0.1
```

The `10.240.0.0/16` you see in the `IPV4_RANGE` column in the output is CIDR notation. CIDR stands for Classless Inter-Domain Routing. When making routing decisions, computers need a way to know if an address is on the same network or a different network. The output here says that any address where the first 16 bits are `10.240` is part of the `default` network (i.e., addresses from `10.240.0.0` through `10.240.255.255`).

This tells us why the internal addresses assigned to vm-1 and vm-2 start with `10.240`. However, it doesn't tell us why we are able to `ssh` into our instances from the global Internet, but we cannot make an HTTP request to them without additional steps. To understand that, we need to examine the default firewall rules:

```
$ gcloud compute firewall-rules list
NAME                    NETWORK SRC_RANGES    RULES
default-allow-icmp      default 0.0.0.0/0     icmp
default-allow-internal default 10.240.0.0/16 tcp:1-65535,udp:1-65535,icmp
default-allow-rdp       default 0.0.0.0/0     tcp:3389
default-allow-ssh       default 0.0.0.0/0     tcp:22
http                    default 0.0.0.0/0     tcp:80
```

Here we see five firewall rules listed. The first four, with default in the name, are created for our project automatically. From their names, it's pretty easy to infer that `default-allow-internal` is what allows our instances to communicate, and `default-ssh` is what allows us to `ssh` into our instances from the global Internet. We can confirm this by examining the details of each firewall rule:

```
$ gcloud compute firewall-rules describe default-allow-internal
allowed:
- IPProtocol: tcp
  ports:
  - 1-65535
- IPProtocol: udp
  ports:
  - 1-65535
- IPProtocol: icmp
[..]
sourceRanges:
- 10.240.0.0/16
```

This says that traffic coming from IP addresses matching the network `10.240.0.0/16` is allowed to send TCP and UDP traffic to any port, and additionally that ICMP traffic is allowed. Effectively, this allows most IP traffic to flow between instances. The configuration of the `default-ssh` firewall rule is both more open and more restrictive at the same time:

```
$ gcloud compute firewall-rules describe default-ssh
allowed:
- IPProtocol: tcp
  ports:
  - '22'
[..]
sourceRanges:
- 0.0.0.0/0
```

This says that traffic coming from anywhere (`0.0.0.0/0`) is allowed to reach TCP port 22. TCP port 22 is the well-known port for the secure shell protocol (`ssh`). This is what allows us to use the `ssh` command (usually via `gcloud compute ssh`) to access our instances remotely.

The final firewall rule in the list is the one that we created in Chapter 2 to allow us to access the Apache server we set up on a VM. If you did not follow that example, then you will not see the `http` firewall rule in your list. The rest of the examples in this chapter assume you have created this firewall rule in addition to the default firewall rules just examined. Refer back to Chapter 2 to see how to create this firewall rule if you have not already done so.

Now that we've examined a project's default networking configuration, we're ready to learn more about configuring additional networks and firewall rules.

Configuring Firewall Rules

As discussed in the previous section, by default, each project has one network named `default` and default firewall rules named `default-allow-internal` and `default-ssh`. For many applications, this is a perfectly reasonable setup. For example, if you're using Compute Engine to perform large-scale analysis, then it may be perfectly sufficient to allow your instances to talk to one another, and to use `ssh` to access your instances. However, for many other applications, this will not be sufficient, and you'll want to serve additional protocols from your instances.

A common scenario is to serve HTTP from Compute Engine. For example, you may have an existing application that you've been hosting elsewhere that uses a typical LAMP stack, and you want to start hosting that application on Compute Engine instances.

 LAMP is a term used to refer to a typical open source software stack. The L and A refer to Linux and Apache. The M refers to a database (often MySQL) the P to a programming language (usually PHP, Perl, or Python). For the purposes of this discussion, the relevant components are Linux and Apache.

We touched on this scenario in Chapter 2, where we created a firewall rule to allow the HTTP traffic through to Apache on any Compute Engine instance in the project. While this might be quite sufficient for many applications, in a large scale distributed system, applications are often partitioned into stateless "frontends" that are reached by clients over HTTP, and stateful "backends," which are only accessed by the frontends and often use non-HTTP protocols. In this architecture, it would be good practice to only allow HTTP traffic to flow to the frontend servers so you don't have to worry about the outside world poking at the HTTP interface on your backend servers. Let's show how that can be accomplished in Compute Engine.

First let's create a frontend VM. We'll do this almost exactly like we've done before, but we're going to tag it as a frontend machine via the `--tags` parameter. The word "frontend" in this example is just a string; it has no special meaning to Compute Engine. It simply adds the string `frontend` as a tag on these instances, which we will use later in our firewall-rule configuration:

```
$ gcloud compute instances create frontend1 \
    --tags frontend --zone us-central1-a
[..]
NAME      ZONE          MACHINE_TYPE INTERNAL_IP   EXTERNAL_IP
frontend1 us-central1-a n1-standard-1 10.240.150.32 146.148.76.NN
```

If we examine our newly created instance, we can see that it has indeed been tagged as a frontend:

```
$ gcloud compute instances describe frontend1 --zone us-central1-a
[..]
tags:
  fingerprint: 4s55Dl-6pHw=
  items:
  - frontend
[..]
```

Now let's create a backend VM similarly:

```
$ gcloud compute instances create backend1 --tags backend --zone us-central1-a
[..]
NAME      ZONE          MACHINE_TYPE  INTERNAL_IP    EXTERNAL_IP
backend1 us-central1-a n1-standard-1 10.240.146.NN  146.148.86.NN
```

At this point, we want to sign into our new VMs and install Apache on them, just like we did in Chapter 2. While we're there, we will also customize the *index.html* file to identify the server to make it easier to confirm where our requests are going:

```
$ gcloud compute ssh frontend1 --zone us-central1-a
[..]
frontend1$ sudo apt-get update
[..]
frontend1$ sudo apt-get install apache2
Reading package lists... Done
Building dependency tree
[..]
[ ok ] Starting web server: apache2.
Setting up apache2 (2.2.22-13) ...
Setting up libswitch-perl (2.16-2) ...
frontend1$ hostname > /tmp/index.html
frontend1$ sudo cp /tmp/index.html /var/www/index.html
frontend1$ exit
[..]
$ gcloud compute ssh backend1 --zone us-central1-a
[..]
backend1$ sudo apt-get update
[..]
backend1$ sudo apt-get install apache2
Reading package lists... Done
Building dependency tree
[..]
[ ok ] Starting web server: apache2.
Setting up apache2 (2.2.22-13) ...
Setting up libswitch-perl (2.16-2) ...
backend1$ hostname > /tmp/index.html
backend1$ sudo cp /tmp/index.html /var/www/index.html
backend1$ exit
[..]
```

Wouldn't it be great if there was some way to have Compute Engine run some commands for us, like installing Apache and customizing *index.html*, without having to manually ssh into each instance after we create it? In fact, Compute Engine provides the ability to specify startup scripts and make custom VM images, the details of which we'll discuss in Chapter 7.

Using the IP addresses of your VMs, you can confirm that we can indeed make HTTP requests to both the frontend and backend VMs:

```
$ curl 146.148.76.NN
frontend1
$ curl 146.148.86.NN
backend1
```

This works because in Chapter 2, we set up the http firewall rule to allow traffic to flow from any address to port 80. Let's delete that firewall rule and confirm that indeed, HTTP traffic is blocked:

```
$ gcloud compute firewall-rules delete http
[..]
Deleted [https://[..]/global/firewalls/http].
$ curl 146.148.76.NN
curl: (7) couldn't connect to host
$ curl 146.148.86.NN
curl: (7) couldn't connect to host
```

Now we're in a position to accomplish our goal of selectively allowing HTTP traffic to only flow to our frontend VMs. Of course, Compute Engine doesn't know which of our VMs are designated as frontends, because that's an application concept, which is why we've used tags to mark our VMs as "frontend" or "backend." We can use these tags to define a firewall rule that allows traffic to flow only to some VMs and not others:

```
$ gcloud compute firewall-rules create http-frontend \
    --allow tcp:80 --target-tags frontend
[..]
NAME          NETWORK SRC_RANGES RULES  SRC_TAGS TARGET_TAGS
http-frontend default 0.0.0.0/0  tcp:80          frontend
$ curl 146.148.76.NN
frontend1
$ curl 146.148.86.NN
curl: (7) couldn't connect to host
```

This output shows that our firewall rule only applies to servers that are tagged with "frontend," and we confirm that this is indeed working as expected by sending HTTP requests via curl to frontend1 (which works) and backend1 (which is unable to connect).

Configuring Load Balancing

In the previous section, we configured a firewall that allowed HTTP traffic to flow from the outside world to a frontend virtual machine, while ensuring that the outside world could not send HTTP traffic to our backend machines. This is a great start toward a networking architecture appropriate for a multitier web application, but what happens when our application gets so popular that one web server is not sufficient to handle the load? Or when we need to make a disruptive change to the software running on that web server? The obvious answer is to have multiple web servers providing frontend services, and the interesting question from a networking perspective is how to hide this complexity from our customers. This is where load balancing comes to the rescue.

To experiment with load balancing, let's set up a second frontend machine like we did the first one:

```
$ gcloud compute instances create frontend2 \
    --tags frontend --zone us-central1-b
[..]
NAME      ZONE     MACHINE_TYPE INTERNAL_IP    EXTERNAL_IP    STATUS
frontend2 us-[..]b n1-standard-1 10.240.248.254 130.211.123.NN RUNNING
$ gcloud compute ssh frontend2 --zone us-central1-b
[..]
frontend2$ sudo apt-get update
[..]
frontend2$ sudo apt-get install apache2
Reading package lists... Done
Building dependency tree
[..]
[ ok ] Starting web server: apache2.
Setting up apache2 (2.2.22-13) ...
Setting up libswitch-perl (2.16-2) ...
frontend2$ hostname > /tmp/index.html
frontend2$ sudo cp /tmp/index.html /var/www/index.html
frontend2$ exit
[..]
$ curl 146.148.76.NN
frontend1
$ curl 130.211.123.NN
frontend2
```

Now that we have two frontends, we can set up a load balanced IP address that will balance traffic between them. The first thing we need to do is define which instances will receive traffic sent to the load balanced IP address. This is called a target pool in Compute Engine. Here we define a target pool called "frontends," then we add our instances to it:

```
$ gcloud compute target-pools create frontends --region us-central1
[..]
NAME      REGION       SESSION_AFFINITY BACKUP HEALTH_CHECKS
frontends us-central1 NONE
$ gcloud compute target-pools add-instances frontends \
    --instances frontend1 --zone us-central1-a
Updated [https://[..]/regions/us-central1/targetPools/frontends].
$ gcloud compute target-pools add-instances frontends \
    --instances frontend2 --zone us-central1-b
Updated [https://[..]/regions/us-central1/targetPools/frontends].
```

Note that in the target-pool create command, we provided a region, us-central1, and that all the instances we added to the target pool were in zones that are part of that region. In this particular example, the frontend1 instance is in zone us-central1-a, and the frontend2 instance is in zone us-central1-b. This demonstrates how a target pool can contain instances from more than one zone, as long as they are all part of the same region.

 Google calls the feature discussed in this section "network load balancing." It operates at the TCP level, and as such, can be used for more than just HTTP requests. Google has released a beta of a feature called "HTTP load balancing," which operates only on HTTP requests, and as such is able to do some interesting things based on the URL in the request. It is also able to intelligently load balance across regions, so if you run servers in asia-east1-a, europe-west1-a, and us-central1-a, HTTP load balancing can send requests to the servers closest to the customer. Because the feature is still in beta at this time, it is not discussed further here, but the reader is encouraged to visit *https://cloud.google.com/compute/docs/load-balancing/* to learn more about it.

Now that we have a target pool that defines where we want traffic sent to the load-balanced IP address to go, we can create the actual forwarding rule, which creates the load-balanced IP address itself:

```
$ gcloud compute forwarding-rules create frontends \
    --target-pool frontends --region us-central1
[..]
NAME      REGION       IP_ADDRESS      IP_PROTOCOL TARGET
frontends us-central1 146.148.88.NN TCP         us-central1/targetPools/frontends
```

Note that again, the region must be specified, and it must match the region of the target pool. So what happens when we send an HTTP request to the load-balanced IP address that was assigned to this forwarding rule?

```
$ for i in {1..10}; do curl 146.148.88.NN; done
frontend2
frontend1
frontend1
frontend2
frontend2
frontend1
frontend2
frontend1
frontend1
frontend1
```

Here we can see the requests are being distributed to both frontend1 and frontend2, just as we hoped. Now let's simulate a failure of the frontend2 server by stopping the Apache server and see what happens:

```
$ gcloud compute ssh frontend2 --zone us-central1-b
[..]
frontend2$ sudo apache2ctl -k stop
frontend2$ exit
[..]
$ for i in {1..10}; do curl 146.148.88.NN; done
frontend1
curl: (7) couldn't connect to host
curl: (7) couldn't connect to host
curl: (7) couldn't connect to host
frontend1
curl: (7) couldn't connect to host
frontend1
curl: (7) couldn't connect to host
curl: (7) couldn't connect to host
curl: (7) couldn't connect to host
```

We can see that load balancing is unaware that Apache has been shut down and therefore continues to send traffic to frontend2, which is unable to serve it. If only there was some way that load balancing could detect this situation and automatically adapt to it. Of course, there is, but because load balancing doesn't know by default what our servers are supposed to be able to do, we have to give it some information to make this work. In the case of our extremely simple frontends, the default health check, which simply performs an HTTP GET / request via port 80, is perfectly adequate for testing the health of our servers:

```
$ gcloud compute http-health-checks create frontend
[..]
NAME      HOST PORT REQUEST_PATH
frontend       80   /
```

```
$ gcloud compute target-pools add-health-checks frontends \
    --http-health-check frontend --region=us-central1
Updated [https://[..]/regions/us-central1/targetPools/frontends].
```

Now the load balancer knows how to check for the health of our servers, and so it should only send traffic to servers that are healthy. Let's try it out:

```
$ for i in {1..10}; do curl 146.148.88.NN; done
frontend1
frontend1
frontend1
frontend1
frontend1
frontend1
frontend1
frontend1
frontend1
frontend1
```

Voilà! Compute Engine has now detected that frontend2 is no longer working, and is sending all the requests to frontend1. And if we bring Apache back up on frontend2, we should find that traffic starts being sent to frontend2 again:

```
$ gcloud compute ssh frontend2 --zone us-central1-b
[..]
frontend2$ sudo apache2ctl -k start
frontend2$ exit
[..]
$ for i in {1..10}; do curl 146.148.88.NN; done
frontend2
frontend1
frontend1
frontend2
frontend1
frontend2
frontend2
frontend1
frontend1
frontend2
```

And there we have it! Compute Engine is now distributing traffic sent to a single load balanced IP address across multiple frontend instances and automatically detecting when servers go down and come back up.

In a real-world application, it's good practice to use a different path for health-check requests and actual requests. Compute Engine allows you to specify the path of the health check via the --request-path flag on the gcloud compute http-health-checks operation. The path we used in our example is simply the default value. By keeping the health-check requests separate from the actual requests, you can implement what's sometimes called a "lame duck" state on your server, where your server fails health-check requests, causing the load balancer to stop sending new requests to the server, but continues to serve actual requests for some period of time. This prevents your server from failing any requests already in flight when the server begins to shut down and also allows it to serve any requests that arrive in the seconds it takes for the load balancer to notice the health check is failing and direct traffic elsewhere. In other words, it allows you to cleanly shut down a server without causing any customer visible errors.

As discussed in an earlier section, we would never expect our customers to use a raw IP address to access our web application. We would instead register a domain name, configure an "A" (address) record to point to the correct IP address, and advertise that name to our customers. For example, we registered the gce-orielly.com domain in this way, and configured an "A" record to point www.gce-orielly.com to the IP address assigned to our forwarding rule:

```
$ dig www.gce-oreilly.com
; <<>> DiG 9.8.3-P1 <<>> www.gce-oreilly.com
;; global options: +cmd
;; Got answer:
;; ->>HEADER<<- opcode: QUERY, status: NOERROR, id: 14586
;; flags: qr rd ra; QUERY: 1, ANSWER: 1, AUTHORITY: 0, ADDITIONAL: 0
;; QUESTION SECTION:
;www.gce-oreilly.com.          IN     A
;; ANSWER SECTION:
www.gce-oreilly.com.    900    IN     A     146.148.88.NN
;; Query time: 137 msec
;; SERVER: 172.16.255.1#53(172.16.255.1)
;; WHEN: Thu Oct  9 09:57:11 2014
;; MSG SIZE  rcvd: 53
$ for i in {1..10}; do curl www.gce-oreilly.com; done
frontend1
frontend2
frontend1
frontend2
frontend2
frontend1
frontend1
frontend1
frontend1
frontend1
```

Reserving External IP Addresses

External addresses that are automatically assigned, such as the one assigned to the forwarding rule in the previous section, are called *ephemeral* addresses in Compute Engine. This means that they are assigned to a resource, like an instance or a forwarding rule, and will remain assigned to that resource for its lifetime, but if you delete and recreate the instance or forwarding rule, it will likely be assigned a different external address.

Depending on your application's design, it may not be a problem that IP addresses could change over time. For example, if you decide you want to tear down and build up a new forwarding rule to replace the one in our example, you would want to bring the new forwarding rule up (which would get a new external address), update DNS to point to that new address, and only turn down the old forwarding rule after the new DNS information has propagated, and there is almost no traffic going to the old forwarding rule. Note that DNS information is heavily cached by servers and clients, so it can take a while for traffic to stop arriving at the old address.

 A DNS entry has a timeout associated with it, called the time to live (TTL), after which both servers and clients are supposed discard the information from their cache. The organization running the authoritative DNS server for your domain (which is often the retail domain registrar you used to obtain the domain) may allow you to adjust the TTL to reduce the amount of time it takes for an updated entry to propagate. Unfortunately, there are some poorly behaved DNS servers and clients that may take much longer to flush the stale information than the TTL specifies, so you may continue to see a trickle of traffic to an old external address, even after the TTL is long expired. Unfortunately, there's not much you can do about it.

If you are uncomfortable with the idea of your external addresses being ephemeral, you do have the option to reserve them. The downside is that reserved external addresses may incur an additional cost (pricing can change over time, so check the current price sheet to be sure). For example, this is how we could promote the ephemeral address that was assigned to our forwarding rule to a reserved address:

```
$ gcloud compute addresses create frontends \
    --address 146.148.88.NN --region us-central1
[..]
NAME      REGION      ADDRESS      STATUS
frontends us-central1 146.148.88.NN IN_USE
```

Notice how at this point, the status of the frontends address is IN_USE. This is because we promoted the address that was already assigned to the forwarding rule.

Now that we've reserved the IP address, we can delete and re-add our forwarding rule and ensure that it gets the same address when we're done. As observed earlier, it would be a bad idea to do this if the forwarding rule was handling production traffic, as it would cause a service interruption, but during development, this might be convenient:

```
$ gcloud compute forwarding-rules delete frontends --region us-central1
[..]
Deleted [https://[..]/regions/us-central1/forwardingRules/frontends].
$ gcloud compute addresses list
NAME      REGION      ADDRESS       STATUS
frontends us-central1 146.148.88.NN RESERVED
```

Note how the status of the frontends address has changed from IN_USE to RESERVED now that we deleted the forwarding rule that was using it. Now we can recreate the forwarding rule and use the --address parameter to specify the reserved address we would like to use:

```
$ gcloud compute forwarding-rules create frontends \
    --address 146.148.88.NN --target-pool frontends --region us-central1
[..]
NAME      REGION      IP_ADDRESS     IP_PROTOCOL TARGET
frontends us-central1 146.148.88.NN TCP
$ gcloud compute addresses list
NAME      REGION      ADDRESS       STATUS
frontends us-central1 146.148.88.NN IN_USE
```

Note how the status of the address has once again returned to IN_USE.

Similar to how we promoted the ephemeral external address assigned to a forwarding rule, you can also promote the ephemeral external address assigned to a particular instance to a reserved address. However, if you find yourself doing so, it may be a sign that you need to examine your application's network architecture a little more closely. Reserving an external address implies that you expect other computers to rely on that address not changing. Doing that for an address that corresponds to a single instance instead of the load balanced IP address assigned to a load balancing forwarding rule means that the reliability of your application could be completely dependent on the status of a single instance, which is rarely a good idea for applications that are serving production traffic.

Configuring Networks

So far, all our examples have used the "default" network that was created automatically for our project and that all our instances are automatically connected to. Many projects can do everything they need using just the default network. However, if your project has a need to isolate one set of instances from another set of instances, then you may want to create additional networks for that purpose. Note that separate networks can still communicate, but they do so like any other network on the Internet (i.e., they use one another's external addresses, and cannot send traffic directly to their internal network addresses).

 Traffic sent between Compute Engine networks is billed just like traffic being sent to the Internet, which is to say, is more costly than traffic sent within a network. If your instances are going to exchange more than just a trickle of traffic, you probably want them on the same Compute Engine network.

One scenario where it might be reasonable to use multiple networks is to create separate, isolated environments for testing and production use. In this example, we will create two networks, called test and prod, for this purpose.

First, we create the two networks:

```
$ gcloud compute networks create test
[..]
NAME IPV4_RANGE     GATEWAY_IPV4
test 10.240.0.0/16 10.240.0.1
$ gcloud compute networks create prod
[..]
NAME IPV4_RANGE     GATEWAY_IPV4
prod 10.240.0.0/16 10.240.0.1
```

Note that we did not need to provide a zone or region. Compute Engine networks span regions and can contain instances from any zone in any region.

Let's create a couple of frontend instances attached to each of our new networks:

```
$ gcloud compute instances create frontend-test-1 frontend-test-2 \
    --network test --tags frontend --zone us-central1-a
[..]
NAME            ZONE         MACHINE_TYPE  INTERNAL_IP    EXTERNAL_IP
frontend-test-1 us-central1-a n1-standard-1 10.240.91.238  146.148.81.N
frontend-test-2 us-central1-a n1-standard-1 10.240.133.43  23.236.50.N

$ gcloud compute instances create frontend-prod-1 frontend-prod-2 \
    --network prod --tags frontend --zone us-central1-a
[..]
NAME            ZONE         MACHINE_TYPE  INTERNAL_IP    EXTERNAL_IP
frontend-prod-1  us-central1-a n1-standard-1 10.240.69.NN   130.211.120.N
frontend-prod-2  us-central1-a n1-standard-1 10.240.129.NN 146.148.71.NN
```

Now let's ssh into one of our instances and see what we can and can't do:

```
$ gcloud compute ssh frontend-test-1 --zone us-central1-a
ssh: connect to host 146.148.81.N port 22: Connection refused
ERROR: (gcloud.compute.ssh) [/usr/local/bin/ssh] exited with return code [255].
```

Pardon me? Why can't we access our instance? Recall that not only was the default network created for us automatically, but several firewall rules were also created for us, one of which allows us to use ssh to reach our instances from the outside world. These firewall rules are *not* created automatically for any networks we create manually; we must do this ourselves for our new networks:

```
$ gcloud compute firewall-rules create test-ssh --network test --allow tcp:22
[..]
NAME      NETWORK SRC_RANGES RULES  SRC_TAGS TARGET_TAGS
test-ssh  test    0.0.0.0/0  tcp:22
$ gcloud compute firewall-rules create prod-ssh --network prod --allow tcp:22
[..]
NAME      NETWORK SRC_RANGES RULES  SRC_TAGS TARGET_TAGS
prod-ssh  prod    0.0.0.0/0  tcp:22
```

Now that we've created a firewall rule to allow connections from the outside world into our test and prod networks, we can ssh into our new instances and poke around the network a bit:

```
$ gcloud compute ssh frontend-test-1 --zone us-central1-a
[..]
frontend-test-1$ ping -c 1 frontend-test-2
PING frontend-test-2.c.gce-oreilly.internal (10.240.133.43) 56(84) bytes of data.
--- frontend-test-2.c.gce-oreilly.internal ping statistics ---
1 packets transmitted, 0 received, 100% packet loss, time 0ms
```

Once again, this confirms that by default, a brand new network doesn't allow any traffic. We need to create the equivalent of the default-allow-internal firewall rule that was created for us on the default network:

```
$ gcloud compute firewall-rules create test-allow-internal \
    --network test --allow tcp:1-65535 udp:1-65535 icmp \
    --source-ranges 10.240.0.0/16
NAME                NETWORK SRC_RANGES      RULES                        [..]
test-allow-internal test    10.240.0.0/16 tcp:1-65535,udp:1-65535,icmp
$ gcloud compute firewall-rules create prod-allow-internal \
    --network prod --allow tcp:1-65535 udp:1-65535 icmp \
    --source-ranges 10.240.0.0/16
NAME                NETWORK SRC_RANGES      RULES                        [..]
prod-allow-internal prod    10.240.0.0/16 tcp:1-65535,udp:1-65535,icmp
```

Now we should be able to ssh in and ping one test frontend from another, and indeed we can:

```
$ gcloud compute ssh frontend-test-1 --zone us-central1-a
[..]
frontend-test-1$ ping -c 1 frontend-test-2
PING frontend-test-2.c.gce-oreilly.internal (10.240.133.43) 56(84) bytes of data.
64 bytes  from  frontend-test.c.gce-oreilly.internal  (10.240.133.43):
icmp_req=1 ttl=64 time=0.927 ms
--- frontend-test-2.c.gce-oreilly.internal ping statistics ---
```

```
1 packets transmitted, 1 received, 0% packet loss, time 0ms
rtt min/avg/max/mdev = 0.927/0.927/0.927/0.000 ms
```

However, we can also confirm that we cannot currently ping a production frontend from a test frontend:

```
frontend-test-1$ ping -c 1 130.211.120.NN
PING 130.211.120.NN (130.211.120.NN) 56(84) bytes of data.
--- 130.211.120.NN ping statistics ---
1 packets transmitted, 0 received, 100% packet loss, time 0ms
```

We can't do this because there is no firewall rule on the prod network that allows ICMP through from addresses outside the prod network. In general, it's a good idea to let ICMP through, because the proper functioning of the Internet relies on ICMP, so you should probably set up the equivalent of the default-icmp firewall rule on any networks you create, if you want them to be reachable from the outside world.

We could continue with this example and configure separate target pools for our test and prod frontends, set up a load balancing forwarding rule for those target pools, and set up DNS names such as test.gce-oreilly.com and prod.gce-oreilly.com to point to these load-balanced IP addresses, but this is left as a straightforward exercise for the reader. Aside from adding the --network flag and changing some names, the commands would be the same as what we saw in the section on load balancing.

Understanding Networking Costs

Pricing in the cloud business changes frequently, but there are some common themes that have been relatively stable for some time, and are important to understand when you are architecting your application. These themes will probably still be accurate at the time you're reading this, but you should of course check Google's current pricing to be sure there hasn't been some major change since this book was published.

First, ingress is free. Ingress means packets that flow into your instances. It's the packets that you send from your instances that could end up costing you money. Generally speaking, the cost of sending a packet will differ depending on where that packet is going.

Currently Google does not charge for sending traffic from one instance to another instance within the same zone via the internal address. Google also allows you to send packets to certain other Google services, under certain circumstances, free of charge. You do have to be careful here, however. For example, you can currently send traffic to Cloud Storage for free, but only if the Cloud Storage bucket is on the same continent as the instance. Cloud Storage buckets can currently be stored in Europe or the United States, so uploading an object to a Cloud Storage bucket in the United States from an instance in the us-central1 region would be free of charge, but uploading that same object to the same bucket from europe-west1 would not.

After "same zone" and "nearby Google services," the hierarchy is roughly "same region" then "same continent," then "the rest of the world." There are wrinkles to this, as the cost of providing network services differs in different places in the world, but if you design your application to try as much as possible to keep network traffic within a zone, then within a region, then within a continent, you will reap the dual benefits of lower cost and higher performance.

Understanding Routing

So far, we haven't worried about routing, even for the two nondefault networks we created in an earlier section. This is because every time we create a network, two routes are created for us automatically which in most cases do everything we want. Let's have a look at these routes:

```
$ gcloud compute routes list
NAME                     NETWORK    DEST_RANGE     NEXT_HOP              PRIORITY
default-route-2e[..] default    10.240.0.0/16                         1000
default-route-4a[..] test       0.0.0.0/0      default-internet-[..] 1000
default-route-79[..] prod       10.240.0.0/16                         1000
default-route-7b[..] default    0.0.0.0/0      default-internet-[..] 1000
default-route-ac[..] test       10.240.0.0/16                         1000
default-route-ff[..] prod       0.0.0.0/0      default-internet-[..] 1000
$ gcloud compute routes describe default-route-4a1c564f4dc16b9c
creationTimestamp: '2014-10-09T10:35:43.594-07:00'
description: Default route to the Internet.
destRange: 0.0.0.0/0
id: '8062926538286370827'
kind: compute#route
name: default-route-4a1c564f4dc16b9c
network: https://[..]/global/networks/test
nextHopGateway: https://[..]/global/gateways/default-internet-gateway
priority: 1000
selfLink: https://[..]/global/routes/default-route-4a1c564f4dc16b9c
$ gcloud compute routes describe default-route-ac954b680a54ddf7
creationTimestamp: '2014-10-09T10:35:43.573-07:00'
description: Default route to the virtual network.
destRange: 10.240.0.0/16
id: '5790468215044274952'
kind: compute#route
name: default-route-ac954b680a54ddf7
network: https://[..]/global/networks/test
nextHopNetwork: https://[..]/global/networks/test
priority: 1000
selfLink: https://[..]/global/routes/default-route-ac954b680a54ddf7
```

Here we can see two routes for each of our networks, and the details for the two routes associated with the test network we created in a previous section.

These routes are pretty self-explanatory. One routes local traffic to the local network (nextHopNetwork = .../networks/test), and the other routes nonlocal traffic to the Internet (nextHopGateway = .../gateways/default-internet-gateway). There is one thing that bears explaining. A destination address like 10.1.2.3 matches both 0.0.0.0/0 and 10.0.0.0/8. How does Compute Engine decide which route to use? First it chooses the most specific route. In this case, 10.0.0.0/8 is more specific than 0.0.0.0/0, so it wins. If there was another route that applied to 10.1.2.3/16, that would be more specific, and it would be applied. The priority field you see in there is only used to break ties between two routes that are equally specific, which is an unusual situation.

You can of course create custom routes in Compute Engine. This can sometimes be useful if you want to set up a virtual private network (VPN) or perform some special kind of network address translation (NAT), but for most projects, the default routes will do what you expect and are all that you need. If you're a seasoned network administrator who needs to do something special, by all means investigate setting up some custom routes, but most readers do not fall into that category and are unlikely to need these more advanced features.

Selecting an Access Mode

The examples in this chapter have all used gcloud compute, but Compute Engine's networking functionality can also be configured via the Cloud Console or even automated in your own code via the Compute Engine API. Unlike starting and stopping instances, configuring networking is usually a relatively rare operation. Typically, you will choose a network architecture early on in your application's development, set it up, and updates to that configuration will be rare. Thus using an interactive method such as the command line or Cloud Console is appropriate. However, if you find yourself needing to automate any portion of the network setup, be aware that you have the ability to do so using the Compute Engine API.

Summary

We began this chapter with a short background primer on computer networking, then quickly dove into how Compute Engine instances communicate with one another and with the outside world in the default scenario. We then began to see how to customize that networking by adding firewall rules to permit additional traffic flows and configuring load balancing to enable our applications to be scalable and fault tolerant. We then quickly touched on the issue of reserving external IP addresses before diving into the subject of adding nondefault networks to a project, discovering along the way how convenient the default network configuration is. We touched briefly on cost considerations before concluding with a peek under the hood of Compute Engine's network routing.

Up Next

In the next chapter, we will examine some more advanced features that can help you get the most out of Compute Engine.

## CHAPTER 7

Advanced Topics

Now that you have an understanding of the basics of Compute Engine, let's take a look at some of the more advanced features of Compute Engine, including *startup scripts*, *custom images*, and the *metadata server*.

Both startup scripts and custom images allow you to customize your Compute Engine instances with specific software, configurations, or even operating systems. The metadata server provides an instance access to information about itself, its owning project, and customizable key/value pairs.

Startup Scripts

In Chapter 1, you started a VM, logged into the machine, and installed Apache. Wouldn't this process be much easier if you could avoid the manual software installation step? One way to avoid manual setup is through the use of a *startup script*. A startup script is a bash script that runs as the last step when a Compute Engine instance boots or restarts. The startup script can contain any number of commands that install software or libraries, create files, or update system users, with all commands running as the root user.

Let's take a look at how to start an instance with a startup script first using `gcloud compute` and then the Compute Engine API.

gcloud compute

The `gcloud compute instances create` command allows you to start a Compute Engine VM with a startup script. The manner in which your script is stored influences how the command is used. The script can be stored in one of four ways: it can be provided as a literal string value within the command itself, it can be saved as a local file, it can be stored as an object on Google Cloud Storage, or it can be available at any public location online. We'll take a look at how to use a startup script using each approach.

Literal-Value Approach

The most straightforward option is to simply pass the startup script as the string value of the `metadata` flag in the `gcloud compute instances create` command. The `metadata` flag allows you to set custom *metadata* for your instance. Metadata are string key/value pairs associated with instances and projects and will be discussed in more detail later in this chapter.

In the `gcloud compute instances create` command, the metadata key is set to `startup-script` and the value is the string startup script. For example, run the following `gcloud compute` command to start an instance, update the packages on the VM, and install Apache:

```
$ gcloud compute instances create startup-script-1 \
--tags frontend \
--metadata startup-script="#! /bin/bash
apt-get update
apt-get install -y apache2
echo Done installing apache"
```

The `tags` flag is set to `frontend` in this command to account for the firewall rule created in Chapter 6. The firewall rule allowed external traffic to flow to port 80 on any instances with a `frontend` tag. We'll continue to use this flag throughout the remainder of this chapter in any example that uses Apache, which allows for ease in testing Apache's installation.

As the instance starts, the script runs as the last step in the instance-boot process. All output from the startup script is saved to a file called *startupscript.log* under the */var/log/* directory.

To verify that the startup script has run properly, log in to the machine as you normally would. View the contents of the */var/log/startupscript.log* file:

```
startup-script-1$ tail -10 /var/log/startupscript.log
Aug 12 20:17:57 startup-script-1 startupscript: Enabling module authz_groupfile.#015
Aug 12 20:17:57 startup-script-1 startupscript: Enabling module authn_file.#015
Aug 12 20:17:57 startup-script-1 startupscript: Enabling module authz_host.#015
Aug 12 20:17:57 startup-script-1 startupscript: Enabling module reqtimeout.#015
Aug 12 20:17:57 startup-script-1 startupscript: Setting up apache2-mpm-worker
(2.2.22-13+deb7u3) ...#015
Aug 12 20:17:58 startup-script-1 startupscript: [....] Starting web server:
apache2#033[?25l#033[?1c#0337#033[1G[#033[32m ok #033[39;49m
#0338#033[?25h#033[?0c.#015
Aug 12 20:17:58 startup-script-1 startupscript: Setting up apache2 (2.2.22-
```

```
13+deb7u3) ...#015
Aug 12 20:17:58 startup-script-1 startupscript: Setting up ssl-cert (1.0.32)
...#015
Aug 12 20:17:59 startup-script-1 startupscript: Done installing apache
Aug 12 20:17:59 startup-script-1 startupscript: Finished running startup
script /var/run/google.startup.script
```

All the output from the startup script was logged in this file, including the output from the Apache installation and the echo from the last line of the startup script (in **bold**). If you don't see the "Done installing apache" message, it's possible that the startup script is still running. Try viewing the tail of the file again after a minute or two.

You can also test the installation of Apache by visiting the instance's external IP in a browser. The external IP is available in the output displayed when the instance was created.

Placing the string value of the startup script in the gcloud compute command itself can make for a very lengthy command and makes it hard to reuse. It would be more convenient to store the script in a file, which is covered in the next few sections.

When using the command-line approach, there is also a 32,768-byte limit to the length of the startup script. If your startup script is longer than 32,768 bytes, consider using Cloud Storage or an online public file instead. We'll cover both options later in this chapter.

Local-File Approach

If your startup script is too long to conveniently fit as the string value of the metadata flag, you can store the startup script in a local file. Let's see how this works. First, create a file called *startup.sh* on your local machine. Add the following code to the file and save the changes:

```
#!/bin/bash
apt-get update
apt-get install -y apache2
echo Done installing apache
```

To start an instance with this startup script, run the gcloud compute instances cre ate command using the metadata-from-file flag. Notice we're using metadata again, but this time the metadata is saved in a local file. gcloud compute reads the contents of the file and sends the script as a string. The key is again called startup-script and the value is the path to the locally saved startup script:

```
$ gcloud compute instances create startup-script-2 \
--tags frontend \
--metadata-from-file startup-script=startup.sh
```

Instance startup proceeds the same as when passing the startup script via the string value of the metadata flag. The script is run as the last step in the instance-boot process. You can verify that the startup script ran properly by logging into the machine and viewing the contents of the */var/log/startupscript.log* file or by visiting the instance's external IP address in a browser.

When using the local-file approach, there is a 32,768-byte limit to the length of the startup script. If your startup script is longer than 32,768 bytes, consider using Cloud Storage or an online public file instead. We'll cover both options next.

Cloud-Storage Approach

If your script is longer than 32,768 bytes, you can no longer use a local file or pass the script as a string in the `gcloud compute instances create` command. One option is to store the script on Google Cloud Storage. During instance startup, you provide the URL of the file on Cloud Storage. Compute Engine downloads the file to a temporary location as the instance starts or reboots and runs the script as the last step in the startup process.

 In order to store files on Cloud Storage, you will need to activate Google Cloud Storage and enable billing on your Developers Console project.

Let's give it a try.[1] Upload the *startup.sh* file you created earlier in this chapter to a Cloud Storage bucket. This can be done via the Cloud Storage UI or using `gsutil` (see Chapter 4 for more details on these options).

At this point, it is important to make sure that Compute Engine has permission to access the file on Cloud Storage. This can be accomplished in one of two ways: you can give the Cloud Storage object public-read access or you can provide the Cloud Storage scope in the `gcloud compute instances create` command. The second method is generally preferred as public-read access grants anyone access to your startup script. Because this is the preferred method, we will cover using scopes only.

---

[1] In this exercise, it is assumed that Google Cloud Storage has been activated and enabled on your Developers Console project and `gsutil` has been installed and authorized.

To start an instance with a startup script stored on Cloud Storage, use the following command:

```
$ gcloud compute instances create startup-script-3 \
--tags frontend \
--metadata startup-script-url=url \
--scopes storage-ro
```

Notice the flags used in this command: `metadata` and `scopes`. The key name provided in the metadata flag is `startup-script-url`, which indicates that the startup script is available via a URL. The value of the key is the URL of the object on Cloud Storage. The URL can be formatted in one of two ways:

- *gs://<bucket>/<object>*
- *https://storage.googleapis.com/<bucket>/<object>*

Replace <bucket> and <object> with the name of your Cloud Storage bucket and object, respectively.

The `scopes` flag is used to provide the instance access to the object on Cloud Storage (more information about scopes can be found in Chapter 2). A scope of `storage-ro` grants the instance read-only access to the object.

Once the instance has started, you can verify that the startup script ran properly by logging into the machine and viewing the contents of the */var/log/startupscript.log* file or by visiting the instance's external IP address in a browser.

Publicly Available Approach

If the first three options don't fit your needs, you can also store your startup script in a location publicly available online. The syntax for starting the instance with the `gcloud compute instances create` command is nearly identical to the syntax used when using a startup script on Cloud Storage, minus the `scopes` flag:

```
$ gcloud compute instances create startup-script-4 \
--metadata startup-script-url=url
```

The URL in this case is the URL to the file stored online.

API Approach

Startup scripts can also be applied to instances created using the API. Taking a look at the instance dictionary in the code from Chapter 2, we can apply a startup script to the instance by adding a metadata object to the instance dictionary (in **bold**):

```
BODY = {
  'name': 'test-vm',
  'machineType': '%s/zones/%s/machineTypes/%s' % (
```

```
        PROJECT_URL, ZONE, MACHINE_TYPE),
  'disks': [{
    'boot': True,
    'type': 'PERSISTENT',
    'mode': 'READ_WRITE',
    'zone': '%s/zones/%s' % (PROJECT_URL, ZONE),
    'initializeParams': {
      'sourceImage': '%s/global/images/%s' % (IMAGE_PROJECT_URL, IMAGE_NAME)
    },
  }],
  'networkInterfaces': [{
    'accessConfigs': [{
      'name': 'External NAT',
      'type': 'ONE_TO_ONE_NAT'
    }],
    'network': PROJECT_URL + '/global/networks/default'
  }],
  'scheduling': {
    'automaticRestart': True,
    'onHostMaintenance': 'MIGRATE'
  },
  'serviceAccounts': [{
    'email': 'default',
    'scopes': [
      'https://www.googleapis.com/auth/compute',
      'https://www.googleapis.com/auth/devstorage.full_control'
    ]
  }],
  'metadata': {
    'items': [{
      'key': 'script-type',
      'value': 'script-or-url'
    }]
  }
}
```

Similar to using gcloud compute, metadata is used to pass our startup script to the instance. The API uses a metadata object within the instance dictionary to represent the metadata key/value pairs.

Also similar to using gcloud compute, there are various storage options available to your startup script. You can pass the script as a string directly in the metadata object or you can store your script online in Cloud Storage or any public location. If you're passing the script as a string, replace script-type with the string startup-script and replace script-or-url with the script itself. If you're storing the script online, replace script-type with the string startup-script-url and replace script-or-url with the URL of the script. The same limitations and URL formats noted for gcloud compute usage apply here.

Let's see this in action using the startup script you saved on Cloud Storage earlier in this chapter. You can start with the complete code in the gce-oreilly GitHub repository (*https://github.com/GoogleCloudPlatform/gce-oreilly/blob/master/ch7-1.py*). If you prefer to do some typing, copy the *ch1-1.py* file you downloaded in Chapter 1, and rename it to *ch7-1.py*. Using your favorite text editor, open the *ch7-1.py* source file and comment out this line (by prepending the line with the Python comment character #):

```
# print 'Success! Now add code here.'
```

Insert the following code directly below the commented-out print statement (making sure to preserve indentation consistently with the containing file):

```
# Set project, zone, and other constants.
URL_PREFIX = 'https://www.googleapis.com/compute'
API_VERSION = 'v1'
PROJECT_ID = 'your-project-id'
PROJECT_URL = '%s/%s/projects/%s' % (URL_PREFIX, API_VERSION, PROJECT_ID)
INSTANCE_NAME = 'startup-script-api'
ZONE = 'us-central1-a'
MACHINE_TYPE = 'n1-standard-1'
IMAGE_PROJECT_ID = 'debian-cloud'
IMAGE_PROJECT_URL = '%s/%s/projects/%s' % (
    URL_PREFIX, API_VERSION, IMAGE_PROJECT_ID)
IMAGE_NAME = 'debian-7-wheezy-v20140807'
STARTUP_SCRIPT_URL = 'gs://bucket/object'

BODY = {
  'name': INSTANCE_NAME,
  'tags': {
    'items': ['frontend']
  },
  'machineType': '%s/zones/%s/machineTypes/%s' % (PROJECT_URL, ZONE, MACHINE_TYPE),
  'disks': [{
    'boot': True,
    'type': 'PERSISTENT',
    'mode': 'READ_WRITE',
    'zone': '%s/zones/%s' % (PROJECT_URL, ZONE),
    'initializeParams': {
      'sourceImage': '%s/global/images/%s' % (IMAGE_PROJECT_URL, IMAGE_NAME)
    },
  }],
  'networkInterfaces': [{
    'accessConfigs': [{
      'name': 'External NAT',
      'type': 'ONE_TO_ONE_NAT'
    }],
    'network': PROJECT_URL + '/global/networks/default'
  }],
  'scheduling': {
    'automaticRestart': True,
```

```
      'onHostMaintenance': 'MIGRATE'
    },
    'serviceAccounts': [{
      'email': 'default',
      'scopes': [
        'https://www.googleapis.com/auth/compute',
        'https://www.googleapis.com/auth/devstorage.full_control'
      ]
    }],
    'metadata': {
      'items': [{
        'key': 'startup-script-url',
        'value': STARTUP_SCRIPT_URL
      }]
    }
  }
}

# Build and execute instance insert request.
request = service.instances().insert(
    project=PROJECT_ID, zone=ZONE, body=BODY)
try:
  response = request.execute()
except Exception, ex:
  print 'ERROR: ' + str(ex)
  sys.exit()

# Instance creation is asynchronous so now wait for a DONE status.
op_name = response['name']
operations = service.zoneOperations()
while True:
  request = operations.get(
      project=PROJECT_ID, zone=ZONE, operation=op_name)
  try:
    response = request.execute()
  except Exception, ex:
    print 'ERROR: ' + str(ex)
    sys.exit()
  if 'error' in response:
    print 'ERROR: ' + str(response['error'])
    sys.exit()
  status = response['status']
  if status == 'DONE':
    print 'Instance created.'
    break
  else:
    print 'Waiting for operation to complete. Status: ' + status
```

Whether you downloaded the complete code from GitHub or manually typed it, replace *your-project-id* with the name of your project, **bucket** with the name of your Cloud Storage bucket, and **object** with the name of your Cloud Storage object. Run the script using the following command:

```
$ python ch7-1.py
```

Verify that Apache was installed by visiting the external IP address of the instance in a browser.

Custom Images

In addition to startup scripts, custom images provide another option for customizing your Compute Engine instances. Custom images are helpful if you need a specific operating system or software package installed on your instances. Similar to startup scripts, they allow you to avoid manual installation of software but with much better performance as all packages and configurations are already downloaded, set, and ready to go.

Starting with one of Compute Engine's standard images, you can customize the image through software installation or other system configurations and then use an image created from that instance to start other instances. You can also build an image from scratch using the operating system of your choice, as long as the image is compatible with Compute Engine's hardware manifest as described in the online documentation: *https://developers.google.com/compute/docs/building-image#providedkernel*. In either case, the image you create is a raw block file that can be deployed on one or more Compute Engine instances.

Custom images are global resources that can be used by any Compute Engine instance that has access to the project owning the image. You can also use images from any project to which you have access. An example of this is the set of images available within the debian-cloud and centos-cloud projects (see Chapter 2).

Creating a Custom Image

Let's take a look at how to create a custom image using one of Compute Engine's standard images.[2] Continuing the web server example, we'll create a custom image with Apache installed. To begin, start a new, default Compute Engine instance in any zone with any machine type and Debian image. This instance will be used as the reference instance with which we'll create our custom image:

```
$ gcloud compute instances create custom-image-reference \
--scopes storage-rw
```

Notice that the Google Cloud Storage read-write scope is added to this command. This is because we will be uploading our image file to Cloud Storage, and the Cloud

---

[2] See the online documentation (*https://developers.google.com/compute/docs/images#buildingimage*) for information on how to build an image from scratch using any operating system: *https://developers.google.com/compute/docs/images#buildingimage*.

Storage read-write scope provides the authorization we need to access Cloud Storage from our instance:

When the instance has started, log in to the machine. Run these two commands to install Apache:

```
custom-image-reference$ sudo apt-get update
custom-image-reference$ sudo apt-get install -y apache2
```

Now let's also update the Apache index page. Using a text editor, make some changes to the *index.html* file in the */var/www* directory, and save the changes. For example, you can use the following HTML code:

```
<!DOCTYPE html>
<html>
  <head>
    <title>Compute Engine demo</title>
  </head>
  <body>
    <h1>Compute Engine demo</h1>
    <p>Have a nice day!</p>
  </body>
</html>
```

At this point, you could also edit system-configuration settings, create new files on the instance's disk, or install more packages, and all customizations would be available in the image created from this instance, but let's make an image using the current setup. To do so, run the *gcimagebundle* script found on the Compute Engine instance:

```
custom-image-reference$ sudo gcimagebundle \
-d /dev/sda -o /tmp/ --log_file=/tmp/image.log
```

The script creates a raw block file with the OS, any installed packages, and all files stored on the instance's disk. The raw block image file is stored within the */tmp* directory as *<hex-number>.image.tar.gz*. You can find the hex number by listing the contents of the */tmp* directory:

```
custom-image-reference$ ls -ltr /tmp
```

A log file is also created in the */tmp* directory as *image.log*.

When the image has been created, the image file must be uploaded to Cloud Storage[3] (more information about Cloud Storage can be found in Chapter 4). To simplify object transfer to Cloud Storage, Compute Engine instances come with gsutil preinstalled. Because we used the read-write Cloud Storage scope when creating our instance, no authentication or configuration is required before using gsutil. If you

---

3 This step assumes you have enabled Cloud Storage on your project.

don't already have a bucket on Cloud Storage, go ahead and create one now with the `gsutil mb` command:

```
custom-image-reference$ gsutil mb gs://<bucket>
```

Then transfer your image to the Cloud Storage bucket with the `gsutil cp` command, replacing `<hex-number>` with the hex number of your image file, `<bucket>` with your Cloud Storage bucket, and `<image-name>` with any name you want to give to your image:

```
custom-image-reference$ gsutil cp /tmp/<hex-number>.image.tar.gz \
gs://<bucket>/<image-name>.image.tar.gz
```

When the image has been successfully transferred to Google Cloud Storage, log out of the machine by entering the `exit` command.

Now you can add this image to the images collection within your project using the `gcloud compute images create` command. The syntax of the command is:

```
$ gcloud compute images create  image-name --source-uri image-url
```

An image name and the URL of the image are both required. The image name can be any unique string name for the image within your project and doesn't have to correspond to the file name. The image URL is a path to the image you stored on Cloud Storage and can be one of the following:

- *gs://<bucket>/<image-name>.image.tar.gz*
- *https://storage.googleapis.com/<bucket>/<image-name>.image.tar.gz*

Run the `gcloud compute images create` command shown earlier, substituting *image-name* with <apache-image> and *image-url* with the URL to your image on Cloud Storage. When the operation is complete, verify that the image has been added to your project by running the `gcloud compute images list` command:

```
$ gcloud compute images list
```

Example output (custom image in **bold**):

```
NAME                                     PROJECT          DEPRECATED STATUS
apache-image                             gce-oreilly                 READY
centos-6-v20140718                       centos-cloud                READY
coreos-alpha-402-2-0-v20140807           coreos-cloud                READY
coreos-beta-367-1-0-v20140715            coreos-cloud                READY
coreos-stable-367-1-0-v20140724          coreos-cloud                READY
backports-debian-7-wheezy-v20140807 debian-cloud                READY
debian-7-wheezy-v20140807                debian-cloud                READY
opensuse-13-1-v20140711                  opensuse-cloud              READY
rhel-6-v20140718                         rhel-cloud                  READY
sles-11-sp3-v20140712                    suse-cloud                  READY
```

Using a Custom Image

gcloud compute

Let's now start an instance using the Apache custom image. Run the `gcloud compute images create` command, this time with an `image` flag set equal to the name of our newly created image:

```
$ gcloud compute instances create apache-instance \
--tags front-end \
--image apache-image
```

Verify that Apache is installed on the instance by visiting the external IP of the instance in a browser (see Chapter 2 for more details).

API

Custom images can also be applied to instances created using the API. Let's review the instance dictionary from our code in Chapter 2. Within the list of disks, there's an `initializeParams` object where a `sourceImage` is specified (see the following code example). To use a custom image, set the value of the `sourceImage` key (in **bold**) with the image resource URL of your custom Compute Engine image (recall from Chapter 1 that the image resource URL has the syntax https://www.googleapis.com/compute/v1/projects/<project>/global/images/<image-name>, for example https://www.googleapis.com/compute/v1/projects/gce-oreilly/global/images/apache-image):

```
BODY = {
  'name': 'test-vm',
  'machineType': '%s/zones/%s/machineTypes/%s' % (
      PROJECT_URL, ZONE, MACHINE_TYPE),
  'disks': [{
    'boot': True,
    'type': 'PERSISTENT',
    'mode': 'READ_WRITE',
    'zone': '%s/zones/%s' % (PROJECT_URL, ZONE),
    'initializeParams': {
      'sourceImage': 'image-url'
    }
  }],
  'networkInterfaces': [{
    'accessConfigs': [{
      'name': 'External NAT',
      'type': 'ONE_TO_ONE_NAT'
    }],
    'network': PROJECT_URL + '/global/networks/default'
  }],
  'scheduling': {
    'automaticRestart': True,
    'onHostMaintenance': 'MIGRATE'
  },
```

```
    'serviceAccounts': [{
      'email': 'default',
      'scopes': [
        'https://www.googleapis.com/auth/compute',
        'https://www.googleapis.com/auth/devstorage.full_control'
      ]
    }]
  }
```

What does the complete code look like? As usual, you can either download the entire sample from the gce-oreilly GitHub repository (*https://github.com/GoogleCloudPlatform/gce-oreilly/blob/master/ch7-2.py*). If you prefer to do some typing, copy the *ch1-1.py* file, and rename it to *ch7-2.py*. Using your favorite text editor, open the *ch7-2.py* source file and comment out this line (by prepending the line with the Python comment character #):

```
# print 'Success! Now add code here.'
```

Insert the following code directly below the commented-out print statement (making sure to preserve indentation consistently with the containing file):

```
# Set project, zone, and other constants.
URL_PREFIX = 'https://www.googleapis.com/compute'
API_VERSION = 'v1'
PROJECT_ID = 'your-project-id'
PROJECT_URL = '%s/%s/projects/%s' % (URL_PREFIX, API_VERSION, PROJECT_ID)
INSTANCE_NAME = 'custom-image-api'
ZONE = 'us-central1-a'
MACHINE_TYPE = 'n1-standard-1'
IMAGE_NAME = 'apache-image'

BODY = {
  'name': INSTANCE_NAME,
  'tags': {
    'items': ['frontend']
  },
  'machineType': '%s/zones/%s/machineTypes/%s' % (
      PROJECT_URL, ZONE, MACHINE_TYPE),
  'disks': [{
    'boot': True,
    'type': 'PERSISTENT',
    'mode': 'READ_WRITE',
    'zone': '%s/zones/%s' % (PROJECT_URL, ZONE),
    'initializeParams': {
      'sourceImage': '%s/global/images/%s' % (PROJECT_URL, IMAGE_NAME)
    }
  }],
  'networkInterfaces': [{
    'accessConfigs': [{
      'name': 'External NAT',
      'type': 'ONE_TO_ONE_NAT'
    }],
```

```
      'network': PROJECT_URL + '/global/networks/default'
    }],
    'scheduling': {
      'automaticRestart': True,
      'onHostMaintenance': 'MIGRATE'
    },
    'serviceAccounts': [{
      'email': 'default',
      'scopes': [
        'https://www.googleapis.com/auth/compute',
        'https://www.googleapis.com/auth/devstorage.full_control'
      ]
    }]
  }

# Build and execute instance insert request.
request = service.instances().insert(
    project=PROJECT_ID, zone=ZONE, body=BODY)
try:
  response = request.execute()
except Exception, ex:
  print 'ERROR: ' + str(ex)
  sys.exit()

# Instance creation is asynchronous so now wait for a DONE status.
op_name = response['name']
operations = service.zoneOperations()
while True:
  request = operations.get(
      project=PROJECT_ID, zone=ZONE, operation=op_name)
  try:
    response = request.execute()
  except Exception, ex:
    print 'ERROR: ' + str(ex)
    sys.exit()
  if 'error' in response:
    print 'ERROR: ' + str(response['error'])
    sys.exit()
  status = response['status']
  if status == 'DONE':
    print 'Instance created.'
    break
  else:
    print 'Waiting for operation to complete. Status: ' + status
```

Whether you downloaded the complete code from GitHub or manually typed it, replace *your-project-id* with the name of your project. Run the code using the following command:

```
$ python ch7-2.py
```

Verify that the new instance has Apache installed.

Metadata

All instances have metadata associated with them. Metadata is essentially a set of key/value string pairs called metadata entries. The metadata entries provide information about your instance (e.g., its zone and machine type), an instance's owning project (e.g., the project ID), and custom data.

Metadata can be retrieved programmatically by the instance or via the API. This allows for some interesting and complex use cases. For example, an instance can discover its own external IP to broadcast to other devices, custom metadata can be used to control a startup script's flow of execution, or your business' contact information can be stored for easy access from any instance within your project.

Metadata Server

Metadata entries are available via Compute Engine's metadata server. Direct access to the server is only available from Compute Engine instances. The syntax for the root URL of the metadata server is:

http://metadata/computeMetadata/<version>/

The API version must be specified in the URL. The current version is v1 and will be used in the metadata URLs throughout the remainder of this book. To find the latest version of the metadata API version, see the online documentation (*https://develop ers.google.com/compute/docs/metadata#metadataserver*).

Metadata entries exist as subpaths under this root URL. For example, an instance's project ID can be found at the URL:

http://metadata/computeMetadata/v1/project/project-id

Because the metadata entries are available via a web server, you can programmatically retrieve the values of the entries using an HTTP request. Let's run through a quick example.

First, start an instance called `metadata-test` using `gcloud compute`, selecting your preferred zone. When the instance is up and running, log in to the machine. Make an HTTP request to the metadata server using curl (*http://curl.haxx.se/*) with the `Metadata-Flavor` header set to Google:

```
metadata-test$ curl http://metadata/computeMetadata/v1/project/project-id \
-H "Metadata-Flavor: Google"
```

The `Metadata-Flavor` header indicates that the request is being made intentionally from a secure source. The output displays the ID of the project owning the instance. For example:

```
gce-oreilly
```

Throughout the remainder of this chapter, we will continue to use curl in requests to the metadata server; but almost any programming language can be used.

There is no newline character at the end of the response to queries for metadata key values. When making the curl request to retrieve the project ID, for example, your project ID will be displayed on the same line as the prompt. The prompt has been removed to simplify the output throughout this chapter. We recommend adding ; echo to the end of your curl requests to add a line between the response and prompt.

Metadata Entries

Metadata entries consist of *directories* and *keys* (a.k.a. *endpoints*), analogous to the directories and files in a hierarchical filesystem. A directory contains other metadata entries, whereas a key is equal to a specific value. Directories can be identified by the trailing slash at the end of the entry name. You can see examples of directories and keys in Table 7-1 and Table 7-2.

The metadata server provides both project and instance information. Project metadata contains information about the project owning the instance. Instance metadata provides information about the current instance.

Project Metadata

Project metadata is relative to the path:

http://metadata/computeMetadata/v1/project/

Table 7-1 lists the project-level metadata available on your Compute Engine instances.

Table 7-1. Project-level metadata

Metadata entry	Description	Full URL
attributes/	A directory containing a list of custom metadata values assigned to the project.	http://metadata/computeMetadata/v1/project/attributes/
attributes/ sshKeys	An endpoint providing a list of ssh keys that can be used to connect to instances in the project.	http://metadata/computeMetadata/v1/project/attributes/sshKeys
numeric-project-id	A key providing the numeric project ID of the project owning the instance.	http://metadata/computeMetadata/v1/project/numeric-project-id

Metadata entry	Description	Full URL
project-id	A key providing the string project ID of the project owning the instance.	http://metadata/ computeMetadata/v1/project/ project-id

Let's take a look at all the project metadata available on the `metadata-test` instance you started earlier in this chapter. If the instance is no longer running, start it again using the `gcloud compute instances create` command, and log in to the instance.

Once logged in to the machine, use the following curl command to retrieve all the information about the instance's owning project:

```
metadata-test$ curl http://metadata/computeMetadata/v1/project/?recursive=true \
-H "Metadata-Flavor: Google"
```

Before we discuss the output, first notice the *recursive* parameter. This parameter tells the metadata server to recursively return all the content under the project directory. The recursive parameter can be used with any HTTP request to any directory, and the resulting output will contain all the metadata keys and values under that directory.

The output is a JavaScript Object Notation (JSON) structure with the metadata entry names as keys, and the metadata entry values as the key values:

```
{"attributes":{"sshKeys":"kbrisbin:ssh-rsa AAA[..]Q1 kbrisbin@mydomain.com"},
"numericProjectId":134224180845,"projectId":"gce-oreilly"}
```

The structure of the JSON response reflects the hierarchical structure of the metadata entries. Directories are represented as JSON objects within the metadata server response. This is true even when the directory is a subdirectory of the requested metadata entry. In the preceding output, *attributes* is a subdirectory within the project directory. In the JSON response, the value of the `attributes` key is a nested JSON object.

Instance Metadata

Instance metadata is relative to the path:

http://metadata/computeMetadata/v1/instance

Table 7-2 lists the instance-level metadata available on your Compute Engine instances.

Table 7-2. Instance-level metadata

Metadata entry	Description	Full URL
`attributes/`	A directory containing a list of custom metadata values assigned to the instance.	http://metadata/ computeMetadata/v1/ instance/attributes/
`description`	A key providing the description of the instance.	http://metadata/ computeMetadata/v1/ instance/description
`disks/`	A directory listing the disks attached to the instance	http://metadata/ computeMetadata/v1/ instance/disks/
`hostname`	A key providing the host name of the instance.	http://metadata/ computeMetadata/v1/ instance/hostname
`id`	A key providing the ID of the instance. This ID is a unique value assigned by Compute Engine.	http://metadata/ computeMetadata/v1/ instance/id
`image`	A key providing the fully qualified name of the image applied to the instance.	http://metadata/ computeMetadata/v1/ instance/image
`machine-type`	A key providing the fully qualified name of the machine-type used by the instance.	http://metadata/ computeMetadata/v1/ instance/machine-type
`network-interfaces/`	A directory containing a list of network interfaces for the instance.	http://metadata/ computeMetadata/v1/ instance/network-interfaces
`network-interfaces/ <index>/ forwarded-ips/`	A directory listing the external IPs that are currently pointing to this virtual machine instance as determined by the network interface at <index>.	http://metadata/ computeMetadata/v1/ instance/network-interfaces/<index>/ forwarded-ips/
`scheduling/`	A directory with the scheduling options for the instance.	http://metadata/ computeMetadata/v1/ instance/scheduling/
`scheduling/on-host-maintenance`	A key providing the instance's scheduled maintenance event behavior setting (equal to MIGRATE or TERMINATE).	http://metadata/ computeMetadata/v1/ instance/scheduling/on-host-maintenance
`scheduling/ automatic-restart`	A key indicating the instance's automatic restart setting (equal to TRUE or FALSE).	http://metadata/ computeMetadata/v1/ instance/scheduling/ automatic-restart

Metadata entry	Description	Full URL
maintenance-event	A key indicating that a scheduled maintenance event is affecting this instance (equal to NONE or MIGRATE_ON_HOST_MAINTENANCE).	http://metadata/ computeMetadata/v1/ instance/maintenance-event
project-id	A key providing the string project ID of the project owning the instance.	http://metadata/ computeMetadata/v1/ instance/project-id
service-accounts/	A directory listing the service accounts associated with the instance.	http://metadata/ computeMetadata/v1/ instance/service-accounts/
tags	A key providing a list of string tags applied to the instance.	http://metadata/ computeMetadata/v1/ instance/tags
zone	A key providing the fully qualified name of the zone in which the instance resides.	http://metadata/ computeMetadata/v1/ instance/zone

Let's view all the instance metadata available on the `metadata-test` instance. Log in to the `metadata-test` instance if you haven't done so already, and use the following curl command to retrieve all the information about the instance's owning project:

```
metadata-test$ curl http://metadata/computeMetadata/v1/instance/?recursive=true \
-H "Metadata-Flavor: Google"
```

You should see output similar to the project directory output. It is a JSON structure with the metadata entry names as keys, and the metadata entry values as the key values. To make the output easier to digest, here's the output formatted for legibility:

```
{
  'attributes': {},
  'description': '',
  'disks': [{
    'deviceName': 'persistent-disk-0',
    'index': 0,
    'mode': 'READ_WRITE',
    'type': 'PERSISTENT'}],
  'hostname': 'metadata-test.c.gce-oreilly.internal',
  'id': 9622837067820057050L,
  'image': '',
  'machineType': 'projects/134224180845/machineTypes/n1-standard-1',
  'maintenanceEvent': 'NONE',
  'networkInterfaces': [{
    'accessConfigs': [{
      'externalIp': '107.178.211.NNN',
      'type': 'ONE_TO_ONE_NAT'}],
    'forwardedIps': [],
    'ip': '10.240.84.188',
    'network': 'projects/134224180845/networks/default'}],
```

```
  'scheduling': {
    'automaticRestart': 'TRUE',
    'onHostMaintenance': 'MIGRATE'},
  'serviceAccounts': {
    '134224180845@developer.gserviceaccount.com': {
      'aliases': ['default'],
      'email': '134224180845@developer.gserviceaccount.com',
      'scopes': [
        'https://www.googleapis.com/auth/devstorage.read_only']},
    'default': {
      'aliases': ['default'],
      'email': '134224180845@developer.gserviceaccount.com',
      'scopes': ['https://www.googleapis.com/auth/devstorage.read_only']}},
  'tags': [],
  'zone': 'projects/134224180845/zones/us-central1-a'
}
```

Data Formats

Each metadata endpoint returns data in a specific format. For example, the project ID metadata endpoint is returned as text. Any directory request with the recursive parameter set to `true` returns as JSON. When the recursive parameter is not present or is set to `false`, the directory request returns as text. You can specify which format you want returned by adding the `alt` parameter to the end of the URL. Supported formats currently include text or JSON.

Let's take a look at how the `alt` parameter can change the return data format of a directory endpoint. Log in to your `metadata-test` instance. Run a curl request to recursively retrieve the instance directory contents again, but this time add the `alt` parameter to the end of the URL and set it equal to `text`:

```
metadata-test$ curl 'http://metadata/
computeMetadata/v1/instance/
?recursive=true&alt=text' \
-H "Metadata-Flavor: Google"
```

The output is a list of metadata keys with the corresponding metadata values in plaintext format:

```
description
disks/0/device-name persistent-disk-0
disks/0/index 0
disks/0/mode READ_WRITE
disks/0/type PERSISTENT
hostname metadata-test.c.gce-oreilly.internal
id 9622837067820057050
image
machine-type projects/134224180845/machineTypes/n1-standard-1
maintenance-event NONE
network-interfaces/0/access-configs/0/external-ip 107.178.211.143
network-interfaces/0/access-configs/0/type ONE_TO_ONE_NAT
```

```
network-interfaces/0/ip 10.240.84.188
network-interfaces/0/network projects/134224180845/networks/default
scheduling/automatic-restart TRUE
scheduling/on-host-maintenance MIGRATE
service-accounts/134224180845@developer.gserviceaccount.com/aliases default
service-accounts/134224180845@developer.gserviceaccount.com/email
134224180845@developer.gserviceaccount.com
service-accounts/134224180845@developer.gserviceaccount.com/scopes
https://www.googleapis.com/auth/devstorage.read_only
service-accounts/default/aliases default
service-accounts/default/email 134224180845@developer.gserviceaccount.com
service-accounts/default/scopes
https://www.googleapis.com/auth/devstorage.read_only
zone projects/134224180845/zones/us-central1-a
```

Default Versus Custom

Compute Engine metadata consists of default and custom metadata entries. Default metadata is set by the Compute Engine metadata server and cannot be updated. Examples include the instance's zone and machine type. Custom metadata can be any arbitrary key/value pair (up to a length of 32,768 bytes). Custom metadata can be applied at both the project and instance level. Let's take a look at both project-level and custom-level metadata in more detail.

Project-Level Custom Metadata

Project-level custom metadata is useful when you want to share a piece of information or data with all instances running in a single project. Continuing with the Apache example, we'll store a couple HTML files for a website on Google Cloud Storage and use project-level metadata to save the Cloud Storage bucket name. Any instances we create within our project will be able to retrieve the name of the bucket from the metadata server. Using a startup script, the instance can then download the files from the Cloud Storage bucket to Apache's default *www* directory during instance creation.

Developers Console

Let's see this in action first using the Google Developers Console. To begin, create a new bucket on Cloud Storage using `gsutil` and add two files to it: *index.html* and *about.html*. For the purposes of this example, we'll make the file content very simple:

index.html

```
<!DOCTYPE html>
<html>
  <head>
    <title>Home</title>
  </head>
  <body>
```

```
    <h1>Home</h1>
    <p><a href="about.html">About</a></p>
  </body>
</html>
```

about.html

```
<!DOCTYPE html>
<html>
  <head>
    <title>About</title>
  </head>
  <body>
    <h1>About</h1>
    <p><a href="index.html">Home</a></p>
  </body>
</html>
```

Now, set the bucket name as custom project metadata. Open up your project in the Google Developers Console (*https://console.developers.google.com/*). Select Compute > Compute Engine in the left navigation, then select Metadata. On this page, you can add custom, project-level metadata to your project (see Figure 7-1).

Figure 7-1. Metadata page in the Developers Console

Click the Edit button. Enter the key `cloud-storage-bucket` into the key field on the left, and the name of your bucket in the value field on the right. Add the metadata to your project by clicking the Done button. The new project-level, custom metadata will be added to your project and is programmatically accessible to any instances within your project. Take a look at Table 7-1 again. The *attributes* directory contains all the custom project-level metadata entries.

Let's view the custom project-level metadata on our `metadata-test` machine. Log in to the instance and run the following curl command to retrieve the metadata entries under the *attributes* directory:

```
metadata-test$ curl http://metadata/computeMetadata/v1/project/attributes/ \
-H "Metadata-Flavor: Google"
```

The output displays a list of custom, project-level metadata keys assigned to the project, as seen in Example 7-1[4].

Example 7-1. Project-level Metadata Key List

```
cloud-storage-bucket
sshKeys
```

Now, run the curl command again to retrieve the value of the `cloud-storage-input` metadata entry:

```
metadata-test$  curl http://metadata/computeMetadata/v1/project/attributes/\
cloud-storage-bucket \
-H "Metadata-Flavor: Google"
```

Your bucket name should be displayed as output.

Let's continue with our Apache example. We have a Cloud Storage bucket storing our two HTML files, and we saved the name of the bucket as project-level metadata. Now we'll create a startup script that downloads the HTML files to Apache's *www* directory on an instance during instance creation. First, log out of the `metadata-test` instance, and save the following script in a local file called *apache-startup-v1.sh*:

```
#!/bin/bash
BUCKET=$(curl http://metadata/computeMetadata/v1/project/attributes\
cloud-storage-bucket -H "Metadata-Flavor: Google")
gsutil cp gs://$BUCKET/* /var/www
```

This script uses curl to retrieve the name of our Cloud Storage bucket from the metadata server. It then uses `gsutil cp` to copy the contents of that bucket to Apache's *www* directory. Start a new instance with this startup script using `gcloud compute instances create`:

```
$ gcloud compute instances create apache-server \
--tags frontend \
--metadata-from-file startup-script=apache-startup-v1.sh \
--image apache-image \
--scopes storage-ro
```

---

4 sshKeys are set when `gcloud compute instances create` or `gcloud compute ssh` is run.

The `--metadata-from-file` flag in this command specifies the locally saved startup script. The `image` flag selects your own custom image to use when booting the instance, which we set to the `apache-image` image you created earlier in this chapter. Finally, the `scopes` flag gives the instance access to the HTML files on Cloud Storage.

Once the instance is running, verify that the Apache server has been set up properly by visiting the external IP of the instance in a browser.

gcloud compute

`gcloud compute` can also be used to set project-level, custom metadata. To create a custom, project-level metadata key/value entry for our Cloud Storage bucket, use the `gcloud compute project-info add-metadata` command along with the `--metadata` flag, substituting *bucket-name* with the name of your bucket:

```
$ gcloud compute project-info add-metadata \
--metadata cloud-storage-bucket= bucket-name
```

You can also use the `metadata-from-file` flag to set a custom metadata key equal to the contents of a locally stored file. The syntax for using the `metadata-from-file` flag is as follows:

```
$ gcloud compute project-info add-metadata \
--metadata-from-file key=path-to-file
```

To view the new custom, project-level metadata, use the `gcloud compute project-info describe` command:

```
$ gcloud compute project-info describe --format json
```

Here's the output (metadata in **bold**):

```
{
  "commonInstanceMetadata": {
    "fingerprint": "oMVjqg6qRC8=",
    "items": [
      {
        "key": "cloud-storage-bucket",
        "value": "gce-oreilly"
      },
      {
        "key": "sshKeys",
        "value": "gce_oreilly..."
      }
    ],
    "kind": "compute#metadata"
  },
  "creationTimestamp": "2014-01-10T13:04:30.298-08:00",
  "description": "",
  "id": "83060252553376467278",
  "kind": "compute#project",
```

```json
    "name": "gce-oreilly",
    "quotas": [
      {
        "limit": 1000.0,
        "metric": "SNAPSHOTS",
        "usage": 0.0
      },
      {
        "limit": 5.0,
        "metric": "NETWORKS",
        "usage": 3.0
      },
      {
        "limit": 100.0,
        "metric": "FIREWALLS",
        "usage": 8.0
      },
      {
        "limit": 100.0,
        "metric": "IMAGES",
        "usage": 1.0
      },
      {
        "limit": 100.0,
        "metric": "ROUTES",
        "usage": 6.0
      },
      {
        "limit": 50.0,
        "metric": "FORWARDING_RULES",
        "usage": 1.0
      },
      {
        "limit": 50.0,
        "metric": "TARGET_POOLS",
        "usage": 1.0
      },
      {
        "limit": 50.0,
        "metric": "HEALTH_CHECKS",
        "usage": 1.0
      },
      {
        "limit": 50.0,
        "metric": "TARGET_INSTANCES",
        "usage": 0.0
      }
    ],
    "selfLink": "https://www.googleapis.com/compute/v1/projects/gce-oreilly"
}
```

API

Custom, project-level metadata can be retrieved, set, and updated via the API.

Retrieve. To retrieve project-level metadata, issue an HTTP GET request to the project resource URL.[5] The response is a project resource, which consists of a dictionary representing the project with the following structure:

```
{
  "kind": "compute#project",
  "selfLink": string,
  "id": unsigned long,
  "creationTimestamp": string,
  "name": string,
  "description": string,
  "commonInstanceMetadata": {
    "kind": "compute#metadata",
    "fingerprint": bytes,
    "items": [
      {
        "key": string,
        "value": string
      }
    ]
  },
  "quotas": [
    {
      "metric": string,
      "limit": double,
      "usage": double
    }
  ],
  "usageExportLocation": {
    "bucketName": string,
    "reportNamePrefix": string
  }
}
```

The project-level metadata is within the value of the `commonInstanceMetadata` key (in **bold**) and consists of a list of objects representing metadata key/value pairs. Notice that the `commonInstanceMetadata` key also has a `fingerprint`. The `finger print` is the hash of the metadata list. To successfully update the metadata, you must provide the most current value of the fingerprint. Compute Engine checks the provided fingerprint value against current version. If the two values do not match, Compute Engine will not update the metadata and an error response of `CONDITION_NOT_MET` will be returned. This mechanism allows for a lock to be placed

---

5 The Compute Center API details, including resource URLs, query parameters, and JSON elements are all documented online at *https://developers.google.com/compute/docs/api/getting-started*.

on the metadata so only one person or application can update the metadata at any one time.

Let's see how to do this using the Python Google API Client Library. You can start with the complete sample in the gce-oreilly GitHub repository (*https://github.com/ GoogleCloudPlatform/gce-oreilly/blob/master/ch7-3.py*). If you would rather do some typing, copy the *ch1-1.py* file and rename it to *ch7-3.py*. Using your favorite text editor, open the *ch7-3.py* source file and comment out this line (by prepending the line with the Python comment character #):

```
# print 'Success! Now add code here.'
```

Insert the following code directly below the commented-out `print` statement (making sure to preserve indentation consistently with the containing file):

```
PROJECT_ID = 'your-project-id'
# Build a request to get the specified project using the Compute Engine API.
request = service.projects().get(project=PROJECT_ID)
try:
  # Execute the request and store the response.
  response = request.execute()
except Exception, ex:
  print 'ERROR: ' + str(ex)
  sys.exit()
print response['commonInstanceMetadata']
```

Whether you downloaded the complete code from GitHub or manually typed it, substitute your project ID for the string *your-project-id*. Run the sample app from a shell or Terminal window using the command:

```
$ python ch7-3.py
```

The project-level metadata should be displayed as output.

Set/update. To set and/or update project-level metadata via the API, we must first retrieve the value of the metadata fingerprint, then send an HTTP POST request to the project `setCommonInstanceMetadata` URL (substitute <project> with the name of your project):

```
POST https://www.googleapis.com/compute/v1/projects/<project>/setCommonInstanceMetadata
```

The body of the request consists of an object similar to the value of the `commonInstan ceMetadata` key in the project resource:

```
{
  'fingerprint': 'fingerprint',
  'items': [{
    'key': 'your-metadata-key',
    'value': 'your-metadata-value'
  }]
}
```

Let's take a look at the code to set/update our `cloud-storage-bucket` key. You can find the complete code in the GitHub repo (*https://github.com/GoogleCloudPlatform/ gce-oreilly/blob/master/ch7-4.py*). If you prefer to type out the code, copy the *ch1-1.py* file again, and rename it to *ch7-4.py*. Using your favorite text editor, open the *ch7-4.py* source file and comment out this line (by prepending the line with the Python comment character #):

```
# print 'Success! Now add code here.'
```

Insert the following code directly below the commented-out `print` statement (making sure to preserve indentation consistently with the containing file):

```
PROJECT_ID = 'your-project-id'
METADATA = {
  'key': 'cloud-storage-bucket',
  'value': 'bucket'
}

# First retrieve the current metadata.
request = service.projects().get(project=PROJECT_ID)
try:
  response = request.execute()
except Exception, ex:
  print 'ERROR: ' + str(ex)
  sys.exit()

# Use the commonInstanceMetadata dictionary as the body
# of the request, and add or update the cloud-storage-bucket
# metadata entry in the list of items in the dictionary.
BODY = response['commonInstanceMetadata']
for item in BODY['items']:
  if item['key'] == METADATA['key']:
    item['value'] = METADATA['value']
    break
else:
  BODY['items'].append(METADATA)

# Build and execute the set common instance metadata request.
request = service.projects().setCommonInstanceMetadata(
    project=PROJECT_ID, body=BODY)
try:
  response = request.execute()
except Exception, ex:
  print 'ERROR: ' + str(ex)
  sys.exit()

# Metadata setting is asynchronous so wait for an operation status of DONE.
op_name = response['name']
operations = service.globalOperations()
while True:
  request = operations.get(project=PROJECT_ID, operation=op_name)
```

```
try:
  response = request.execute()
except Exception, ex:
  print 'ERROR: ' + str(ex)
  sys.exit()
if 'error' in response:
  print 'ERROR: ' + str(response['error'])
  sys.exit()
status = response['status']
if status == 'DONE':
  print 'Project-level metadata updated.'
  break
else:
  print 'Waiting for operation to complete. Status: ' + status
```

To run the code, replace *your-project-id* with your own project ID. In addition, replace **bucket** with the name of your Cloud Storage bucket. Run the code using the command:

```
$ python ch7-4.py
```

Check your project-level metadata to make sure that the `cloud-storage-bucket` key has been set to the provided value.

Let's take a closer look at the code in this sample, as it's a little more complex than the other samples. As mentioned earlier, a fingerprint is required to set or update the metadata values. To account for this fact, we first send a request to the project endpoint to retrieve the current fingerprint:

```
# First retrieve the current metadata.
request = service.projects().get(project=PROJECT_ID)
try:
  response = request.execute()
except Exception, ex:
  print 'ERROR: ' + str(ex)
  sys.exit()
```

We then add our new metadata key/value pair to the list of metadata entries:

```
# Use the commonInstanceMetadata dictionary as the body
# of the request, and add the new cloud-storage-bucket
# metadata entry to the list of items in the dictionary.
BODY = response['commonInstanceMetadata']
BODY['items'].append(METADATA)
```

Finally, the updated list of metadata entries is sent as the body of the request to the `setCommonInstanceMetadata` endpoint:

```
# Build and execute the set common instance metadata request.
request = service.projects().setCommonInstanceMetadata(
    project=PROJECT_ID, body=BODY)
try:
  response = request.execute()
```

```
  except Exception, ex:
    print 'ERROR: ' + str(ex)
    sys.exit()
```

Instance-Level Custom Metadata

Custom metadata can also be set at the instance level. Instance-level custom metadata is helpful when you want to apply unique data to each individual instance. Using our Apache example, let's say we have both production and staging versions of our website stored in different buckets on Cloud Storage. Instead of using custom project-level metadata to specify the bucket, we can use custom instance-level metadata to indicate whether an instance is a production or a staging server.

gcloud compute

Let's see this in action using gcloud compute. We'll first create some files for our staging server. You can use the HTML files from earlier and add the text Staging in the title and header:

index.html

```
<!DOCTYPE html>
<html>
  <head>
    <title>Staging Home</title>
  </head>
  <body>
    <h1>Staging Home</h1>
    <p><a href="about.html">About</a></p>
  </body>
</html>
```

about.html

```
<!DOCTYPE html>
<html>
  <head>
    <title>Staging About</title>
  </head>
  <body>
    <h1>Staging About</h1>
    <p><a href="index.html">Home</a></p>
  </body>
</html>
```

We'll use the existing bucket for the production server and create a new bucket on Cloud Storage for the staging server. Use the same bucket name with the string "-staging" appended to the end. Upload the staging files to this new staging bucket.

Similar to the custom, project-level metadata, custom, instance-level metadata is found under an *attributes/* metadata directory on the metadata server (see Table 7-2).

This allows us to use the same startup script that we created earlier, but with one change: replace the string `project` with `instance` in the metadata URL. Save this new script as *apache-startup-v2.sh*:

```
#!/bin/bash
BUCKET=$(curl http://metadata/computeMetadata/v1/instance/attributes/\
cloud-storage-bucket -H "Metadata-Flavor: Google")
cd /var/www
gsutil cp gs://$BUCKET/* .
```

Now that we have our staging files available on Cloud Storage, and we updated our startup script, let's start a staging server instance and apply custom, instance-level metadata that designates it as a staging server. We're going to use the `metadata` flag in the `gcloud compute instances create` command to set the instance-level metadata. For the purposes of this exercise, simply set a key called `cloud-storage-bucket` equal to your staging Cloud Storage bucket name:

```
$ gcloud compute instances create apache-server-staging \
--metadata-from-file startup-script=apache-startup-v2.sh \
--metadata cloud-storage-bucket=<bucket-name>-staging \
--image apache-image \
--scopes storage-ro
```

You can verify that the custom metadata has been set by using the `gcloud compute instances describe` command:

```
$ gcloud compute instances describe apache-server-staging --format json
```

Here's the output:

```
{
  "canIpForward": false,
  "creationTimestamp": "2014-08-15T11:01:14.762-07:00",
  "disks": [
    {
      "autoDelete": true,
      "boot": true,
      "deviceName": "persistent-disk-0",
      "index": 0,
      "kind": "compute#attachedDisk",
      "mode": "READ_WRITE",
      "source": "https://www.googleapis.com/compute/v1/projects/gce-oreilly/zones/us-
central1-a/disks/apache-server-staging",
      "type": "PERSISTENT"
    }
  ],
  "id": "1667502912688517705",
  "kind": "compute#instance",
  "machineType": "https://www.googleapis.com/compute/v1/projects/gce-oreilly/zones/us-
central1-a/machineTypes/n1-standard-1",
  "metadata": {
    "fingerprint": "WdSqV7Z0YQE=",
```

```
      "items": [
        {
          "key": "cloud-storage-bucket",
          "value": "gce-oreilly-staging"
        },
        {
          "key": "startup-script",
          "value": "#!/bin/bash\nBUCKET=$(curl
http://metadata/computeMetadata/v1/instance/attributes/cloud-storage-bucket -H
\"Metadata-Flavor: Google\")\ncd /var/www\ngsutil cp gs://$BUCKET/* .\n"
        }
      ],
      "kind": "compute#metadata"
    },
    "name": "apache-server-staging",
    "networkInterfaces": [
      {
        "accessConfigs": [
          {
            "kind": "compute#accessConfig",
            "name": "external-nat",
            "natIP": "146.148.40.147",
            "type": "ONE_TO_ONE_NAT"
          }
        ],
        "name": "nic0",
        "network": "https://www.googleapis.com/compute/v1/projects/gce-
oreilly/global/networks/default",
        "networkIP": "10.240.19.9"
      }
    ],
    "scheduling": {
      "automaticRestart": true,
      "onHostMaintenance": "MIGRATE"
    },
    "selfLink": "https://www.googleapis.com/compute/v1/projects/gce-oreilly/zones/us-
central1-a/instances/apache-server-staging",
    "serviceAccounts": [
      {
        "email": "134224180845@developer.gserviceaccount.com",
        "scopes": [
          "https://www.googleapis.com/auth/devstorage.read_only"
        ]
      }
    ],
    "status": "RUNNING",
    "tags": {
      "fingerprint": "42WmSpB8rSM="
    },
    "zone": "https://www.googleapis.com/compute/v1/projects/gce-oreilly/zones/us-
central1-a"
}
```

Notice how the metadata property contains a key called `cloud-storage-bucket` with a value equal to your Cloud Storage staging bucket name (in **bold**).

To start a production instance, use the same command, but set the key `cloud-storage-bucket` equal to your production Cloud Storage bucket:

```
$ gcloud compute instances create apache-server-production \
--metadata-from-file startup-script=apache-startup-v2.sh \
--metadata cloud-storage-bucket=<bucket-name> \
--image apache-image \
--scopes=storage-ro
```

Updating instance-level, custom metadata

Custom metadata can be updated or added at any time, even while the instance is running. This can be handy if, for example, the name of the production or staging Cloud Storage bucket changes. To change instance-level custom metadata while the instance is still running, use the `gcloud compute instances add-metadata` command. The syntax of the command is as follows:

```
$ gcloud compute instances add-metadata <instance-name> \
--metadata <key>=<value>
```

API

Custom, instance-level metadata can also be retrieved, set, and updated via the API.

Retrieve.   To retrieve instance-level metadata, issue an HTTP GET request to the instance resource URL (substitute <project> with the name of your project, <zone> with the instance's zone, and <instance> with the name of your instance):

```
GET https://www.googleapis.com/compute/v1/projects/<project>/zones/<zone>
/instances/<instance>
```

The response is an instance resource, which consists of a dictionary representing the instance with the following structure:

```
{
  "kind": "compute#instance",
  "id": unsigned long,
  "creationTimestamp": string,
  "zone": string,
  "status": string,
  "statusMessage": string,
  "name": string,
  "description": string,
  "tags": {
    "items": [
      string
    ],
    "fingerprint": bytes
```

```
    },
    "machineType": string,
    "canIpForward": boolean,
    "networkInterfaces": [
      {
        "network": string,
        "networkIP": string,
        "name": string,
        "accessConfigs": [
          {
            "kind": "compute#accessConfig",
            "type": string,
            "name": string,
            "natIP": string
          }
        ]
      }
    ],
    "disks": [
      {
        "kind": "compute#attachedDisk",
        "index": integer,
        "type": string,
        "mode": string,
        "source": string,
        "deviceName": string,
        "boot": boolean,
        "initializeParams": {
          "diskName": string,
          "sourceImage": string,
          "diskSizeGb": long,
          "diskType": string
        },
        "autoDelete": boolean,
        "licenses": [
          string
        ]
      }
    ],
    "metadata": {
      "kind": "compute#metadata",
      "fingerprint": bytes,
      "items": [
        {
          "key": string,
          "value": string
        }
      ]
    },
    "serviceAccounts": [
      {
        "email": string,
```

```
      "scopes": [
        string
      ]
    }
  ],
  "selfLink": string,
  "scheduling": {
    "onHostMaintenance": string,
    "automaticRestart": boolean
  }
}
```

The instance-level metadata (in **bold**) can be found as the value of the `metadata` key. The value contains a list of dictionary items representing metadata key/value pairs. Notice that the `metadata` key also has a fingerprint. The fingerprint is the hash of the metadata and must be provided when updating metadata via the API.

Let's take a look at a code sample. As usual, you can either start with the complete sample in the gce-oreilly GitHub repository (*https://github.com/GoogleCloudPlatform/gce-oreilly/blob/master/ch7-5.py*); or, if you prefer to do some typing, copy the *ch1-1.py* file and rename it to *ch7-5.py*. Using your favorite text editor, open the *ch7-5.py* source file and comment out this line (by prepending the line with the Python comment character #):

```
# print 'Success! Now add code here.'
```

Insert the following code directly below the commented-out `print` statement (making sure to preserve indentation consistently with the containing file):

```
# Set project, zone, and other constants
PROJECT_ID = 'your-project-id'
ZONE = 'us-central1-a'
INSTANCE_NAME = 'apache-server-staging'

# Retrieve project-level metadata.
request = service.instances().get(
    project=PROJECT_ID, zone=ZONE, instance=INSTANCE_NAME)
try:
  response = request.execute()
except Exception, ex:
  print 'ERROR: ' + str(ex)
  sys.exit()

print response['metadata']
```

Before running the code, replace **your-project-id** with your own project ID. Run the code using the command:

```
$ python ch7-5.py
```

The metadata dictionary will be displayed as output.

Set. Custom, instance-level metadata can be set when the instance is first created. We've already seen this in action when we used a startup script. The metadata key was added to the instance dictionary. Take a look at the code again (you should be able to find it in *ch7-1.py*), and see if you can update the code to set the metadata key cloud-storage-bucket equal to the Cloud Storage bucket name. The complete sample is in the gce-oreilly GitHub repository (*https://github.com/GoogleCloudPlatform/gce-oreilly/blob/master/ch7-6.py*).

Update. Updating metadata on an existing instance is similar to setting project-level custom metadata. To update instance-level metadata, we must first retrieve the value of the metadata fingerprint, then send an HTTP POST request to the instance setMetadata endpoint (substitute <project> with the name of your project, <zone> with the instance's zone, and <instance> with the name of your instance):

```
POST https://www.googleapis.com/compute/v1/projects/
<project>/zones/<zone>/instances/<instance>/
setMetadata
```

The body of the request consists of an object similar to the value of the metadata key in the instance resource:

```
{
  'fingerprint': 'fingerprint',
  'items': [{
    'key': 'your-metadata-key',
    'value': 'your-metadata-value'
  }]
}
```

Here's the code to update our instance-level cloud-storage-bucket key. You should be familiar with the process now: either start with the complete sample in the gce-oreilly GitHub repository (*https://github.com/GoogleCloudPlatform/gce-oreilly/blob/master/ch7-7.py*), or copy the *ch1-1.py* file, and rename it to *ch7-7.py*. Using your favorite text editor, open the *ch7-7.py* source file and comment out this line (by prepending the line with the Python comment character #):

```
# print 'Success! Now add code here.'
```

Insert the following code directly below the commented-out print statement (making sure to preserve indentation consistently with the containing file):

```
PROJECT_ID = 'your-project-id'
ZONE = 'us-central1-a'
INSTANCE_NAME = 'instance-metadata-api'
METADATA = {
  'key': 'cloud-storage-bucket',
  'value': 'bucket'
}

# First retrieve the current metadata fingerprint.
```

```python
request = service.instances().get(
    project=PROJECT_ID, zone=ZONE, instance=INSTANCE_NAME)
try:
  response = request.execute()
except Exception, ex:
  print 'ERROR: ' + str(ex)
  sys.exit()

# Create the body of the request using the response.
BODY = response['metadata']
for item in BODY['items']:
  if item['key'] == METADATA['key']:
    item['value'] = METADATA['value']
    break
else:
  BODY['items'].append(METADATA)

# Build and execute set common instance data request.
request = service.instances().setMetadata(
    project=PROJECT_ID, zone=ZONE, instance=INSTANCE_NAME, body=BODY)
try:
  response = request.execute()
except Exception, ex:
  print 'ERROR: ' + str(ex)
  sys.exit()

# Metadata setting is asynchronous so now wait for response.
op_name = response['name']
operations = service.zoneOperations()
while True:
  request = operations.get(project=PROJECT_ID, zone=ZONE, operation=op_name)
  try:
    response = request.execute()
  except Exception, ex:
    print 'ERROR: ' + str(ex)
    sys.exit()
  if 'error' in response:
    print 'ERROR: ' + str(response['error'])
    sys.exit()
  status = response['status']
  if status == 'DONE':
    print 'Instance-level metadata updated.'
    break
  else:
    print 'Waiting for operation to complete. Status: ' + status
```

Before running the code, replace **your-project-id** with your own project ID and **bucket** with the name of your bucket. Run the code using the command:

```
$ python ch7-7.py
```

wait_for_change URL parameter

Not only can you update custom metadata on your exiting instances, but you can also issue a hanging GET request to the metadata server that doesn't return until the specified metadata key value has changed. Using our Apache server as an example, you can write a script that redownloads the contents of the Cloud Storage bucket if the value of the `cloud-storage-bucket` metadata key changes. To send an HTTP request that waits until the value of the requested metadata entry has changed, add the `wait_for_change` parameter to the metadata entry URL, and set the parameter equal to `true`.

The best way to see this in action is to open two Terminal windows, one of which is logged into your `apache-server-staging` instance. In the window logged into the instance, use curl to issue an HTTP request to retrieve the `cloud-storage-bucket` value, but this time add the `wait_for_change` parameter to the end of the URL:

```
apache-server-staging$ curl http://metadata/computeMetadata/v1/instance/\
attributes/cloud-storage-bucket?wait_for_change=true \
-H "Metadata-Flavor: Google"
```

The command should not return, because the HTTP request is waiting for a change to occur to `cloud-storage-bucket`. Now, in the other window, use the `gcloud com pute instances add-metadata` command to set a new `cloud-storage-bucket` value:

```
$ gcloud compute instances add-metadata apache-server-staging \
--metadata cloud-storage-bucket=<new-bucket-name>
```

Once the value of `cloud-storage-bucket` has been updated, you should see the result display in the other window.

Summary

In this chapter, you learned how to use custom images and startup scripts to customize your Compute Engine instances. You also learned how to use the metadata server to retrieve information about your project and instances and also set custom metadata values at both the project and instance level.

Up Next

In the preceding chapters, we've covered everything from the basics of getting started to the more advanced topics of networking and instance customization. Now it's time to put all the pieces together and build a complete, fully functional application.

## CHAPTER 8

A Complete Application

In this chapter, we'll integrate most of what we've learned so far about Google Compute Engine into a complete cloud application, which we'll deploy and test. In so doing, we'll review and extend concepts from earlier chapters and explore a few new concepts, including the use of containers using Docker and automated deployment using a simple shell script.

Application Concept

When evaluating cloud-computing services (or physical-computing resources, for that matter), it's often important to understand the relevant performance characteristics. In this chapter, we'll create an application to run distributed tests that tell us something useful about the performance of a compute cluster.

In addition to helping us evaluate performance, this application illustrates several of the concepts presented earlier, such as virtual-machine creation, persistent disks, network configuration, images, and metadata. We'll also learn about some powerful open source tools and we'll see how easy it is to use open source software with Google Compute Engine.

Requirements

Before jumping into our application design, let's take a moment to reflect on the problem we're trying to solve. Here's a list of requirements for the app we'll build in this chapter:

Distributed

The app should support distributed performance tests (i.e., it should be able to run tests in parallel on an arbitrary number of servers).

Scalable

The app should enable efficient testing of reasonably large compute clusters, on the order of 1,000 virtual machines.

Elastic

The app should dynamically and seamlessly accommodate new virtual machines (i.e., new test subjects), even while a test is in progress. The end user should be able to add one or more new virtual machines to the cluster (with some specific set of characteristics to indicate inclusion), without requiring explicit central administration.

Life-cycle tooling independence

The app should not require the use of any particular tool for creating or destroying virtual machines in the cluster. Any tool that supports virtual machine life-cycle operations, from service providers like Rightscale and Scalr, to open source projects, like Chef, Puppet, Vagrant, Ansible, and Salt, should interoperate with this app without requiring source-code modifications.

Computing-platform independence

The app should be usable with any cluster of virtual (or physical) machines, including Google Compute Engine or any other cloud-computing service provider's virtual machines.

Stateless

The app should gracefully tolerate test requests from web clients that may come and go freely without warning and with no explicit session termination.

Let's also give our app a name. The word *perfuse* means to permeate or suffuse. Because this app is designed to distribute performance test requests throughout a network of servers, we'll call our application "perfuse." It's also convenient that this name starts with "perf," which is a good fit for an application focused on performance testing.

Figure 8-1 shows us what our app will look like when we've finished step 7.

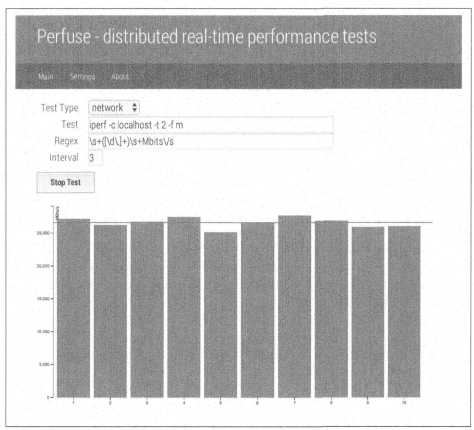

Figure 8-1. Perfuse in action

Open Source Software Used in This Chapter

Because Google Compute Engine provides an open framework for deploying any software we like, we're going to make extensive use of open source software in our application. This will serve two purposes: it gives us access to a rich ecosystem of existing components, and it illustrates how easy it is to use open source software on Google Compute Engine. In this section, we provide a summary of the open source tools and projects we'll use in building our application:

- Node.js is a popular, high performance, scalable, server-side implementation of Chrome's V8 JavaScript engine. In this chapter, we'll build our server components (including our web server) using Node.js as our development platform and JavaScript as our primary implementation language.

- Docker is a containerization system for encapsulating an application and its dependencies into a system and language-independent package. Docker containers are much more lightweight than virtual machines, provide modularity (develop and test locally, deploy anywhere), portability (no lock-in to a particular hardware platform or service provider), and consistency (the code you test is the code you push to production).

- ZeroMQ is an open source communication library, designed for efficiency and simplicity. It abstracts the underlying communication mechanism (typically sockets) and makes it easy to write applications using point-to-point message passing, broadcast messaging, publish/subscribe and other common messaging patterns. In this chapter, we'll use ZeroMQ to distribute requests from a master to multiple slaves and to send results from the slaves back to the master.

- Web Starter Kit[1] is a collection of HTML, CSS, JavaScript, and supporting tools that make it easy to start a new website with a great multidevice user experience, following the Web Fundamentals[2] guidelines. We'll use the Web Starter Kit to quickly build a nice looking user interface for our application that looks and works great on desktops, mobile phones, tablets and other devices.

- AngularJS is a popular framework for extending HTML and building dynamic websites with two-way data binding. We'll use AngularJS for managing the form data in our application.

- WebSocket is a protocol for sending asynchronous, full-duplex messages between a web client (i.e., a browser) and a web server, without requiring a new connection for each request. We'll use WebSocket in this application to send performance test requests from the browser to the compute cluster and for receiving test results in real time, as they become available.

- D3.js is a powerful and flexible data-driven JavaScript visualization library. We'll use D3 to graphically display our performance test results.

Application Information Flow

Figure 8-2 illustrates the flow of information through the perfuse application.

---

1 *https://developers.google.com/web/starter-kit/*
2 *https://developers.google.com/web/fundamentals/*

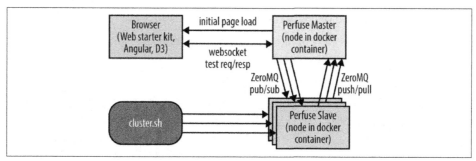

Figure 8-2. Perfuse information flow

The browser sends performance tests to the perfuse master, which distributes those requests to a collection of slave servers. Each slave server runs the requested performance test independently and transmits the results back to the master, which relays the results back to the browser as they arrive from the slaves. The browser displays those results graphically, in real time, as they arrive from the master.

Building Our App Step by Step

In this section, we'll build, test, and deploy an application in the cloud. We'll create a special development virtual machine and do our coding and deployment from there.

Step 0: Create Your Development VM and Clone the Sample App

Using the `gcloud compute instances create` command, create a new virtual machine with the following syntax:

```
$ gcloud compute instances create perfuse-dev \
    --image-project google-containers           \
    --image container-vm-v20140826              \
    --zone your-preferred-zone                  \
    --machine-type n1-standard-1                \
    --scopes compute-rw
```

We're using a special container-optimized image,[3] which comes with Docker baked right in, so there's no additional installation step required. We're also specifying the following instance attributes:

- Name: `perfuse-dev`
- Image project: `google-containers`

---

3 See *https://developers.google.com/compute/docs/containers/container_vms* for more information about Compute Engine's container-optimized images.

- Image: latest version of `container-vm-*`

- Zone: choose any zone you like (use the `gcloud compute zones list` command to see the list of available zones)

- Machine type: `n1-standard-1`

- Scopes: `compute-rw` (provides preauthenticated access to the Compute Engine API on the new VM)

Wait for that request to complete successfully, then use the `gcloud compute ssh` command to log in to your new development machine:

```
$ gcloud compute ssh perfuse-dev --zone your-preferred-zone
[..]
perfuse-dev$
```

You now have a home development environment, which you'll use to do all the work for this chapter's exercise.

The source code for this application is stored in GitHub and organized into seven steps. Let's clone the repo locally so that you have all the code you'll need on your new development server. Do that by issuing the following `git clone` command:

```
perfuse-dev$ git clone https://github.com/GoogleCloudPlatform/gce-oreilly.git
Cloning into 'gce-oreilly'...
remote: Counting objects: 60, done.
remote: Total 60 (delta 0), reused 0 (delta 0)
Unpacking objects: 100% (60/60), done.
```

You now have a local copy of the book repo, under the *gce-oreilly* directory tree. For the remainder of this tutorial, we'll use this local repo to build, test, and deploy the perfuse application, step by step.

Step 1: Create a Docker image for your app

Docker gives us the ability to programmatically create an environment in which to run our application. We call the result a Docker image (not to be confused with a Compute Engine image). A Docker image is a stored representation of a container and its current state. In this step, we'll create a Docker image, which we'll use to encapsulate our application and all of its dependencies. This Docker image will form the basic building block for deploying our application on Compute Engine. Because Docker can be used on nearly any virtual or real server, this gives us a way to deploy our application anywhere we like and to move our application from one service to another.

Change to the directory containing all the steps of this exercise by executing the command `cd gce-oreilly/ch8`. You should see several files and directories there:

1, 2, ..., 7

These directories contain files that are specific to a particular step. The current directory (the one we just changed to) contains files that are shared across all steps.

Dockerfile

This file is a blueprint for constructing your image. It tells Docker about your operating environment, instructions on how to install your dependencies, and tells Docker how to run your application:

```
# We use debian as our base distro for this container.
FROM debian:latest
# Refresh apt-get.
RUN apt-get update
# Install some utilities needed by node, npm, and ZeroMQ.
RUN apt-get install -y curl make g++
# Install Node.js and npm.
RUN curl -sL https://deb.nodesource.com/setup | bash -
RUN apt-get install -y npm
# Install ZeroMQ libs.
RUN apt-get install -y libzmq-dev
# Install some perf test tools.
RUN apt-get install -y fio iperf
# Install required npm packages.
ADD package.json /package.json
RUN npm install
# Set /src as the working directory for this container.
WORKDIR /src
# Open up external access to port 80.
EXPOSE  80
# Run startup command.
CMD ["node", "/src/scripts/server.js"]
```

This file arranges for the creation of a Docker image including support for Node.js and npm (the Node.js package manager) and some other packages we'll need later in this chapter.

package.json

This file contains a JSON document which describes your application to Node.js. This includes things like the name of your app, the version string, and any required Node.js packages:

```
{
  "name": "perfuse",
  "private": true,
  "version": "1.0.0",
  "description": "Distributed dynamic performance test tool",
  "author": "Marc Cohen <marcccohen@google.com>",
  "dependencies": {
    "express": "3.2.4",
    "zmq": "2.7.0",
    "ws": "0.4.31"
```

```
        }
    }
```

wsk

> This directory containers assets generated by the Web Starter Kit, including images, fonts, CSS files, and other goodies. These assets are shared by all the steps in this chapter.

1/scripts/server.js

> This step-1-specific file (hence located under the 1 directory tree) is a Node.js application that uses express.js to generate a simple web page. This app displays the contents of the index.html file to anyone who navigates their browser to your container's IP address and port 80:

```
var express = require('express');
// Constants
var PORT = 80;
// App
var app = express();
app.get('/', function (req, res) {
    res.sendfile('/src/index.html');
});
app.listen(PORT);
console.log('Running on port ' + PORT);
```

1/index.html

> This file (also step 1 specific) provides the HTML content to be displayed by your node.js app. The step 1 version of this file contains only the static string "Hello World!"

Let's now build a Docker image by running the following command:

```
perfuse-dev$ sudo docker build -t perfuse/test . # Don't miss the dot!
[..]
```

Let's verify our new image exists by running the following command:

```
perfuse-dev$ sudo docker images
REPOSITORY     TAG      IMAGE ID        CREATED        VIRTUAL SIZE
perfuse/test   latest   aee4af3c0502    5 seconds ago  272.3 MB
[..]
```

Here we see an image named *perfuse/test*, which is the image you just created.

Now let's test your image by running the step 1 app inside a Docker container with the following command:

```
perfuse-dev$ sudo docker run -p 80:80 -v $PWD/1:/src -d perfuse/test
ed4721f0e90632628debf1f3e4ade4d5576718b10a1b19c69fde65173487f37f
```

The -p 80:80 option tells Docker to map external port 80 (on the host VM) into the same port number inside the running container. This makes life easy because the

---

server code we write and the external port number we connect to in order to test our application will be the same (80), but we could just as easily use the -p option to map any arbitrary external port on the host to any desired internal port inside the container.

The -v option tells Docker to create a volume, which is a container directory that is accessible outside the container. The characters after the -v option ($PWD/1:/src) tell Docker to map the step 1 directory on the host to the */src* path in the container. This makes the current directory accessible to code running inside the container. This is a shared, read-write volume, so any changes made to the contents of this directory from either the host or the container will be immediately visible in both environments.

The -d option tells Docker to run the container in "detached mode," independent of the I/O streams from the terminal that started the container. You can think of -d as being loosely analogous to use of the "&" symbol to run a Unix/Linux shell command in the background. If we don't use -d, our container will run in the foreground in our terminal window and wait for input.

Let's run the sudo docker ps command to verify that we now have a running container:

```
perfuse-dev$ sudo docker ps
CONTAINER ID  IMAGE     COMMAND    CREATED STATUS  PORTS
bdf05a55ef9b  per[..]  "node[..]/s 4sec[..] Up 3[..] 0.0.0[..]
[..]
```

There we see our running container along with some of its attributes, like its container ID, when it was created, the image name, the run command, and the configured port mapping. Everything looks good, so we're nearly ready to test the application by pointing our web browser to the Node.js application running inside our container.

But first, we have one more thing to configure. Remember, we've been working on a Compute Engine VM, so we need to open up external access to the desired port (80) on our virtual machine. We already did this in Chapter 6 by creating a firewall rule, so you should have already configured your project to allow HTTP access. If you need to recreate that firewall rule, you can do so by running this command:

```
perfuse-dev$ gcloud compute firewall-rules create http --allow tcp:80
[..]
http default 0.0.0.0/0  tcp:80
```

Now we're ready to test our application, which should now be running inside the Docker container you started earlier. First we need to find the external IP address associated with your VM, which you can obtain by executing the gcloud compute instances list command (look for the external address associated with the perfuse-dev virtual machine):

```
perfuse-dev$ gcloud compute instances list
NAME        ZONE         MACHINE_TYPE INTERNAL_IP   EXTERNAL_IP    STATUS
perfuse-dev europe-west1-a n1-standard-1 10.240.104.25 23.251.NNN.NNN RUNNING
[..]
```

Now, simply point your browser to the discovered IP address and you should see a screen that looks like Figure 8-3.

Figure 8-3. Hello World user interface

Just to assure ourselves that we're actually communicating with the container running on our virtual machine (and not some random resource on the web that happens to display "Hello World"), let's change the message we display and verify that refreshing our browser page displays the changed message.

Using your favorite text editor, modify the message contained in *index.html* (e.g., you could change it to display "Hello from Docker!"):

```
# Modify 1/index.html to display 'Hello from Docker!\n'
perfuse-dev$ vi 1/index.html  # Use your favorite text editor here
[..]
```

Now reload the browser page you previously used to verify this step and you should see the modified message you just inserted into the *1/index.html* file.

Before moving on to the next step, make sure to stop the running container by using sudo docker ps to find the desired container ID, and then sudo docker stop short-id to stop the running container (where short-id is the first four characters of the container ID).

Step 2: Build the UI framework

For this step, we've generated several boilerplate files and stored them in a shared directory tree (*gce-oreilly/ch8/wsk*). These files will suffice for all of the steps in this chapter, but you can generate similar boilerplate files for your own sites by visiting the Web Starter Kit at *https://developers.google.com/web/starter-kit/*. The Web Starter Kit files give our simple Hello World app several advantages:

- A more compelling, more professional look and feel
- A mobile-first, multidevice, responsive framework
- Optimized for performance right from the start

In order to take advantage of these capabilities, we need a modified *index.html* file, which you can find in the *gce-oreilly/ch8/2* directory. This file was generated for us automatically by the Web Starter Kit. Our new *index.html* file requests some CSS, JavaScript, and image files, so have a modified Node app in *2/scripts/server.js* to serve those files along with the root path we served in the previous step.

We could do that by adding an additional `app.get` call using a regular expression to match the new resource types we want to serve. But instead of repeating the app.get call and its associated logic, let's refactor that code into a common function, which we'll call `route`:

```
function route(app, regex, prefix) {
    app.get(regex, function (req, res) {
        var type = req.params[0];
        var path = req.params[1];
        var file = prefix + type + '/' + path
        res.sendfile(file);
    });
}
```

The first argument to `app.get()` is a regular expression, which is a special kind of string that matches many possible comparison strings and captures certain matching substrings. With this function, we can replace this block of code:

```
app.get(/^\/(styles)\/(.*)/, function (req, res) {
    res.sendfile('/wsk/');
});
```

with a single call to our `route` function:

```
route(app, /^\/(styles)\/(.*)/, '/wsk/');
```

The first argument is a reference to an express.js `app` object, and the second argument is a regular expression that matches the desired URLs. This regular expression says we're looking for a slash followed by the string `styles`, followed by another slash and any remaining text. The parentheses enable us to capture two matching substrings. The third argument specifies a prefix to the filesystem path containing the desired content.

The resulting step 2 version of our *server.js* file is shown here:

```
function route(app, regex, prefix) {
    app.get(regex, function (req, res) {
        var type = req.params[0];
        var path = req.params[1];
```

```
            var file = prefix + type + '/' + path
            res.sendfile(file);
        });
    }
    var express = require('express');
    // Constants
    var PORT = 80;
    // App
    var app = express();
    app.get('/', function (req, res) {
        res.sendfile('/src/index.html');
    });
    route(app, /^\/(scripts)\/(.*)/, '/src/');
    route(app, /^\/(styles|styleguide|images|fonts)\/(.*)/, '/wsk/');
    app.listen(PORT);
    console.log('Running on port ' + PORT);
```

With these changes, we've enabled our application to serve the Web Starter Kit CSS, JavaScript, font, and image files, along with an *index.html* file that integrates those resources into a simple page. Let's now rerun our Docker image, but we'll change the directory mapped to */src* from $PWD/1 to $PWD/2, and we'll add a second volume to share the Web Starter Kit files at */wsk* in the container:

```
# Run container with shared /src and /wsk volumes.
perfuse-dev$ sudo docker run -p 80:80 -v $PWD/2:/src \
            -v $PWD/wsk:/wsk -d perfuse/test
[..]
```

Now, simply point your browser to the discovered IP address and you should see a screen that looks like Figure 8-4.

Figure 8-4. Web Starter Kit user interface

Before moving on to the next step, make sure to stop the running container by using `sudo docker ps` to find the desired container ID, and then `sudo docker stop short-id` to stop the running container (where `short-id` indicates the first four characters of the desired container ID).

Step 3: Build the user interface

In this step, most of the supporting files (Dockerfile, *server.js*, Web Starter Kit resource files) remain the same, but we've substantially modified the main *index.html* file to provide a skeletal UI for our perfuse application. Let's take a look at that file section by section.

We start with some boilerplate:

```
<!doctype html>
<html ng-app>
  <head>
    <meta charset="utf-8">
    <meta http-equiv="X-UA-Compatible" content="IE=edge">
    <meta name="description" content="A front-end template that helps you build
fast, modern mobile web apps.">
    <meta name="viewport" content="width=device-width, initial-scale=1">
```

```
<title>Perfuse</title>
<!-- Add to homescreen for Chrome on Android -->
<meta name="mobile-web-app-capable" content="yes">
<link rel="icon" sizes="196x196" href="images/touch/chrome-touch-icon-
196x196.png">
<!-- Add to homescreen for Safari on iOS -->
<meta name="apple-mobile-web-app-capable" content="yes">
<meta name="apple-mobile-web-app-status-bar-style" content="black">
<meta name="apple-mobile-web-app-title" content="Web Starter Kit">
<!-- Tile icon for Win8 (144x144 + tile color) -->
<meta name="msapplication-TileImage" content="images/touch/ms-touch-icon-
144x144-precomposed.png">
<meta name="msapplication-TileColor" content="#3372DF">
<!-- SEO: If your mobile URL is different from the desktop URL, add a
canonical link to the desktop page
https://developers.google.com/webmasters/smartphone-sites/feature-phones -->
<!--
<link rel="canonical" href="http://www.example.com/">
-->
```

Nearly all of this text was automatically generated by the Web Starter Kit, with the exception of our app's title, which we've customized and marked in boldface type.

Next, we have some markup to include the Web Starter Kit CSS files:

```
<!-- build:css styles/components/main.min.css -->
<link rel="stylesheet" href="styles/h5bp.css">
<link rel="stylesheet" href="styles/components/components.css">
<link rel="stylesheet" href="styles/main.css">
<link rel="stylesheet" href="styles/perfuse.css">
<!-- endbuild -->
</head>
```

Again, we're using boilerplate markup, except for the line shown in bold, which includes our application-specific CSS file (*perfuse.css*).

Now we've completed the head of our HTML document and we move on to the body. The body starts with some headings and a list of elements that allow us to display navigation links at the top of our page. These links will initially be nonfunctional; we'll populate them later:

```
<body>
  <header class="app-bar promote-layer">
    <div class="app-bar-container">
      <button class="menu"><img src="images/hamburger.svg" alt="Menu">
      </button>
      <h1 class="logo">Perfuse - distributed real-time performance tests</h1>
      <section class="app-bar-actions">
      <!-- Put App Bar Buttons Here -->
      </section>
    </div>
  </header>
  <nav class="navdrawer-container promote-layer">
```

```
    <h4>Navigation</h4>
    <ul>
      <li><a href="#main">Main</a></li>
      <li><a href="#about">About</a></li>
    </ul>
  </nav>
```

Again, the one deviation from the markup generated by Web Starter Kit is shown in bold. Here we've customized a level-one heading to be displayed on our main page.

Next we define a form for requesting different types of performance tests. The elements here are using AngularJS to populate and manage the data selected on this form. By specifying the ng-model attribute, we're defining a two-way data binding relationship between form elements here and some JavaScript code we'll see later:

```
<main>
  <div id="main">
    <br />
    <div class="form" ng-controller="MyCntrl">
      <div align="left">
        <label>Test Type</label>
        <select ng-model="test" ng-options="c.name for c in tests">
        </select>
      </div>
      <div align="left">
        <label>Test</label>
        <input class="form" type="text" size="55" ng-model="test.cmd"
          placeholder="Enter perf test command">
      </div>
      <div align="left">
        <label>Regex</label>
        <input class="form" type="text" size="55" ng-model="test.regexp"
          placeholder="Enter regular express for parsing test output">
      </div>
      <div align="left">
        <label>Interval</label>
        <input class="form" type="text" ng-model="test.interval" size="2"
          placeholder="Enter refresh interval">
      </div>
      <div align="left">
        <button class="button" id="start-test-button"
          ng-click="start_test()">Start Test</button>
      </div>
    </div>
  </div>
```

Next, we define a div that is initially empty but will eventually contain the graphical performance test results once the user starts a test. We give this element a special name (perf-graph), which will have meaning in the JavaScript code we'll add later to display the results. We also add some descriptive text about our app for the About button:.

```
        <div id="perf-graph" style="display: none"></div>
        <div id="about">
    Perfuse is an example application from Chapter 8 of "Google Compute Engine"
    from O'Reilly Media, by Marc Cohen, Kathryn Hurley, and Paul Newson.
    Perfuse distributes performance test requests to a cluster of servers
    and summarizes the results graphically and dynamically, as they stream in
    from the test machines.
        <div>
    </main>
```

Finally, we terminate the body of our HTML document by including all the required JavaScript files and we add the terminating body and html tags:

```
    <!-- build:js scripts/main.min.js -->
    <script src="scripts/main.js"></script>
    <!-- endbuild -->
    <!-- Google Analytics: change UA-XXXXX-X to be your site's ID -->
    <script>
(function(i,s,o,g,r,a,m){i['GoogleAnalyticsObject']=r;i[r]=i[r]||function(){
    (i[r].q=i[r].q||[]).push(arguments)},i[r].l=1*new
Date();a=s.createElement(o),
m=s.getElementsByTagName(o)[0];a.async=1;a.src=g;m.parentNode.insertBefore(a,m)
    })(window,document,'script','//www.google-
analytics.com/analytics.js','ga');
    ga('create', 'UA-XXXXX-X');
    ga('send', 'pageview');
    </script>
    <script src="http://code.angularjs.org/1.2.0/angular.min.js"></script>
    <script type="text/javascript" src="scripts/client.js"></script>
    <script>
      var perfuse = new Perfuse();
    </script>
    <!-- Built with love using Web Starter Kit -->
  </body>
</html>
```

In addition to the modified *index.html*, we've added the new file *3/scripts/client.js*. This file contains JavaScript code for our client-side (i.e., browser) logic. The primary function of this code is to provide the runtime logic to bind a JavaScript data structure with the form fields we created in our *index.html* file. We use AngularJS to do this, which prescribes the creation of a controller function we've defined here:

```
function MyCntrl($scope) {
    $scope.tests = [
        {
            name:'random',
            cmd:'random',
            interval: '3',
            regexp: '',
            label: '',
        },
        {
```

```
            name:'randread',
            cmd:'fio --name=foo --rw=randread --size=10m --blocksize=4k -
    -iodepth=64 --direct=1',
            interval: '4',
            regexp: '  read :.* iops=(.*) ,',
            label: 'IOPs',
        },
        {
            name:'randwrite',
            cmd:'fio --name=foo --rw=randwrite --size=10m --blocksize=4k
    --iodepth=64 --direct=1',
            interval: '3',
            regexp: 'write:.* iops=(.*) ,',
            label: 'IOPs',
        },
        {
            name:'seqread',
            cmd:'fio --name=foo --rw=read --size=300m --blocksize=1m --
    iodepth=16 --direct=1',
            interval: '9',
            regexp: ' READ:.* aggrb=(.*)KB\/s, minb=',
            label: 'KB/s',
        },
        {
            name:'network',
            cmd:'iperf -c localhost -t 2 -f m',
            interval: '3',
            regexp: '\\s+([\\d\\.]+)\\s+Mbits\\/s',
            label: 'MBits/s',
        },
    ];
    $scope.test = $scope.tests[0];
    $scope.start_test = function () {
        var name = $scope.test.name;
        var cmd = $scope.test.cmd;
        var interval = $scope.test.interval;
        var regexp = $scope.test.regexp;
        var label = $scope.test.label;
        Perfuse.perfToggle(name, cmd, interval, regexp, label);
    };
}
/**
 * Perfuse class.
 * @constructor
 */
var Perfuse = function() { };
```

With these changes, we've created an initial user-interface structure for our application. Let's now rerun our Docker container, but this time we'll connect the */src* volume to our step 3 files, like this:

```
# Run container with shared /src and /wsk volumes.
perfuse-dev$ sudo docker run -p 80:80 -v $PWD/3:/src \
             -v $PWD/wsk:/wsk -d perfuse/test
[..]
```

Now, simply point your browser to the discovered IP address and you should see a screen that looks like Figure 8-5.

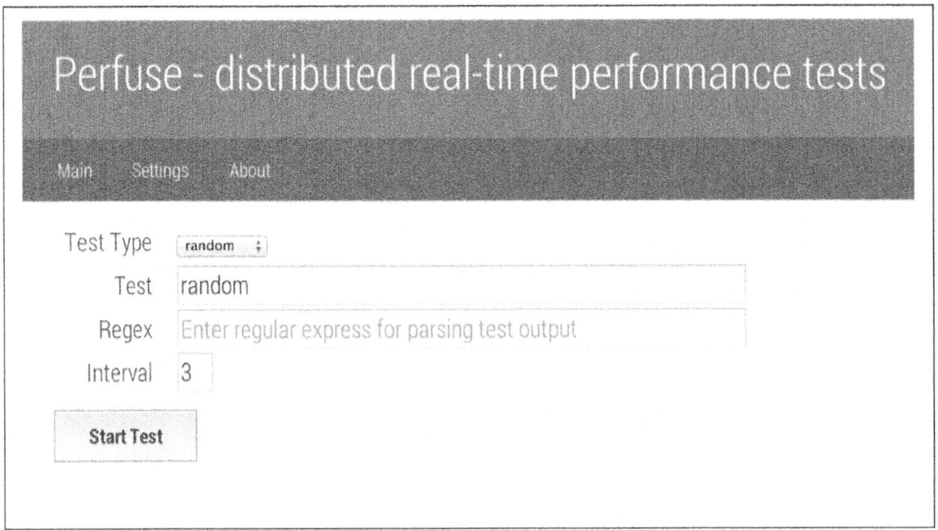

Figure 8-5. Perfuse user interface

Before moving on to the next step, make sure to stop the running container by using sudo docker ps to find the desired container ID, and then sudo docker stop short-id to stop the running container (where short-id indicates the first four characters of the desired container ID).

Step 4: Implement the master

Our *server.js* script will eventually have two personalities, one for the perfuse master, which distributes performance-test requests to one or more slaves, and one for the slave, which executes the requested tests and returns the corresponding results to the master. The version of *server.js* in this step (*gce-oreilly/ch8/4/scripts/server.js*) is limited to the logic required to implement the master. In the next step, we'll add the slave logic to this file.

Let's examine the step 4 version of *server.js*, one logical block at a time.

We'll skip over the definition of our route function, which we've already discussed.

We start by defining some constants and application-specific variables, encapsulated in an object for modularity:

```
var PERFUSE = (function() {
    // Initialize some private variables.
    var os = require('os');
    var express = require('express');

    // Return object encapsulating public variables.
    return {
        // Initialize some public constants.
        MASTER: 'perfuse-master', // Master's hostname
        WEB_PORT: '80',           // Port num to use for web content
        WS_PORT: '8080',          // Port num to use for websockets
        REQ_PORT: '3000',         // Port num to use for pub requests
        RES_PORT: '3001',         // Port num to use for pull responses

        // Initialize some public variables.
        app: express(),
        zmq: require('zmq'),
        hostname: os.hostname(),
        web_sock_server: require('ws').Server,
        web_sock: null
        }
}());
```

Then we add conditional logic to support the master. This block of code looks quite similar to our previous *server.js* file:

```
if (PERFUSE.hostname == PERFUSE.MASTER) {
    console.log('Master running');

    // Serve main page.
    PERFUSE.app.get('/', function(req, res){
        res.sendfile('/src/index.html');
    });

    // Serve js, css, and image files.
    route(PERFUSE.app, /^\/(scripts)\/(.*)/, '/src/');
    route(PERFUSE.app, /^\/(styles|styleguide|images|fonts)\/(.*)/, '/wsk/');

    // Start web server listening.
    PERFUSE.app.listen(PERFUSE.WEB_PORT);
    console.log('Listening on port ' + PERFUSE.WEB_PORT);
```

Next, we open communication channels for sending requests to the slaves and receiving responses back from the slaves. We do this by defining a ZeroMQ "pub" socket for broadcasting incoming performance-test requests to all registered slaves and a ZeroMQ "pull" socket for receiving individual test results back from each slave:

```
    // Init ZeroMQ pub socket for fanning out requests, and
    // pull socket for receiving point-to-point responses.
    var sock_send = PERFUSE.zmq.socket('pub');
    sock_send.bindSync('tcp://*:' + PERFUSE.REQ_PORT);
    var sock_recv = PERFUSE.zmq.socket('pull');
    sock_recv.bindSync('tcp://*:' + PERFUSE.RES_PORT);
```

At this point, we add support for WebSockets. WebSockets are useful here because we want these performance tests to be run asynchronously—we'd like the browser to be able to send a stream of periodic tests to the server and have those tests started without having to wait for the results. We'd also like to be notified about the results as soon as they are available. WebSockets is ideal for this sort of asynchronous messaging pattern between a web browser and a service provider.

The following block of code instantiates a new WebSocketServer object (using our desired port), and defines some logic to handle incoming connections, received messages, and connection-close indications. The message-handler logic parses the received message, which is expected to be encoded in JSON and sends the test request over a broadcast (pub side of ZeroMQ pub/sub) socket, which fans the request out to all currently registered slaves:

```
// Open a server side websocket connection.
wss = new PERFUSE.web_sock_server({port: PERFUSE.WS_PORT});

// Define behavior for handling websocket connection requests.
wss.on('connection', function(ws) {
    console.log('new websocket connected');
    PERFUSE.web_sock = ws;
    // Define behavior for receiving websocket messages.
    ws.on('message', function(msg) {
        try {
            console.log('received from ws client: ' + msg);
            m = JSON.parse(msg);
            msg = JSON.stringify(m);
            try {
                // Perf test request received. Distribute too all slaves
                // via the ZeroMQ pub socket.
                sock_send.send(msg);
            } catch(e) {
                console.log("error " + e);
            }
        } catch(e) {
            console.log("error " + e);
        }
    });

    // Define behavior for handling closed websocket connection.
    ws.on('close', function(ws) {
        console.log('websocket disconnected');
        PERFUSE.web_sock = null;
    });
});
```

Finally, we define the logic for handling messages received by the pull socket we defined. These messages represent test responses from the slaves. For each message received on this socket, we parse the (JSON formatted) message, and we route the test results, as they arrive, to the client via the WebSocket connection:

```
    // Define behavior for handling test responses.
    sock_recv.on('message', function(msg) {
        try {
            var ev = JSON.parse(msg);
            if (ev.type == 'perf') {
                console.log('event received from slave: ' + msg);
                // We received a perf test response from a slave. If we
                // have a websockets connection, forward the result to
                // the client so that it can be presented to the user.
                if (PERFUSE.web_sock) {
                    try {
                        PERFUSE.web_sock.send(msg.toString());
                    } catch(e) {
                        console.log("error " + e);
                    }
                }
            } else {
                console.log('unknown event received from slave: ' + msg);
            }
        } catch(e) {
            console.log("error " + e);
        }
    });
```

Now that we've given our server the ability to receive performance tests via WebSockets, we'll add some client-side logic to request a performance test, and thereby exercise the logic we've just added to *server.js*. In order to do that, we've added some code to our client JavaScript source file, *client.js*. Let's examine those changes in logical blocks.

First, we define some constants and application-specific variables:

```
var Perfuse = function() {
    this.wsPort = '8080';
    this.ipAddr = location.host.split(':')[0];
    this.perfState = false;
    this.webSock = null;
    this.repeatingTests = null;
    this.reqCount = 0;
    this.data = [];
    this.active = {};
    this.resetBars = false;
};
```

Next, we augment our `Perfuse` object, which we defined in step 3, to include a `perf Toggle` method, which is run whenever our Start/Stop Test button is pressed. This method inspects the current state of the button and reverses (i.e., toggles) its state. If a test was running, it stops the test in progress. If a test was not running, it starts one.

The Stop Test action clears a JavaScript interval timer that drives the test repetitions, calls a function to delete the bar chart we are currently displaying for the test in progress (this function call is commented out until we add our visualization in a later step), hides the bar graph HTML element, changes the test state to `false`, closes the WebSocket connection to the perfuse master, and changes the button text from Stop Test to Start Test to indicate the system is ready to start a new test:

```
Perfuse.prototype.perfToggle = function (type, cmd, interval, regexp, label) {
    var id = 'perf-graph';
    if (this.perfState) {
        clearInterval(this.repeatingTests);
        //del_bar_chart();
        document.getElementById(id).style.display = 'none';
        this.perfState = false;
        this.webSock.close();
        this.reqCount = 0;
        document.getElementById('start-test-button').innerHTML = 'Start Test';
```

The Start Test action does an inverse set of actions. It displays the HTML element containing the performance graph, clears the data stored for test results, and calls a function to generate an initial, empty bar chart (this function call is commented out until we add our visualization in a later step). This function then opens a WebSocket connection to the perfuse master, sets up appropriate handler logic to dynamically redraw bars in the bar graph when test results begin streaming in, schedules repeated test invocations (at a frequency specified by the user), changes the test state to true, and changes the button text from Start Test to Stop Test to indicate a test is now running and the button may now be used to stop the running test:

```
    } else {
        document.getElementById(id).style.display = 'block';
        this.data = [];
        this.resetBars = true;
        //gen_bar_chart(label);
        this.perfState = true;
        if (('WebSocket' in window) && this.ipAddr) {
            var url = 'ws://' + this.ipAddr + ':' + this.wsPort + '/';
            this.webSock = new WebSocket(url);
            this.webSock.onmessage = function(event) {
                var res = JSON.parse(event.data);
                if (res.type == 'perf') {
                    var host_num = res.host - 1;
                    var index = null;
                    var new_val = parseInt(res.host, 10);

                    if (res.host in this.active) {
                        index = this.active[res.host];
                    } else {
                        index = 0;
                        for (i in this.data) {
                            var old_val = parseInt(this.data[i].host, 10);
                            if (old_val > new_val) {
                                break;
```

```
                }
                index++;
            }
            this.data.splice(index, 0, {});
            this.resetBars = true;
        }
        this.data[index] = {
                        host: res.host,
                        value: parseFloat(res.value, 10)
                };
        for (i in this.data) {
            this.active[this.data[i].host] = i;
        }
        if (this.reqCount >= 0) {
            //redraw_bars(this.data, this.resetBars, this.reqCount);
            this.resetBars = false;
        }
    }
}.bind(this);
this.webSock.onopen = function() {
    var req = {};
    req.type = type;
    req.cmd = cmd;
    req.regexp = regexp;
    var req_str = JSON.stringify(req);
    this.webSock.send(req_str);
    this.repeatingTests = setInterval(function() {
        this.reqCount++;
        this.webSock.send(req_str);
    }.bind(this), interval * 1000);
}.bind(this);
    }
    document.getElementById('start-test-button').innerHTML = 'Stop Test';
    }
};
```

Now it's time to try our step 4 application. With the preceding changes, we've created enough logic to run repeated performance tests from the client, which are sent to the server via WebSockets. Let's now rerun our Docker container, but this time we'll connect our step 4 files to the */src* volume, like this:

```
# Run container with shared /src and /wsk volumes.
perfuse-dev$ sudo docker run -p 80:80 -p 8080:8080 \
  -v $PWD/4:/src -v $PWD/wsk:/wsk -h perfuse-master \
  -d perfuse/test
[..]
```

Notice two important differences in how we're running our Docker container for this step:

- In addition to the -p 80:80 option, which we needed to map port 80 on the host server to port 80 in the container, we add another port mapping: -p 8080:8080.

This maps host port 8080 to container port 8080, which is needed in order to route WebSocket connections into our running container.

- We add the `-h perfuse-master` option to set the desired hostname inside our container. If we don't do that, our container will end up with a random hostname generated by Docker. Why do we suddenly care about our container's hostname? You may recall that in this step, we introduced a bit of logic in *server.js* to determine whether our server should think of itself as a master or a slave. We based that decision on the server's hostname: we assume the perfuse master has a special name: `perfuse-master`. Any other server running this JavaScript code will assume it should take on the role of a perfuse slave.

We need to make one more change before we can test our app: we must add a new firewall rule to tell Compute Engine that it's OK to route WebSocket requests into our master server. We do that by creating a firewall rule in our default network allowing traffic from any source to `tcp:8080`, using this command:

```
perfuse-dev$ gcloud compute firewall-rules create http --allow tcp:8080
[..]
http default 0.0.0.0/0  tcp:8080
```

Now point your browser to your `perfuse-dev` VM's external IP address and you should see a screen like the one we saw earlier in Figure 8-4, except this time the page will be a bit more functional—we should be able to run a test and see the test requests being received by the master via WebSockets. In order to verify those received requests, let's examine logging output for the Docker container running the master. We do this by finding the container id using `sudo docker ps`, and then running `sudo docker logs -f short-id` (where `short-id` indicates the first four characters of the desired container ID) to view the container's log output. The `-f` option requests continuous output, until interrupted by user action:

```
perfuse-dev$ sudo docker ps
CONTAINER ID   IMAGE      COMMAND      CREATED    STATUS    PORTS
808799[..] marc/step[..] node js/[..] 7 sec[..] Up 7 s[..] 0.0.0[..]
NAMES
clever_brattain
perfuse-dev$ sudo docker logs -f 8087
Master running
Listening on port 80
```

Now we're ready to start a test. In your web browser, click the Start Test button and you should see an incoming WebSocket connection reported by the `perfuse-master` container, followed by a stream of test requests. If you then click the Stop Test button, you should see the request stream stop, along with an indication that the WebSocket connection was closed by the client. The resulting log output should look similar to the following transcript:

```
Master running
Listening on port 80
[Start Test button clicked here]
new websocket connected
received from ws client: {"type":"random","cmd":"random","regexp":""}
received from ws client: {"type":"random","cmd":"random","regexp":""}
received from ws client: {"type":"random","cmd":"random","regexp":""}
received from ws client: {"type":"random","cmd":"random","regexp":""}
received from ws client: {"type":"random","cmd":"random","regexp":""}
[Stop Test button clicked here]
websocket disconnected
```

You've now verified that you can send performance tests from your web client to the perfuse-master container running on your development VM. In the next step, we'll add the logic for the perfuse slaves, the entities that actually run the tests.

Before moving on, make sure to stop the running container by using sudo docker ps to find the desired container ID, and then sudo docker stop short-id to stop the running container (where short-id indicates the first four characters of the desired container ID).

Step 5: Implement the slave

In this step, we'll add the slave personality to our *server.js* file in the step 5 directory (*gce-oreilly/ch8/5*). Let's examine the modifications to *server.js*, one logical block at a time.

We start by adding an else branch to the if statement that distinguished between master and slave personalities. Once inside this branch, we define a ZeroMQ "sub" (subscriber) socket for receiving performance test requests, and a ZeroMQ "push" socket for sending the results back to the master. These are the corresponding sides of the "pub" and "pull" sockets created on the master:

```
} else {
    console.log('Slave running');
    // Init ZeroMQ sub socket for receiving pub requests, and
    // push socket for sending point-to-point responses to master.
    sock_recv = PERFUSE.zmq.socket('sub');
    sock_recv.connect('tcp://perfuse-dev' + ':' + PERFUSE.REQ_PORT);
    sock_send = PERFUSE.zmq.socket('push');
    sock_send.connect('tcp://perfuse-dev' + ':' + PERFUSE.RES_PORT);
```

Next, we define the logic for handling messages received by the "sub" socket we just defined. For each message received on this socket, we parse the (JSON formatted) message, run the command associated with the requested performance test, parse the command response using a regular expression sent by the client, encode the result in a JSON document, and send the JSON text back to the master for forwarding on to the client via WebSocket:

```
// Define behavior for handling test requests.
sock_recv.on('message', function(msg){
    try {
        console.log('received from master: ' + msg);
        var msg = JSON.parse(msg);
        var args = msg.cmd.split(" ");
        console.log('args: ' + JSON.stringify(args));
        var cmd = args.shift();
        var regexp = new RegExp(msg.regexp);
        if (msg.type === 'random') {
            cmd = msg.type;
        }
        // Run the perf test command and send results
        // to sock_send (ZeroMQ push socket).
        run_cmd(PERFUSE.hostnum, cmd, args, regexp, sock_send);
    } catch(e) {
        console.log("error " + e);
    }
});
```

Next, we define a utility function for running the requested performance test on the slave server. This logic parses the test request, spawns the associated command with the requested arguments, scans the resulting output line by line using the regular expression provided by the client, assembles the results in a JSON document, and sends the results back to the master via the ZeroMQ push socket:

```
// Run a perf test command. Caller passes command to run,
// arguments, regexp to use to extract result, and socket
// on which to send JSON encoded result.
function run_cmd(hostnum, cmd, args, regexp, sock) {
    var resp = null;
    var resp_str = null;
    console.log('running cmd: ' + cmd + ' w/ args: ' + args);
    if (cmd == 'random') {
        resp = { type: 'perf', host: PERFUSE.hostnum,
        value: Math.random() };
        resp_str = JSON.stringify(resp);
        console.log('response: ' + resp_str);
        try {
            sock.send(resp_str);
        } catch(e) {
            console.log("error " + e);
        }
        return;
    }
    // Start running test command and process returned data asynchrously.
    var proc = PERFUSE.spawn(cmd, args);
    // Handle data received from test command one line at a time.
    proc.stdout.on('data', function (data) {
        console.log('stdout: ' + data);
        // Match passed regexp against each line of data from test command.
        var match = regexp.exec(data);
```

```
                console.log('running', regexp, 'on', data, 'yielded', match);
                if (match) {
                    // If we match a line, JSON format result and send to master.
                    resp = { type: 'perf', host: PERFUSE.hostnum,
                    value: match[1] };
                    resp_str = JSON.stringify(resp);
                    console.log('response: ' + resp_str);
                    try {
                        sock.send(resp_str);
                    } catch(e) {
                        console.log("error " + e);
                    }
                }
            }
        });
        // Log test exec errors to console.
        proc.stderr.on('data', function (data) {
            console.log('stderr: ' + data);
        });
        // Handle command completion event.
        proc.on('close', function (code) {
            console.log('child process exited with code ' + code);
        });
    };
```

Finally, we call the ZeroMQ subscribe function to start this slave listening to pub/sub events from the master:

```
        sock_recv.subscribe('');
    }
```

Now let's try our step 5 application. With the preceding changes, we've created enough logic to run repeated performance tests exercising the complete information flow from client to master to slaves, with results returned to the master and forwarded back to the client. We haven't yet implemented our visualization, but that's coming in the next step.

Let's rerun our perfuse-master container, but this time we'll connect our step 5 files to the /src volume and we'll add identical port mapping for the ports we're using for ZeroMQ (3000 and 3001), like this:

```
# Run perfuse-master container.
perfuse-dev$ sudo docker run                              \
  -p 80:80 -p 8080:8080 -p 3000:3000 -p 3001:3001    \
  -v $PWD/5:/src -v $PWD/wsk:/wsk -h perfuse-master \
  -d perfuse/test
[..]
```

Let's also start a container slave. There are three differences in how we start the slaves: we don't need to make any port assignments (because the slaves don't accept incoming connections), we don't need to connect a volume to the /wsk directory (because the slaves don't serve any web content), and we need to specify a different hostname (to instruct the container to adopt the slave role):

```
# Run slave 1 container.
perfuse-dev$ sudo docker run -v $PWD/5:/src -h perfuse-1 -d perfuse/test
[..]
```

In order to verify received requests, let's view the output logs for our two containers in parallel. We do this by finding the container IDs for the master and the slave using sudo docker ps. Then, in two separate windows, we run sudo docker logs -f short-id to view the output from both containers at the same time, as illustrated here:

```
perfuse-dev$ sudo docker ps
CONTAINER ID   IMAGE     COMMAND     CREATED STATUS PORTS     NAMES
e600[..]    mcohen/[..] node js[..] minute Up minute 80/tcp thir[..]
15f4[..]    mcohen/[..] node js[..] minute Up minute 0.0[..] trust[..]
perfuse-dev$ sudo docker logs -f 15f4
Master running
Listening on port 80
```

[in a separate window..]

```
perfuse-dev$ sudo docker logs -f e600
Slave running
```

In addition to the master and slave logs, if you're using the Chrome browser, you can open the JavaScript console by selecting Menu->Tools->JavaScript Console to verify the last hop—the performance test results are received all the way back at the browser.

Once again, point your browser to your perfuse-dev VM's external IP address. Now we're ready to start a test. In your web browser, click the Start Test button. You should see an incoming WebSocket connection reported by the Docker container running the master, followed by a stream of test requests from the browser to the master, each of which is forwarded from the master to the slave.

You should also see the slave report the received test requests, run a test command, and send the result back to the master. You should see the master report receiving the result from the slave and forwarding the result asynchronously to the browser via WebSockets. If you have the Chrome JavaScript console open, you should also see evidence of the test result being received by the browser.

If you then click the Stop Test button, you should see the request stream stop, along with an indication that the WebSocket connection was closed by the client. The resulting log output should look similar to the following transcript:

```
[Master container log...]
Master running
Listening on port 80
```

```
[Start Test button clicked here]
new websocket connected
received from ws client: {"type":"random","cmd":"random","regexp":""}
event received from slave: {"type":"perf","host":"1","value":0.7852813333738595}
received from ws client: {"type":"random","cmd":"random","regexp":""}
event received from slave: {"type":"perf","host":"1","value":0.05954153626225889}
received from ws client: {"type":"random","cmd":"random","regexp":""}
event received from slave: {"type":"perf","host":"1","value":0.2834956750739366}
[Stop Test button clicked here]
websocket disconnected

[Slave container log...]
Slave running
[Start Test button clicked here]
received from master: {"type":"random","cmd":"random","regexp":""}
args: ["random"]
running cmd: random w/ args:
response: {"type":"perf","host":"1","value":0.8582024811767042}
received from master: {"type":"random","cmd":"random","regexp":""}
args: ["random"]
running cmd: random w/ args:
response: {"type":"perf","host":"1","value":0.3966985512524843}
[Stop Test button clicked here]
```

Now that we're seeing our basic design working on an end-to-end basis with a client, a master, and a slave, let's add the final piece of the puzzle, a nice looking interactive visualization using the D3.js library. With this addition, we'll be able to verify end-to-end functionality without needing to monitor container logs or the Chrome Java-Script console.

Disconnect the running docker logs commands by entering Crtl-C. Before moving on to the next step, make sure to stop the running containers by using sudo docker ps to find the desired container IDs, and then sudo docker stop short-ids to stop the master and slave containers (where short-id indicates the first four characters of the desired container ID).

Step 6: Add our visualization

In this step, we add the new *ch8/6/cripts/vis.js* file, which uses the powerful d3.js Java-Script visualization library to graph our performance test results as they arrive. Let's examine this file in logical blocks.

First, let's define some variables inside a JavaScript object (to appropriately limit their scope):

```
var Perfuse_vis = function() {
    this.svg = null;
    this.width = null;
    this.height = null;
    this.x = null;
```

```
        this.x2 = null;
        this.y = null;
        this.xAxis = null;
        this.yAxis = null;
        this.globalMax = 0;
    }
```

The gen_bar_chart() function draws the initial, empty bar chart and prepares the view for displaying real-time results. This is useful when the end user starts running a new test:

```
Perfuse_vis.prototype.gen_bar_chart = function(label) {
    var margin = {top: 20, right: 20, bottom: 30, left: 40};
    this.width = 960 - margin.left - margin.right,
    this.height = 500 - margin.top - margin.bottom;
    this.x = d3.scale.ordinal().rangeRoundBands([0, this.width], .1);
    this.x2 = d3.scale.ordinal().rangeBands([0, this.width], 0);
    this.y = d3.scale.linear().range([this.height, 0]);
    this.xAxis = d3.svg.axis().scale(this.x).orient("bottom");
    this.yAxis = d3.svg.axis().scale(this.y).orient("left");
    // append to hide y axis labels
    //.tickFormat("");
    this.svg = d3.select("#perf-graph").append("svg")
            .attr("width", this.width + margin.left + margin.right)
            .attr("height", this.height + margin.top + margin.bottom)
            .append("g")
            .attr("transform", "translate(" + margin.left + "," +
            margin.top + ")");
    this.svg.append("g")
            .attr("class", "x axis")
            .attr("transform", "translate(0," + this.height + ")")
            .call(this.xAxis);
    this.svg.append("g")
            .attr("class", "y axis")
            .call(this.yAxis)
            .append("text")
            .attr("transform", "rotate(-90)")
            .attr("y", 6)
            .attr("dy", ".71em")
            .style("text-anchor", "end")
            .text(label);
    this.svg.append("path").attr("class", "avg-line")
};
```

The del_bar_chart() function removes the bar chart from view, which is useful when the end user stops a running test:

```
Perfuse_vis.prototype.del_bar_chart = function() {
    d3.select("#perf-graph").select("svg").remove();
    this.svg = null;
    this.globalMax = 0;
}
```

Next, we define the `redraw_bars()` function. This function takes the latest test results received from the active slaves (passed via the `data` object), along with a flag indicating whether to reset the bars (or to update the bars in an existing graph), and a request count. The reset bars flag is used whenever a new slave joins (or an existing slave leaves) the cluster. The request count is used to tell whether this is the first or a subsequent result. If the latter, we use d3.js animation to move the existing bar to a new position. This results in a pleasing real-time animation effect as the user can watch the bars adjust to her new values over time:

```
Perfuse_vis.prototype.redraw_bars = function(data, reset_bars, req_count) {
    var max = d3.max(data, function(d) { return d.value; });
    if (max > this.globalMax) {
        this.globalMax = max;
    };
    var avg = d3.sum(data, function(d) { return d.value; }) / data.length;
    this.y.domain([0, this.globalMax]);
    this.x.domain(data.map(function(d) { return d.host; }));
    this.x2.domain(data.map(function(d) { return d.host; }));
    // uncomment next line to have y axis only grow, never shrink
    //this.y.domain([0, max]);
    this.svg.selectAll("g.x.axis").call(this.xAxis);
    this.svg.selectAll("g.y.axis").call(this.yAxis);
    if (reset_bars) {
        this.svg.selectAll("rect").remove();
        this.svg.selectAll(".bar")
          .data(data)
          .enter().append("rect")
          .attr("class", "bar")
          .attr("x", function(d) { return this.x(d.host); }.bind(this))
          .attr("width", this.x.rangeBand())
          .attr("y", function(d) { return this.y(d.value); }.bind(this))
          .attr("height", function(d) { return this.height - this.y(d.value);
          }.bind(this));
    }
    this.svg.selectAll("rect")
      .data(data)
      .transition()
      .duration(1000)
        .attr("y", function(d) { return this.y(d.value); }.bind(this))
        .attr("height", function(d) { return this.height - this.y(d.value);
        }.bind(this));
    if (req_count > 0) {
        // Animate/adjust average line.
        var line = d3.svg.line()
                    .x(function(d, i) {
                        return (typeof this.x2(i) === 'undefined')?
                        i*this.x2(i) + i
                      }.bind(this))
                    .y(function(d, i) { return this.y(avg); }.bind(this));
        this.svg.selectAll(".avg-line")
          .datum(data)
```

```
            .transition()
            .duration(1000)
            .attr("d", line)
    }
}
```

We can now uncomment the calls to our visualization logic in *client.js*. Specifically, calls to gen_bar_chart(), del_bar_chart(), and redraw_bars(), which we introduced in step 4, can now be exercised.

Finally, we need to include our visualization logic and the d3.js library by adding the following highlighted lines near the bottom of our *index.html* file:

```
<script src="js/bootstrap.min.js"></script>
<script src="http://code.angularjs.org/1.2.0/angular.min.js"></script>
<script type="text/javascript" src="scripts/client.js"></script>
<script type="text/javascript" src="scripts/vis.js"></script>
<script src="http://d3js.org/d3.v3.min.js"></script>
```

Now it's time to try our step 6 application. With the preceding changes, we no longer need to monitor container logs to verify each step of the information flow. We can simply watch our visualization to verify the end-to-end system behavior.

For this step, instead of running our containers by hand, we're going to use a shell script to start and stop containers on our development VM. The script can be found in *ch8/6/run.sh*. Here are the contents of our *run.sh* script:

```
#! /bin/bash
USAGE="run.sh step beg end"
if [ $# != 3 ]
then
  # Make sure user supplied three args: step, start, and end.
  echo $USAGE
  exit 1
fi
STEP=$1
START=$2
END=$3
VOLUMES_MASTER="-v $PWD/$STEP:/src -v $PWD/wsk:/wsk"
VOLUMES_SLAVES="-v $PWD/$STEP:/src"
PORTS_MASTER="-p 80:80 -p 8080:8080 -p 3000:3000 -p 3001:3001"
PORTS_SLAVES=""
IMAGE="perfuse/test"
for i in $(seq $START $END)
do
  if [ $i = "0" ]
  then
    VOLUMES=$VOLUMES_MASTER
    PORTS=$PORTS_MASTER
    HOSTNAME=perfuse-master
  else
    VOLUMES=$VOLUMES_SLAVES
```

```
        PORTS=$PORTS_SLAVES
        HOSTNAME="perfuse-$i"
    fi
    sudo docker run $VOLUMES $PORTS -h $HOSTNAME -d $IMAGE
done
```

Let's start a master container and two slave containers by running this command:

```
$ 6/run.sh 6 0 2
65b97b77ec10e78cc6e6cf6d2bb6361b8f5c0dd12c86be14c83200545d538048
feb729968508348802188d4cb0b4ea40db1c75443eeff20cb24bea1783289b62
fd413b8c953ef73a7fa275ee5af24af54571f74fbde4a104fec063bdd374f32d
```

This tells our script to run the step 6 code, and to start containers 0 (the master) and 1-2 (two slaves). The results are, as you can see, the Docker container IDs for the three containers we started. Now we're ready to start a test. Navigate your web browser to your perfuse-dev server, and click the Start Test button. You should see a graph including the two slaves we just started, as shown in Figure 8-6.

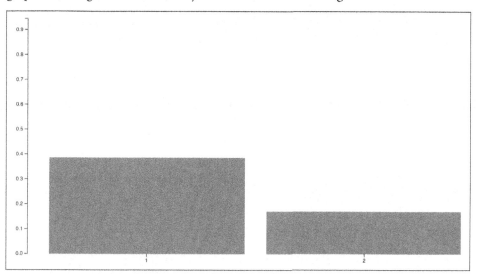

Figure 8-6. A two-slave Node.js cluster running dynamic performance tests

The graph should automatically update to reflect the varying test results in real time —you should see a dynamic, animated bar chart illustrating the results of your requested performance test throughout your two-slave cluster.

Now let's grow the size of our cluster to 10 slaves. Run the run.sh command to start container slaves 3-10, like this:

```
$ 6/run.sh 6 3 10
e6cbee9f07e7d79f5a5e391a3c684650e794e128f3dbcef99931742b3c8d6e78
[..]
df724bd821c4ed750fe25b68174752bed08d282263e8a006d32a7f7d7f39b160
```

Your animated graph should automatically add the newly created slaves without requiring any interaction on the user interface. Your new graph should look like the one shown in Figure 8-7.

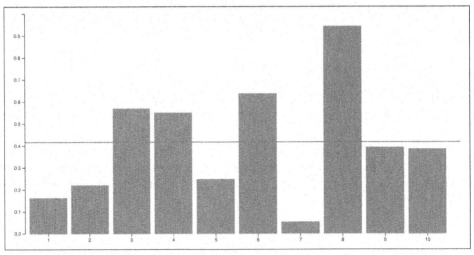

Figure 8-7. A 10-slave Node.js cluster running dynamic performance tests

If you then click the Stop Test button, the test will stop and the visualization will disappear.

Before moving on to the next step, make sure to stop the running containers by using `sudo docker ps` to find the desired container IDs, and then `sudo docker stop short-id` to stop the master-and-slave containers (where `short-id` indicates the first four characters of the desired container ID).

Step 7: Deploy a cluster into production

Now that we've verified the functionality of our application in a test environment, with master and slaves running in containers on a single VM, let's deploy our app into production, with the master and slaves running in one container per VM.

Our step 7 directory contains the following changes:

7/Dockerfile contains the following lines added to the version we used to build our first image in step 1:

```
# Add step 7 and wsk contents into container.
ADD 7 /src
ADD wsk /wsk
```

We want to run our containers on a vanilla VM that hasn't preinstalled our GitHub repo. In other words, our image needs to be completely self-contained. We achieve this by using the ADD directive, which copies the contents of a directory into the image. This is essentially an alternative to using the -v option when we run a container—instead of sharing a directory on the host, we copy the contents of that directory into the image.

We've built an image with this modified Dockerfile and stored it in the public Docker registry under the name marcacohen/perfuse. We'll reference that image name later when we need to start our VMs.

We've added the following line to our *7/scripts/server.js* file:

```
var auth = express.basicAuth('super', 'secret');
```

and modified the routing for the root ('/') service to use the auth function in order to apply a simple login and password prompt:

```
PERFUSE.app.get('/', PERFUSE.auth, function(req, res){
```

You should modify the username and password to suit your preference.

We've also modified the logic for establishing a connection to the master. Instead of assuming a hard-coded hostname (previously perfuse-dev, our development VM), we now obtain the master's hostname and associated ports from a data structure:

```
console.log('connecting to pubsub and p2p @', PERFUSE.MASTER);
sock_recv.connect('tcp://' + PERFUSE.MASTER + ':' +
PERFUSE.REQ_PORT);
sock_send.connect('tcp://' + PERFUSE.MASTER + ':' +
PERFUSE.RES_PORT);
```

Because our app is focused on performance testing, it makes sense to run one container per VM so that performance tests aren't contending for the same virtual machine resources. But we don't want to manually repeat all these steps (clone the perfuse repo, build a container, run a master or slave container, etc.) for every VM in our cluster.

We need a way to stamp out VMs automatically. We'll use the container-optimized image we used in step 0 to build our perfuse-dev development server. We could use any software we like to create and destroy VMs, but to keep things simple, we'll use the following shell script, which is just a thin wrapper around the gcloud compute command:

```
#! /bin/bash
USAGE="cluster.sh start|stop beg end"
ZONE="--zone us-central1-a"
TYPE="--machine-type f1-micro"
MTCE="--maintenance-policy TERMINATE"
META_INIT="--metadata-from-file google-container-manifest="
IMAGE="--image container-vm-v20140826 --image-project google-containers"
QUIET="-q"
PREFIX="perfuse-"
if [ $# != 3 ]
```

```
then
  # Make sure user supplied three args: operation, start, and end.
  echo $USAGE
  exit 1
fi
OP=$1
START=$2
END=$3
for i in $(seq $START $END)
do
  if [ $i = "0" ]
  then
    ID=${PREFIX}master
    META="${META_INIT}master.yaml"
  else
    ID=${PREFIX}$i
    cp slave.yaml $ID.yaml
    echo "        value: $ID" >>$ID.yaml
    META="${META_INIT}$ID.yaml"
  fi
  if [ "$OP" = "start" ]
  then
    gcloud compute instances create $ID $META $ZONE $TYPE $MTCE \
      $IMAGE $QUIET &
  elif [ "$OP" = "stop" ]
  then
    gcloud compute instances delete $ID $ZONE $QUIET &
  else
    echo $USAGE
    exit 1
  fi
done
# All requests above were run in the background, the following wait
# command causes us to wait until all requests have completed before
# exiting this script.
wait
# Clean up per-slave manifest files.
for i in $(seq $START $END)
do
  if [ $i != "0" ]
  then
    rm -f ${PREFIX}$i
  fi
done
```

This script is called *cluster.sh* and can be found in the *gce-oreilly/ch8/7* directory. It provides two operations:

- start creates a range of instances
- stop deletes a range of instances

Now you can use the `start` operation to create a master VM and 20 slave VMs, like this:

```
$ cd 7
$ ./cluster.sh start 0 20
```

Wait a few minutes for all of the VMs to initialize and then navigate your browser to the external IP address associated with the `perfuse-master` VM. You'll find the same UI we saw in step 6, but now when you start a test, you should see dynamic performance results from 20 VMs, as shown in Figure 8-8.

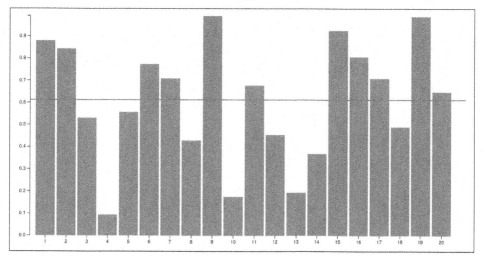

Figure 8-8. A 20-slave Node.js cluster running dynamic performance tests

To illustrate the dynamic, self-configuring nature of this app, while the current test is in progress, add five more VMs with the following command:

```
$ ./cluster.sh start 21 25
```

Wait a little while for the new VMs to start running (and for the agent to start the containers). After a few minutes, you should see the additional five VMs automatically add their test results to the dynamic display.

The `random` test we've been using so far causes the slaves to generate and return a random number, which causes significant visual animation in the bar graphs but is not otherwise meaningful. The other performance tests cause a particular test command to be run on each slave. The results of the command are parsed by a regular expression in order to extract the result, and the result is returned to the master and thence to the JavaScript client via Web Socket. As you can see, the UI allows you to modify the command run for a given test and the regular expression used to parse the test output. Now you can try some of the other performance tests, beside the default random test we've been using so far. Figure 8-1, which we saw at the beginning of this chapter, shows the perfuse app running a network throughput test on a cluster of 10 virtual machines.

Conclusion

In this chapter, we used Google Compute Engine and a variety of open source tools and libraries to build a simple, highly scalable, service-provider–independent performance test application. Along the way, we exercised VM creation, network and firewall configuration, testing and deployment using Docker containers, a container-optimized image, cluster management using a simple shell script, advanced communication using ZeroMQ, and a simple but powerful dynamic bar chart using D3.js. This example application illustrates the power and flexibility of applications written with open source software and deployed on Google Compute Engine.

Index

OWNER role, for ACLs, 86, 88, 89

P

packets, 118, 119
PDs (see persistent disks)
performance
    of instances (virtual machines), 56
    of persistent disks, 56
    testing, example of (see perfuse application example)
perfuse application example
    deploying, 216-220
    development VM for, 187-188
    Docker image for, 188-192
    graphs for, 211-216
    information flow for, 186
    master server for, 200-207
    open source software used in, 185
    requirements for, 183-184
    slave server for, 207-211
    source code for, 188
    UI for, 195-200
    UI framework for, 192-195
permissions, for members, 3
persistent disks (PDs), 4, 53-56
    access scope of, 54
    attaching to a running instance, 64-66, 67
    boot persistent disk, 27, 53, 55, 58-59, 60, 63
    creating
        with API, 67-73
        with Developers Console, 56-59
        with gcloud compute command, 60-63
    creating directories on, 66
    data model for, 54
    detaching from a running instance, 66
    encryption of, 54
    formatting and mounting, 65, 67
    journaling filesystem for, 74
    JSON objects for, 68
    managed, 54
    maximum size of, 54
    mounting to filesystem, 65
    non-bootable, 53, 55, 64
    performance of, 56
    read-only access to, 55
    read/write access to, 55
    redundancy of, 54, 55
    snapshots of, 56, 73-75
    storage scope of, 54
    types of, 55
    unmounting from filesystem, 66
    use cases for, 55
    zone for, 56
ping command, 125
pip tool, 45, 83, 112
planned outages, 7
ports, 119
POST HTTP method, 17
private canned ACL, 86
project ID
    setting, 2
    specifying for Cloud SDK, 12-13
project-private canned ACL, 86
projects, viii-ix, 1
    billing for, enabling, 3
    creating, 2-3
    information about, listing, 13
    members for, adding, 3
    metadata for, 160-161, 165-173
    name of, 2
PROVISIONING state, 34
public-read canned ACL, 86
Python Google API Client Library, 21-24, 44-49, 45, 83-84, 112-115
Python interpreter, 21

Q

Quotas section, Developers Console, 10-11

R

READER role, for ACLs, 87-89
redundancy of storage mechanism, 54
regional resources, 5, 17
regions, 37
resources, viii
    costs incurred by, 3
    managing, 5-24
        with API, 14-24
        with Cloud SDK, 11-14
        with Developers Console, 6-11
    number available and in use, 10
    scopes (levels) of, 5, 17, 54
    types of, 4-5
RESTful interface for API, 15, 44
roles, ACL, 86, 88-89
root account access to instances, 41
routes, 5
routing, 118, 141-142

RUNNING state, 34

S

safe_format_and_mount command, 65, 67
scopes (levels) of resources, 5, 17, 54
scopes, for service accounts, 37-39, 80, 81
scripts run at startup (see startup scripts)
select command, MySQL, 106-108
servers
    Google Authorization Server, 18-20
    health of, checking, 133
    master server, example of, 200-207
    metadata server, 125, 159-160
    slave servers, example of, 207-211
service accounts, 3
    instances, creating, 49-50
    scopes for, 37-39, 80, 81
service object, 22
service-level agreement (SLA), 78
shared core machine types, 35
SLA (service-level agreement), 78
snapshots, 4, 56, 73-75
software, installing, 41
    (see also open source software)
Solid State Device (SSD) drives, 55
source command, MySQL, 106
sql scope, 39
sql-admin scope, 39
SSD (Solid State Device) drives, 55
SSH session to instances, 30, 38, 40-43
STAGING state, 34
standard disk drives, 55
standard machine types, 35
startup scripts, 145-153
    with API, 149-153
    in Cloud Storage, 148-149, 150
    with gcloud compute command, 145-149
    length limit for, 147, 148
    in public online location, 149, 150
    with local files, 147-148
startupscript.log file, 146, 148, 149
states, for instances, 34
static IP address, 40
STOPPING state, 35
storage, x, 53-54
    availability of, 78
    Cloud Datastore (see Cloud Datastore)
    Cloud SQL (see Cloud SQL)
    Cloud Storage (see Cloud Storage)

durability of, 78
    open source database management systems, 115-116
    persistent disks (see persistent disks (PDs))
storage-full scope, 39, 81
storage-ro scope, 39
storage-rw scope, 39
sudo apt-get install command, 41
sudo command, 41, 61
sudo sync command, 74

T

tables, creating in Cloud SQL, 103-106
tags, for instances, 40
taskqueue scope, 39
TCP (Transport Control Protocol), 119-120
TERMINATED state, 35
TLD (top-level domain), 121
Transport Control Protocol (see TCP)

U

umount command, 66
URI syntax, for files and objects, 81, 82
URL, for HTTP requests, 15, 17-18

V

virtual machine manager, 25
    (see also KVM hypervisor)
virtualization, 25
VM (virtual machine) (see instances)
VM instances section, Developers Console, 6, 27-28

W

wait_for_change URL parameter, 182
Web Starter Kit software, 186, 190, 192-195
WebSocket software, 186, 202
WRITER role, for ACLs, 89-89

Z

ZeroMQ software, 186, 201, 207, 209
zonal resources, 5, 17
zones, 37
    cross-zone static data distribution, 75
    planned outages for, 7, 37
Zones section, Developers Console, 7

About the Author(s)

Marc manages Google's Developer Relations Engineering team in London, which helps software developers get the most out of the Google APIs and services in the EMEA region. In a previous life, Marc helped design and build communication systems at Bell Labs and Lucent Technologies. When he's not working, Marc enjoys indie music and films, writing, teaching, and chess.

Kathryn Hurley is a Developer Programs Engineer at Google for Compute Engine. In this role, she helps developers learn how to use the Compute Engine API by developing sample applications. She received an MS in Web Science from the University of San Francisco and a BS in Genetics from the University of California, Davis. Prior work experience includes research in mobile and peer-to-peer computing.

Paul Newson is a Software Engineer at Google. Currently, he is focusing on helping developers harness the power of the Google Cloud Platform to solve their Big Data problems. Prior to his current role in Developer Relations, Paul helped build Google's Cloud Platform as an engineer on Google Cloud Storage. Before joining Google, Paul cofounded a tiny game technology startup and sold it to Microsoft, where he then worked on DirectX, Xbox, Xbox Live, and Forza Motorsport. He then spent some time working on interesting machine learning problems in Microsoft Research. Outside of work Paul enjoys rock climbing, motorcycling, and other activities that demand complete focus.

Colophon

The animal on the cover of *Google Compute Engine* is a *Rufous treepie*. This bird is native to India and other parts of southeast Asia, such as Thailand, Laos, and Pakistan. They find the majority of their diet in trees, feeding on fruits, seeds, and insects among other organisms. They are also known to eat the eggs and young of other birds.

Weight ranges are generally between 90-130 grams for both males and females. They have dark-colored heads that almost look black, but bright, orangish bodies. The eyes are a deep red color.

The rufous treepie is know to be a noisy bird with many calls. Some of these calls have been named by locals, such as the "bob-o-link" or "ko-tree." They're not shy, and will take food from strangers depending on their exposure to co-existing with humans. They have been known to be aggressive in getting food if they see an opportunity.

Many of the animals on O'Reilly covers are endangered; all of them are important to the world. To learn more about how you can help, go to animals.oreilly.com.

The cover image is from *Wood's Animate Creation*. The cover fonts are URW Typewriter and Guardian Sans. The text font is Adobe Minion Pro; the heading font is Adobe Myriad Condensed; and the code font is Dalton Maag's Ubuntu Mono.

Get even more for your money.

Join the O'Reilly Community, and register the O'Reilly books you own. It's free, and you'll get:

- $4.99 ebook upgrade offer
- 40% upgrade offer on O'Reilly print books
- Membership discounts on books and events
- Free lifetime updates to ebooks and videos
- Multiple ebook formats, DRM FREE
- Participation in the O'Reilly community
- Newsletters
- Account management
- 100% Satisfaction Guarantee

Signing up is easy:

1. Go to: oreilly.com/go/register
2. Create an O'Reilly login.
3. Provide your address.
4. Register your books.

Note: English-language books only

To order books online:
oreilly.com/store

For questions about products or an order:
orders@oreilly.com

To sign up to get topic-specific email announcements and/or news about upcoming books, conferences, special offers, and new technologies:
elists@oreilly.com

For technical questions about book content:
booktech@oreilly.com

To submit new book proposals to our editors:
proposals@oreilly.com

O'Reilly books are available in multiple DRM-free ebook formats. For more information:
oreilly.com/ebooks

O'REILLY®

CPSIA information can be obtained at www.ICGtesting.com
Printed in the USA
BVOW08s2231121214

379056BV00004B/5/P